CHALLENGE ACCEPTED

CHALLENGE ACCEPTED

A Finnish Immigrant Response to Industrial America in Michigan's Copper Country

Gary Kaunonen

Michigan State University Press • *East Lansing*

⊜ The paper used in this publication meets the minimum requirements of ANSI/NISO Z39.48-1992 (R 1997) (Permanence of Paper).

Michigan State University Press
East Lansing, Michigan 48823-5245

Printed and bound in the United States of America.

19 18 17 16 15 14 13 12 11 10 1 2 3 4 5 6 7 8 9 10

LIBRARY OF CONGRESS CATALOGING-IN-PUBLICATION DATA
Kaunonen, Gary.
Challenge accepted : a Finnish immigrant response to industrial America in Michigan's copper country / Gary Kaunonen.
p. cm.
Includes bibliographical references and index.
ISBN 978-0-87013-873-7 (paper : alk. paper) 1. Finnish Americans—Michigan—Hancock—History. 2. Immigrants—Michigan—Hancock—History. 3. Finnish Americans—Michigan—Hancock—Social life and customs. 4. Finnish Americans—Michigan—Hancock—Social conditions. 5. Working class—Michigan—Hancock—History. 6. Labor unions—Michigan—Hancock—History. 7. Työmies Publishing Company—History. 8. Hancock (Mich.)—History. 9. Hancock (Mich.)—Social conditions. 10. Hancock (Mich.)—Ethnic relations. I. Title.
F574.H23K386 2009
977.4'00494541—dc22

Cover design by Erin Kirk New
Book design by Charlie Sharp, Sharp Des!gns, Lansing, Michigan
Cover art is a *Lapatossu* cartoon by Konstu Sallinen depicting the awakening of an underground copper mine worker as the Copper Country bosses scramble in the midst of the stirring, 1913. (Finlandia University's Finnish American Historical Archive.)

green press INITIATIVE Michigan State University Press is a member of the Green Press Initiative and is committed to developing and encouraging ecologically responsible publishing practices. For more information about the Green Press Initiative and the use of recycled paper in book publishing, please visit *www.greenpressinitiative.org*.

Visit Michigan State University Press on the World Wide Web at *www.msupress.msu.edu*

Contents

Diagrams, Drawing, and Maps

Diagrams

Drawing

Maps

Preface

> The strongest bond of human sympathy outside the family relation should be one uniting working people; people of all nations and tongues and kindreds.
>
> —Abraham Lincoln

LABOR HISTORY . . . FOR MANY THE TERM ALMOST IMMEDIATELY CONJURES up images of "Commies" infiltrating American unions, or Joseph McCarthy shouting blistering accusations into an HUAC microphone. With all the implications and stigma about labor and the American "Left" that became a part of the American consciousness throughout the Cold War, it is often difficult for entire generations to think of labor history as anything more than the analysis of Soviet ideological seepage into American institutions. There was however, dare I say, a much simpler time in the history of American labor and working-class politics. This was a time before Stalin and the advent of the Cold War—a time when socialism and the labor movement meant the demolition of the capitalist system, and not the annihilation of the world as we knew it.

I hope that as a reader (if I have done my job well enough), you can transport your mind back to a time before we had the collective fears of nuclear missiles flying over our heads. I hope you can read with an open mind, so that the actions of an early twentieth-century immigrant people can be judged not by the standards and stigma of the Cold War era, but rather by the merits and values of the period in which these immigrants tried to proactively shape the world in which they lived. I challenge you to read without recent historical bias.

In that vein, bias and revisionism are terms quite often associated with labor history. Regarding bias, I will admit to you right now that this is a "biased" history, because it examines an aspect of the Finnish immigrant labor and political movement in the early twentieth century on its own terms. If the book is critical of capitalism and large corporations, it is because the historical actors in this book were critical of those entities. I dedicated myself to writing a type of history that would let my bias choose the topic and focus of what I wanted to research and write, but not let that bias filter into my research and writing concerning the actions of the people and organizations about which I write. The Finnish immigrant socialist and union movement did some remarkable and distinctive things in their challenging of the American capitalist system, but they also perpetrated some status quo–like transgressions against African Americans and women, and at times, simply put, just could not get along with one another; both sides of the coin are covered in this book. Additionally, I do not consider this a revisionist history. I have always had a problem with that term because what is called "revisionist" is often just a change of perspective. "Revisionist history" is often just a different viewpoint that affords those who did not have the means, for any number of reasons, a place in the contextual fabric of America's history. This was the impetus and inspiration for this book.

Acknowledgments

As a general note, this book comes out of thesis work done in the Industrial Archaeology program at Michigan Technological University. With the help of the original manuscript readers and the editors and staff at Michigan State University Press, I have hopefully made the contents more readable from the thesis work and more agreeable to book form.

An undertaking such as this has a number of people and places that I must thank for their help in bringing this work to completion. First, and above all else, I would like to thank my family, Denina, Sofia, Niilo, Art, Edie, and Grandma Vienna, for their support and interest in this work and for keeping me grounded. I should also thank my four-legged kids (sled dogs) for letting me bounce many ideas off them when no one else wanted to listen (or perhaps when I was reluctant to talk with two-footers about my ideas). Thank you to Ruutu, V, Robi, Gretzky, Michi, Kivi, Kesä, Laikku, KaBluwie, Karhu, and Musta.

Next, I would like to thank those individuals who helped me along in the research, writing, and editing process. Carol MacLennan, Larry Lankton, Kim

Hoagland, and Christa Walck provided great insight and helped to focus what could have easily been (and almost was) a never-ending thesis. I would also like to thank the entire faculty and staff of the Industrial Archaeology program at Michigan Technological University. I received an incredible education from them, and the lessons learned shape more clearly how I view my surroundings. I would especially like to thank Pat Martin for taking a chance on accepting a late application from Minnesota and thus letting me into the program. In the realm of translating selected works that proved too much for my limited abilities, I would like to thank Anna Leppänen, Jarno Heinilä, Tanja Aho, and Harry Siitonen. Their work was instrumental in getting a complete picture of the subject matter. I would like to thank Kent Randell for his work digitizing sections of the Finnish American Historical Archive's oral history collection. Working with digital was so much better than analog. I would also like to thank Vern Simula for his early reads and enthusiasm on the topic.

Institutionally, I would like to thank the Michigan Tech Archives and Copper Country Historical Collections in the Garden Level of Michigan Technological University's Library. Erik Nordberg, Julia Blair, Christine Holland, and their work-study students were always helpful and willing to assist even with the strangest of requests, namely, the "corduroy book." I would like to thank the Immigration History Research Center on the campus of the University of Minnesota in Minneapolis. Joel Wurl, Donna Gabaccia, Daniel Necas, and staff were instrumental in opening that great collection of Finnish American materials, both through their knowledge and in sponsoring the Michael G. Karni Research Grant (a memorial grant to the late, great Dr. Karni); my thanks go to Karen Karni, Dr. Karni's wife, for her support of labor history as well. I will also take this chance to thank two history Profs at Minnesota State University-Mankato: my social-and labor-history professor at Minnesota State University-Mankato, Charles K. Piehl, and my history department advisor Erwin "Ernie" Grieshaber. They focused my interests, pushed my buttons, and opened my eyes. I would also like to thank the readers of the original manuscript (specifically for their insightful comments and thoughts) and Michigan State University Press. It has been a pleasure working with them, and it is wonderful to see their support of Upper Peninsula history.

Last, but in no way least, I would like to thank the Finnish immigrant working class, of which my grandfather, Neal, was a member. This book is dedicated to them. Their history is remarkable; I only hope that I have fulfilled what I might term my responsibility to them by shedding light on the important contributions they made to the history of Michigan and America.

Introduction

> I came in through the door and went to the back part of the hall and sat down with Mrs. Warminen and took the children in our laps and sat down in the back part of the hall. We were waiting for the program and simply sat there . . . [The program] had singing and dancing. The old people had some kind of a circular dance and some were singing. Could not hear the program in the back part of the hall. It was all full . . . A lady came and announced that the children go through that door and get their presents and then go out through the other [door] . . . A man in Finnish made the same announcement.[1]

INA KARNA, A FINNISH IMMIGRANT AND THE PERSON WHO MADE THE ABOVE statement, was at the Italian Hall Christmas Eve party for striking mineworkers' families in Red Jacket or Calumet, Michigan, that day in 1913. She was one of hundreds of Finnish immigrants who were attending the multiethnic Christmas party for the children of striking Michigan copper workers.

So was Charles Olson, who had just come to the Italian Hall from a funeral only blocks away on Pine Street in Red Jacket. He was looking for his wife and two daughters in the mass of people celebrating at Italian Hall that day. You can almost hear the brogue of an immigrant describing what were to become the horrifying details of a sadly eventful day:

> I come to the hall, I was looking all over and could not see them. My neighbor woman had five or six children and my other brother was there too, and asked that lady if she had seen my wife and child. She said they were just going in. They were going in the door. There was children on both sides by the wall just as tight as could be, standing on chairs and most the seats were pretty close and there was an alley where they pass. There was not very many women, it was mostly children. So I got up on the stool or one of them seats and I began to look out, and could not see them. I said to myself they must be gone through the other side [of the hall] . . .
>
> [I was] in the middle of the hall on the north side looking up here to the door leading to the stage on the north side and then looking at the same time out to the main entrance door, that's the door going to the stairway to see whether or not my children and wife were passing through. When I was standing a fellow come through the door, quite a big man, sealskin cap on and shook his hands and hollered, "FIRE!," "FIRE!," and turned back, and a lady took hold of him by the shoulders and wanted to keep him back but they [the crowd] got so excited they started to run.[2]

Mrs. Mary Lantto was in the Italian Hall from early on that day:

> I went there about two thirty, around that time; and when I went there the hall was full and I had seven children with me and then I stand there near the door for a while with my children, and then a little at a time I went through the crowd [to get] near the stage and then when I got near the stage it was so crowded I had to stand on a chair and put my baby on the edge of the stage and kept my baby there. While I was there for a while again I seen a lady on the side of the hall, right hand side, and she was standing on that desk and was motioning towards the door. That's all I heard her say, "Every-body go out." I did not hear her say fire. I did not understand what was up but I seen the people run towards the door.

> Then I was knocked off [the chair] with my baby from that stage and went on my knees near that heater. Got up from there as fast as I could and tried to hold my baby with one hand and the heater with the other so the crowd would not bring me down with them.[3]

Andrew Saari, who was in the hall with his two boys, one who was almost six years old and the other who was almost eight, heard the cry of fire and witnessed the panicked exodus toward the hall's stairway:

> I hear something like that [cry of fire] but I did not take notice of it. I had a newspaper and started to read that and then I looked inside where they give the candy and see no fire. I thought they were fooling and started to read again but the people were going out so fast I thought there must be some kind of trouble . . . Yes, looks to me as though everybody was going out.[4]

John Aho and his family were in the Italian Hall immediately before the rush to the stairs, and John recalled the events of the charge down the stairs that led toward doom for many:

> When I got in with my wife and children, my wife wanted to go in the hall; she wanted to get some presents for the little youngsters that she had with her . . . I was talking to the children and asked them whether they got any presents or [if they could not go in]. Some children said they had their clothes. [To the others] I says you go in and get your clothes, had the door closed. I opened the door and saw the crowd crowding towards the door. I opened the door and looked inside and there was a man on the stage with his hands raised up high. I did not hear no cry of fire at all.
>
> I went into that stairway. I pulled some of the people into that little room and when I got in I pushed the crowd back and told them to go back in the hall that there was no fire, to go inside. As I got the crowd stopped enough I started to empty the stairway. I had been carrying the boys up into that little room, I don't know whether they were dead but they were injured; great crying done, and they were lying down. I looked there about twenty minutes and I

> got decided, I went and looked for my own children and wife. I found them. I stood with them and got them water.
>
> [When trying to pull bodies from the stairway] it was all filled up . . . They [bodies] were all laying against each others back, crushed, and just as soon as you would take them away some would fall down and some would get stuck, just pick them away from them. Most of those that I carried were children.[5]

Mrs. Anna Wuolukka, who was an organizer of the Christmas party, recalled that the Women's Auxiliary of the Western Federation of Miners union did not buy candles for the festivities in the hall because they were "afraid the children would catch fire." During the panic, Anna yelled to people that there was no fire, but this did not stem the tide of the mass heading toward the stairway. As the dead piled up, she tended to a number of children and tried to revive others that were likely already dead:

> I hollered to the people to come back that there was no fire, and they were all rushing, I could not say no more. After that my little girl come and said, "Ma, everybody is going out the window and there's a fire here" . . . saw they were carrying the dead, but then I did not know what they were doing, and felt those that were dead and cold and tried to carry them and try to make them come to as much as I could.[6]

John Antilla was arriving at the hall just as the panic was occurring. He was unable to get up the stairs of the Italian Hall as the rush of people began to tumble, fall, and clog on the stairway. Antilla remembered, "My intentions were of entering but it was impossible; and did not see any fire and did not see any smoke. Several inside, a couple men I noticed at that time were trying to quiet the people, hollering there was no fire. The [bottom] door was wide open . . . Of course the children and grown-ups were all screaming at the time."[7]

One of those on the bottom of the pile was the previously introduced Andrew Saari. Andrew rushed toward the door that led from the hall to the stairway, keeping his two boys in front of him as the mass of people flowed toward the flight of stairs. Andrew remarked that he tried to keep his boys "in front of me trying to keep them back so nobody would step on them." Andrew and his boys made it to the stairs, but were then engulfed in the mass of people flowing down the steps. Eventually as people fell in the stairwell, body piled on body, and Andrew was swallowed up in the heap of bodies at the bottom of the stairwell. Andrew stated that he made it about six feet away from the door at the bottom of the stairs. "There was a clear place by the door. I was laying with the rest of the people." He remembered that the mass of people "pushed me down. I hollered as long as I could but I fell down and stepped over the two boys." He had to wait for people to be taken from the top of the pile and then some men plucked him from the mass. He lamented about his boys: "One of my boys dead. I thought they would be both dead; but when they were taken up one was living."[8]

Oscar Hietalahti used restraint and sat in the hall during the rush while looking for an alternate way to get out of the hall. He attempted to open a window to get his wife and children out, but when he was unable to open a window, he waited for about a half hour and then headed toward the stairway. At the top of the stairway, Oscar saw a man with a white button, which he described as a Citizens' Alliance button. The Citizens' Alliance was a pro–mining company group formed to thwart the organizational efforts of the Western Federation of Miners' union. Oscar described witnessing the careless, heinous handling of Italian Hall fatalities:

> [I] saw a man with a blue coat and an Alliance button, had the child under his arms and he placed his hands upon the child's neck and threw the child on the floor. I can't say whether he was alive or not, but he hung like it from his [the man's] arms. [The man] just came up through the doorway and threw him in. When my wife and I came they came in and threw a man the same way on the floor. They carried him by the neck, that's around the throat.[9]

The events of Italian Hall did not happen in a vacuum; there was a context in which this tragedy took place. The framework in which the Italian Hall disaster occurred consisted of many significant factors, but one important aspect was the number of Finnish immigrant families attending a Christmas party at the *Italian* Hall. The woeful tally of the dead confirms that there were a large number of "Finns" at Italian Hall. Of the estimated seventy-three to seventy-nine dead, fifty or so were of Finnish ethnicity.[10] At a time when ethnic groups tended to segregate from one another, why were there so many "Finns" at the Italian Hall? Interlocked with the tragic events of Italian Hall and the surge of proletarian consciousness that led to the 1913–14 Michigan Copper Miners' Strike was the radicalization of Finnish immigrant workers in Michigan's Keweenaw Peninsula. This story of an immigrant challenge to the historic socioeconomic order is one important contextual piece in understanding the heightened tensions between labor and capital in Michigan's Copper Country and early twentieth-century America.

For the Copper Country's working class, socioeconomic problems in the Keweenaw Peninsula from the mid-1870s to the first decade of the twentieth century were much like the legendary seasonal weather in Michigan's tempestuous Upper Peninsula. Summer is often sublime—warm days and cool, restful nights. However, fall brings many changes. The nights grow frigid, the winds shift to the north, sleet and early snow pelt the landscape, and the leaves on the deciduous trees flare into brilliant colors only to plummet to the ground, brown, and decay. These leaves become old news, and the legendary snows of a Keweenaw winter cover these symbols of rot and decay. The decomposing leaves lie in a state of suspended animation under heavy layers of snow, unseen for months. As snowstorms and lake-effect snow add layers of white to the landscape, in urban areas the byproducts of industry and development dirty each new layer of snow; but in a Keweenaw winter, there is always another snow that brings a fresh, pure cover of white. Until spring erupts, fast and furious. In cities built on copper dollars, the snows melt, revealing dirty layer after dirty layer; the natural setting struggles back to life; small streams turn into swollen torrents of melt water; and the rotting leaves, forgotten for the winter, are uncovered—emitting a smell of decay. This cycle repeats itself year after year.

This, in a symbolic sense, was proletarian life on the Keweenaw in the late nineteenth and early twentieth centuries; shifting seasons of satisfaction and discontent changed like the weather, but the problems, while for a time covered, never went away. There always seemed to be a fresh layer of white snow to coat the sullied, rotting labor and social problems of yesterday. This was so until a group of immigrants came and waged a definitive challenge to the alternating proletarian seasons. The "Finns" were not the first or lone voices in discontent—help from other ethnic groups fortified the challenge to the Copper Country bosses—but Finns in leadership roles, and in large rank-and-file numbers ardently joined the cause to create what they believed was a more equal, just, and democratic industrial society in the Copper Country. Finnish immigrants were determined to alter the course of Keweenaw labor and social relations and used direct action to confront the underlying problems of the copper-mining industry in Michigan, forcing the forgotten leaves of the Michigan's copper workers' discontent to be uncovered, altering (for a time) a socioeconomic environment that many once thought was as unchangeable as the changing seasons.

The Finnish immigrant collision with the unfamiliar industrial setting of Michigan's Copper Country soured many "Finns" to the American experience. The cultural and social manifestation of this discontent, occurring between 1885 and 1914, was a unique Finnish immigrant movement rooted in proletarian ideology and direct action. This movement was a multifaceted response by a seemingly clannish group of immigrants to the perceived inequality and lopsided distribution of Copper Country prosperity. This response was in essence an answer to an unspoken challenge issued by the Copper Country's mining oligarchy to Finnish immigrants, provoking them to struggle for the betterment of their lives in America. In a sense, the socioeconomic conditions in the Copper Country, ostensibly dominated by the copper-mining companies and the men who controlled them, were a powder keg waiting for a match that would explode the exploitive living, working, and wage conditions. The Finnish immigrant proletarians accepted this tacit challenge from the mining companies, facing great odds. Resistance to the Finnish immigrant proletarians' actions came fast and furious from the mining companies, and at times even from within their own organizations as the movement struggled with creating a focused direction, recognizing a shared guiding ideology and utilizing agreed-upon strategy and tactics.

In accepting this challenge, the upstart Copper Country Finnish immigrants often stumbled and stammered in awkward directions, but seldom wavered in their bold attempt to shape their lives into what they perceived to be a more just and equal existence. Over time, however, the Finnish immigrants' response became highly organized. The foundations for this organization began at the start of the twentieth century, when Finnish immigrants were searching for a direction and effective leadership in their rebuke of Copper Country capitalism. This changed when a talented cadre of organizers known as the "Apostles of Socialism" energized a primed proletarian base. Comprised mostly of unskilled laborers, this base grew in meteoric fashion—growing so fast that within a decade the Finnish immigrant socialist-unionists were ready to take a leading role in a major assault on the hegemony of powerful, established mining companies in the Copper Country.

Before 1910, the Finnish immigrant socialist and unionist groups were a somewhat rag-tag mixture of anarchists, Marxists, social democrats, Christian socialists, utopian theorists, and temperance crusaders. Finnish immigrant socialist and unionist groups were an eclectic bunch, and the term "Finnish immigrant socialist-unionist" best demonstrates the breadth of ideology included within the movement at this time. Within this Finnish immigrant movement, there was a dual affiliation with complementary political and labor union principles, which provided the Finnish immigrant a voice in an unfamiliar land. Many of the Finnish immigrants working in the Copper Country mines were not United States citizens. Thus, they could not vote in federal, state, or local elections, but they certainly could vote in their socialist local or union. The Western Federation of Miners, the union of choice for some Finnish immigrant mineworkers, was supported by the Socialist Party of America, so for many Finnish immigrant socialist-unionists, the dual political-labor union grouping was an affirmative collaboration that gave disenfranchised people a well-deserved voice in a new land.

The mining companies were generally the only game in the Copper Country, and the copper "bosses," as many Copper Country workers knew them, seemed to sit on the assets of a one-industry area. They owned much of the land, machinery, houses, and in some cases local governments, either tacitly or overtly. The Copper Country mine owners had such a hold on the region, they were able to dictate what ethnic groups were allowed work and when. "Big" Jim MacNaughton, general manager of the mighty Calumet and Hecla Mining Company, after suspecting Finnish immigrant workers of labor agitation once wrote the commissioner of immigration at Ellis Island, "We [Calumet and Hecla] do not want Finlanders."[11] In some cases and in many places, the leaders of the Copper Country mining companies wielded absolute power absolutely—hiring and firing whom they wanted, cutting wages as they saw fit, and doling out housing and benefits as they pleased.[12]

Finnish immigrant socialist-unionists in the Copper Country responded to this impact of Copper Country capital by organizing institutions that directly challenged the hegemony, paternalism, and oligarchy of the copper companies in the region. Finnish immigrants were familiar with social subservience to a ruling class from experiences in the czarist-controlled Grand Duchy of Finland. While the Copper Country mine owners' hegemony was different from czarist rule in Finland, it was likely enough of a prompting stimulus to precipitate conflict between socialist-unionist Finnish immigrants and the copper industry's monopoly capital.[13]

Although the majority of Finnish immigrants to the Copper Country were from the northern and western provinces of Finland and unfamiliar with the ways of industrial work and exploitation, there was a cadre of Finnish immigrant socialists who came to the United States possibly prepared for and looking to fight. These early activists and organizers recruited many disaffected and disenfranchised Finnish immigrant laborers into the socialist-unionist movement through Finnish immigrant organizations in America. In 1904, this grassroots organizational effort chose Hancock, Michigan, as a venue to begin a localized challenge to the dangerous, unsanitary, and economically dissonant conditions in the Copper Country mines. These Finnish immigrant socialist-unionists were working to improve "bread-and-butter issues," such as laboring conditions and pay, as well as attempting to transform the Copper Country's social structure by curtailing the hegemony of the "copper bosses."

The first target of the organized Copper Country Finnish immigrant socialist-unionists was the Quincy Mining Company in Hancock, which represented the physical manifestation of a paternalistic hierarchy that watched over the citizens of Hancock from a vigilant perch high atop Quincy Hill. As the Finnish immigrant socialist-unionist movement flourished, the challenge to monopoly capital expanded to other areas of the Copper Country, culminating in the at-times bloody 1913–14 Copper Country Strike. Over the course of a decade, these primed Finnish immigrant proletarians envisioned and implemented a well-organized challenge to Copper Country mine owners, but in the end, the power of the movement disintegrated under the weight of internal ideological disputes regarding the proper course of action against monopoly capital.

In this book, we will examine the Finnish immigrant challenge to Copper Country capitalism; we will frame this challenge as a response to social, economic, and working conditions in the copper mines and community environs of the Keweenaw Peninsula. While the focus of this book is to examine the challenge and response to Copper Country capitalists using the Finnish immigrant socialist-unionists' written record and material culture, two significant subthemes emerge as well. These are: maintenance of Finnish ethnic identity while participating in the broader American labor-political movement, and fractioning within Finnish immigrant cultural organizations.

Analyzing the maintenance of ethnic identity while participating in a broader American social movement is important because Finnish immigrants have often been characterized as clannish; but the examination of Finnish immigrant socialist-unionists in Hancock shows that ethnic identity took a back seat to working-class solidarity during confrontation with American capitalism. The second subtheme, fractioning within the Finnish immigrant socialist-unionist movement, illustrates the division and decline that terminally fractured working-class solidarity in the Finnish immigrant labor-political movement circa 1914. Analysis of this demise is significant when recounting the capabilities and vulnerabilities of immigrant labor and political organizations in the early twentieth century.

While previous works in Finnish American social and labor history were the first of their kind and thus groundbreaking additions to the greater understanding of ethnic, labor, and social history, none have ever overtly examined the course of the Finnish immigrants' socialist-unionist movement in Michigan, as we will through the use of material culture (leftover physical things) as a tool of analysis. Why do this? According to Thomas J. Schlereth, material culture's rubric "is increasingly being used as the most appropriate generic name describing the research, writing, teaching and publishing done by individuals who interpret past human activity largely, although not exclusively, through extant physical evidence."[14]

We will use material culture to expand the Finnish immigrants' archival record and extend the "reach" of historical comprehension. The use of material culture as a companion to the New Social History is a natural combination that effectively fills out the historic record for groups that left little to no documentary record, or communicated in a language foreign to English-speaking historians. Artifacts or tangible objects can work in combination with a group's historical records to illuminate untold elements of the group's history that create a "more democratic, populist, even proletarian history."[15] This combination of material culture with social history is perhaps most important to groups whose historical voice has been disenfranchised, oppressed, and/or suppressed. As Schlereth wrote:

> Both social history and material culture studies challenge the older view of history as past politics, both have sought to demonstrate the great diversity of the American people and their lifestyles, and both have been anxious to expand (some would say explode) the traditional boundaries of American historical scholarship and thereby actually redefine what constitutes American history.[16]

Specifically in this book, we are using the written record and the findings of material culture as our guiding historical "tools"; we will incorporate the analysis of physical things into the historical narrative in an examination of socialist-unionist Finnish immigrants' localized challenge to the Copper Country oligarchy. The buildings, publications, printing presses, ephemera, and machinery of the Finnish immigrant socialist-unionist movement relate more than the historical record could on its own. These things give a more complete, expanded, and unique contextual glimpse into a very significant time in the Copper Country's captivating history.

CHAPTER 1

Finnish Immigration and Settlement in a Hancock, Michigan, Neighborhood

FINNISH IMMIGRANT SOCIALIST-UNIONISTS FOUND LIFE IN MICHIGAN'S Copper Country much like the existence they had left in Finland, but laced with expensive machinery, sometimes pitiful working conditions, and a distinct out-group status. In this chapter, we will examine an author-defined historic neighborhood in Hancock, Michigan, circa 1910. In doing so, we will establish Finnish immigrants in their historic context concerning their unique temporal and spatial framework—affording a "snapshot in time" quality that establishes the period social and cultural demographics of likely people Finnish immigrant socialist-unionists sought to convert into class-conscious workers in the Copper Country between 1904 and 1914.

Emigration from Finland

Between the late 1880s and the early 1900s, the cultural control of czarist Russia, conscription into the Russian army, the influence of Finland's upper class, and the Finnish national church created a paternalistic hierarchy that

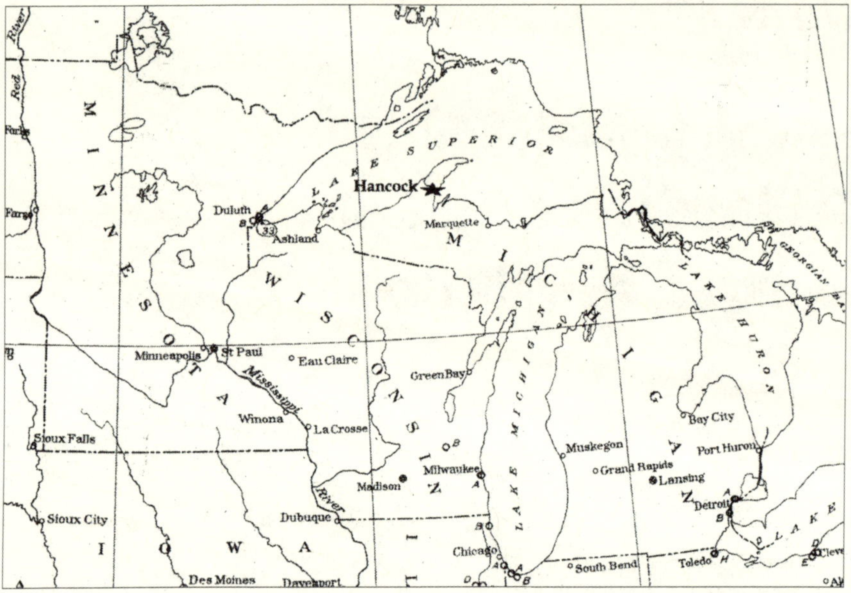

The Upper Great Lakes Region. Map showing Hancock in relation to other urban areas.
(United States Geological Survey, 1915.)

many Finnish proletarians despised. In addition to social tribulations, Finland was also facing periodic agricultural famines that forced many into a search for more fertile environs. In the mind of many Finns, emigration to America was an answer to socioeconomic problems in Finland. The largest numbers of Finnish emigrants came from Finland's western and northern provinces. These emigrants from the west and north were largely farmers, cottagers, and tenant croppers who were poor, disenfranchised, but semiliterate country people. A lesser segment of Finnish emigrants came from Finland's southern urban centers. These emigrants were tradesmen, factory workers, and intellectuals who were wageworkers. Many of these southern wageworkers were ideologically at odds with the autocratic, imperialist rule of the Russian czar, who controlled Finland as a grand duchy of the Russian Empire until 1917.[1]

The common perception in Finnish American labor history is that many leaders, as well as rank-and-filers, of the early Finnish American labor-political movement came from southern, urban-industrialized areas of Finland in 1905 or thereafter. This year, 1905, is significant because it featured an event that was

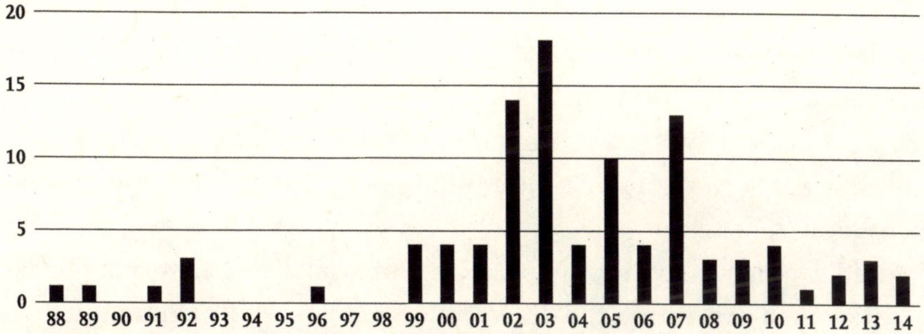

Immigration Years of Finnish Labor-Political Leaders, 1888–1914. This diagram shows that the highest years of immigration for Finnish immigrant labor leaders to the United States or Canada came before the 1905 General Strike or Viapori Rebellion. (Gary Kaunonen.)

the climax of a period of social upheaval in Finland. The 1905 General Strike in Finland and the Viapori (Sveaborg) Rebellion, which occurred the following year, cast a long shadow in radicalizing segments of southern Finland's population. The General Strike of 1905, a weeklong affair, saw Social Democrats in Tampere issue a "Red Declaration," while Red Guards in Helsinki attempted to shut down Stockmann's, one of Finland's largest department stores. The Viapori Rebellion, in 1906, saw proletarian Russian soldiers (including ethnic Finns in the Russian Army) and the Finnish Red Guard attempt to overthrow the Russian czarist government at Sveaborg Castle. This attempt at revolution failed, but set an ideological model for proletarian-minded, southern Finnish citizens.[2]

While much of the revolutionary sentiment seemed to be coming from the south of Finland, Elis Sulkanen's *Amerikan Suomalaisen Työväenliikkeen Historia* indicates that leaders of the Finnish immigrant socialist-unionist movement in America came more from the largely agricultural, nonindustrialized western, northern, and central provinces than from the southern, urban centers. From biographies in Sulkanen's work, of the ninety-one leaders (with birthplaces I was able to identify in Finland) in the Finnish American socialist-unionist movement, fifty-one, or 56 percent, of the leaders came from places in the western, northern, and central regions of Finland. Of this hinterland, thirty-four came from the western and northern provinces of Vaasa and Oulu. Seventeen came from the central/eastern provinces. The balance of the Finnish American labor-political movement's leaders, forty, or roughly 44 percent, came from southern areas, though not necessarily urban or industrial. Whether these people came from the western, northern, or central provinces of Finland as believers in the movement or found this ideology in America is not always clear, but in some cases, people moved from the agricultural hinterland to Finnish cities such as Helsinki, Hämeenlinna, or Tampere prior to making their way to America.[3]

Additionally, it is apparent from Sulkanen's biographies that two years in the early twentieth century saw the largest number of Finnish American socialist-unionist leaders immigrate from Finland, but these two years were not 1905 and 1906. Of the one hundred identified dates of immigration for leaders in the movement from 1888 to 1914, a majority (sixty-four) came within the time span of six years, 1902 through 1907. Of these six years, 1903 (eighteen) and 1902 (fourteen) saw the largest number of immigrant leaders of the Finnish American socialist-unionist movement make their way to America. The years 1907 (thirteen) and then 1905 (eleven) were the next most registered years of immigration from Finland for these labor and political leaders; the years 1904 and 1906 saw only four (each year) of the Finnish immigrant labor-political movement's leaders venture to America.[4] Therefore, characterizing the Finnish immigrant leaders of the Finnish American labor-political movement as having primarily come from the southern, urban centers of Finland during and after 1905 is false. It is more accurate to typify the Finnish immigrant socialist-unionist leaders, and perhaps extrapolate that to the general Finnish immigrant labor-political movement's members as well, by a variety of geographic, occupational, and temporal variables.

As further evidence of the radical movement's permeation of agricultural areas in Finland, Fred Torma, an immigrant to the United States in 1905, stated that he was familiar with socialism from experiences on his father's farm in Parkano parish in the province of Turku-Pori:

> At that time even the rural areas began getting speakers of the socialist thought and theory. We had a big workroom at home . . . Father rented it out—I don't know if he charged any rent actually—but he gave it to those speakers and other travelers, wandering speakers and performers. Maybe he received a markka each time. I wound up being a speaker's assistant there—when they

> wanted a glass of water or something like that . . . It was Marxist doctrine. The original. They kept coming there and I was a helper. My father received a certain education there also.[5]

Finnish Immigration to America and Houghton County, Michigan

To many outsiders, the Finns immigrating to America seemed to share a predisposition toward social and cultural like-mindedness that bonded them together. Finnish immigrants tended to live in the same area with other Finns, get involved in the same occupations as other Finns, and join the same civic, political, and cultural organizations as other Finns. As Finnish American historian Peter Kivisto wrote:

> Finns occupied the status of a definite 'out-group' even though they are White Protestant. They were depicted as "Jack-pine Savages," Mongolians (in 1907, an attempt was made to deny them citizenship by invoking existing anti-Oriental legislation), and violence prone revolutionaries.[6]

Houghton County in Michigan's Upper Peninsula beckoned many of these immigrant Finns. Beginning in the mid-1860s, Finnish immigrants began to settle in Houghton County. These early immigrants did not come in large numbers, nor were they social reformers, but they paved the road into the Copper Country for future waves of Finnish immigrants. Clemens Niemi, a Finnish American historian, wrote: "It was not until about 1861 that we might say the actual immigration from Finland to have begun. At this time, according to the old settlers, a group of Finns from Sweden and Norway where they had been engaged in mining and fishing arrived in Houghton County. These pathfinders came from northern Finland originally and they were followed by friends and relatives."[7] As successive waves of Finnish immigrants arrived in Houghton County starting around the mid-1880s, many newly arrived Finnish immigrants followed their predecessor compatriots into the Lake Superior copper mines. The first Finnish immigrants to arrive in Houghton County in the 1860s were familiar with mining from work in northern Sweden and Norway. As more Finnish immigrants arrived from Finland proper, the level of skill and knowledge in the extractive industries dramatically decreased with the incoming Finnish immigrant population.[8]

The Finnish immigrants streaming into Copper Country industry were a sort of tabula rasa. Finland in the late nineteenth century had little in the way of natural resources besides the tree and accompanying log harvests. Finnish immigrants were unfamiliar with the ways of industrial work, not to mention the intricacies of the mining industry. Many Finnish immigrants in America were receptive to agriculture, but had no land to farm or had to hack some type of farmland out of the dense Upper Peninsula forest. Finnish immigrants found that if they were to make a living in Houghton County, it would first have to be in an unfamiliar industrial world as unskilled labor in copper mines. At the very least, they would have to work the mines long enough to save money for farm ownership.

The majority of Finnish immigrants settled in the upper midwestern states of Michigan, northern Wisconsin, and Minnesota. Some immigrants worked for a while in America and then returned to Finland, but by 1920 there were some 150,000 foreign-born Finns in America. Michigan alone had 30,100, or roughly 20 percent of the foreign-born Finnish population in America.[9] Finnish immigrants inundated Houghton County, Michigan, copper mines and thus Houghton County's municipal areas. According to the 13th Census of the United States, conducted in 1910, foreign-born Finns comprised 11,536 of Houghton County's 88,098 residents. The next largest ethnic populations were the English (Cornish), Italians, and French Canadians.[10] The mass immigration of non-Anglo-Saxon workers into Houghton County precipitated a change in the workforce, especially at larger copper mines such as the Quincy. In the early days, Cornish, Irish, Germans, and French Canadians largely made up most of the company's workforce. In 1885, this began to change as Finns, Italians, "Austrians" (persons from the Austro-Hungarian Empire), and Eastern Europeans began to take unskilled jobs.[11]

The deluge of a cheap labor pool to area copper mines between 1885 and 1900 came at an especially fortuitous time for the Quincy Mining Company. Using copper production in tons as an indicator of success, Quincy was expanding and reaping the benefits of an overall boom during the late nineteenth century. Between 1885 and 1901, Quincy's production of copper rose from 2,924 tons in 1885 to 10,270 tons in 1901. The years of 1901 to 1910 found copper production reaching unprecedented levels, staying at between 8,000 and 11,000 tons.[12]

The Quincy Mining Company was running well in the black and desperately needed to increase its labor force. Of the Quincy Mining Company's new employees between 1890 and 1909, Finnish immigrant workers accounted for nearly half of all new hires. Between 1890 and 1899, there were 55 foreign-born Finns working at the Quincy Mining Company; that number jumped dramatically to 256 foreign-born Finns and 21 first-generation Americans working at the Quincy between 1900 and 1909. This brought Quincy Mining Company's two-decade total to 332 Finns employed between 1890 and 1909. This number made Finns the largest ethnic group working at Quincy, surpassing the size of any other ethnic group by three times.[13]

Finnish Immigrants Settle in Hancock, Michigan

The Quincy Mining Company needed a place to put all these new workers. While the company constructed houses for its workers at locations close to the industrial core, these houses were for preferred employees of favored ethnicities and family men; in general, neither of these two categories included many Finns.[14] In anticipation of adding to its workforce and needing a place to put workers, Quincy platted an addition to the Village of Hancock on June 6, 1900.[15] The newly coined Quincy Hillside Addition (QHA) was previously an unplatted area north of and adjacent to the Village of Hancock, set on a steeply pitched hillside. This hillside border between Quincy's industrial mining core and the Village of Hancock was a haphazard collection of houses, barns, and hovels along winding dirt lanes. This slapdash, ramshackle landscape found its occupants labeled as members in a neighborhood mockingly known as "Shantytown."[16]

The Village of Hancock was experiencing a rapid growth of its own between 1880 and 1910. In a census taken for local businessman and politician A. P. Ruppe, G. Walton Smith tallied the booming Hancock population. In 1880,

Hancock had 1,783 residents; that number declined to 1,772 in 1894, but rose meteorically to 4,050 by 1900 and doubled to 8,981 in 1910. Hancock was fast becoming the commercial and residential center of the Portage Lake Copper District, due to the increased production of copper at the Quincy Mining Company.[17]

Hancock collected an abundance of Finnish immigrants, due to the large number of unskilled jobs at the booming Quincy Mine. As mentioned earlier, by 1910 Quincy employed nearly three times more Finnish immigrants than any other nationality. Hancock's streets and institutions took on a Finnish flair, accommodating the swell of Finnish immigrants to the area. The 1913 Hancock School census confirmed the large Finnish immigrant population in the city. In 1913, there were 546 Finnish children enrolled in Hancock schools. These 546 Finnish students represented an ethnic majority of 38.5 percent of the overall children enrolled in Hancock schools.[18]

The preceding summary of QHA and the Village of Hancock sets the background for a quantitative and qualitative study of the influence of Finnish immigrants in an author-specified Hancock neighborhood. For identification purposes, this neighborhood will be referred to as the Finnish Transitional Neighborhood (FTN). The remainder of this chapter will examine Finnish immigrant settlement in the FTN surrounding Block B of the QHA, using 1910 through 1914 as a temporal period of significance.

A demographic study of the FTN is important because it establishes the Finnish immigrant experience spatially and temporally within the Copper Country during the early twentieth century. As portrayed statistically in this chapter, Finnish immigrants were flooding into the Copper Country during the late nineteenth and early twentieth centuries. Most of these Finnish immigrants were unfamiliar with Copper Country industry, its working conditions, management policies, and landscape. Through efforts of organizational societies, Finnish immigrants created a response to cope with Copper Country industry and oligarchy. Diverse ideological segments formed diverse responses to tangible and intangible conditions of the Copper Country social milieu (this will be examined in chapter 2), but all organizational societies sought to find a voice and sense of being within this industrial setting. An examination of a specific Finnish immigrant neighborhood places the immigrants' individual, social, and material surroundings in a context that illustrates the historic industrial backdrop in which Hancock's socialist-unionist Finns operated.

The period of examination for the FTN, 1910–1914, coincides with the building of the Kansankoti (Peoples' Home) Hall as a meeting place. The Kansankoti housed a Finnish immigrant socialist-unionist group that directly challenged the management policies of Copper Country capitalists. Pursuant to the construction of the Kansankoti Hall, the Työmies Publishing Company, a socialist-unionist printing enterprise, moved its presses and offices to previous structures in Block B of the FTN. I argue that Block B and its Finnish socialist-unionist cultural organizations, located within the FTN, became the center of the Finnish immigrant socialist-unionist activity in Hancock, and eventually the Copper Country, because of demographic characteristics of the FTN—so let us explore those characteristics in detail.

The Finnish Transitional Neighborhood

Within the boundaries of the FTN, there were 351 total residents, according to a 1912 Polk's Houghton County Directory. Of these inhabitants, 160 were Finnish,[19] meaning that close to half the neighborhood's population was of Finnish ethnicity. The next largest ethnicity in the FTN were the Irish—most likely due to the location of the St. Patrick's Roman Catholic Church, Convent, and School at 233 Quincy Street and the Ancient Order of Hibernia at 326 Quincy. Germans were the next most common ethnicity, with their cultural center, the Germania Hall, located at 309–313 Quincy Street.[20]

Indicative of the trend of Finnish immigrants from rural regions settling in the FTN were Maria and Laina Ollila. Maria and Laina came from Kempele parish in Oulu province. Maria was a farmer's wife and Laina her daughter. In Kempele, Maria was a respected sewing teacher, using her domestic skills as a way to supplement her family's farming income.[21] Maria and Laina made the voyage in 1900, when Laina was just fifteen years old. Mother and daughter traveled on the same passport from a port in Helsinki to Ellis Island. They traveled on the passenger ship *Astraea* from Helsinki to Liverpool and took a ship of the White Star Line from England to America. Laina's ticket to the United States cost $59.00 (U.S. currency), enough to earn her a place in crowded steerage's hold.[22] The trip across the Atlantic was probably harrowing, but Maria and Laina were likely looking to improve their lot in life, and looking to do so with the prospects offered in America. Maria and Laina settled in Hancock, just inside the boundaries of the FTN. Maria ran a boarding house at 237 Wright Street in Block H of the Quincy Hillside Addition. Laina helped her mother in the house, and the two women acted as hosts to what was likely a testosterone-infused collection of immigrant mine laborers who spoke Finnish.

While operating a boarding house in Hancock was a popular type of "cottage industry," there were an additional 120 conventional businesses in the FTN. Thirty-seven of these businesses were combination businesses/dwellings with commercial space downstairs and residential space upstairs.[23] Thirty percent of these businesses were Finnish-run businesses. Saloons were the most numerous Finnish businesses, with eleven Finnish-run saloons operating in the FTN. There were also three major hotels in the FTN. They all had Finnish proprietors. The inns were the International Hotel, the Northwestern Hotel, and the Hotel Salo.[24] The Northwestern Hotel building also housed the offices of the Finnish Mutual Life Insurance Agency.[25]

Finnish ownership of land, and thus commercial buildings and dwellings, was disproportionately small compared to the size of its ethnic population in the FTN. While almost 50 percent of the FTN's population was Finnish in 1912, these Finns owned only 14 percent of the land parcels within the neighborhood by 1914.[26] The 1914 percentage of ownership was up from 1909, when Finns owned 13 percent of land parcels in the neighborhood. The disparity between Finnish ethnic population and land ownership in the FTN meant that while there were many Finns in this spatial area, they were likely poor and probably itinerant wageworkers. The Finns in the FTN were in all likelihood mine laborers who did not own much besides their labor. Prominent Hancock names like Funkey, Ryan, Scott, Kauth, Gartner, Ruppe, and Finn (Irish ethnicity) dominated the tax records for the FTN. Of all property owners in the FTN, the German-owned Bosch Brewing Company held the most property titles, with six.[27]

Block B, Lot 1: An Emerging Immigrants' Proletarian Stronghold

There was one exception to minority Finnish ownership of property in the FTN: it was Block B of the QHA.[28] Ownership of lots and buildings on Block B in 1909 was far more representative of the Finnish population that lived in the FTN. Finns owned six lots and non-Finns owned six lots.[29] By 1909, the Kansankoti Real Estate Company, a socialist-unionist affiliated group, owned the largest lot in Block B, holding title over the irregularly shaped Lot 1. The Quincy Mining Company originally sold the lot to the Schulte Estate after the creation of the QHA. The Kansankoti Real Estate Company bought the lot in 1907 or 1908 after associating on September 16, 1907, with capital stock amounting to $15,000 for the purpose of "acquiring, holding, leasing, selling and buying real estate and for the erection of building there on."[30] The significance of this incorporation was that socialist-unionist Finns in the Copper Country now had the ability to finance land acquisition and major construction efforts.

Purchasing land in Block B positioned the Kansankoti Real Estate Company and their publishing association counterpart, the Työmies Publishing Company, as a pivot between the commercial center of Hancock and the burgeoning working-class residential areas of Quincy's hillside.[31] This brought the socialist and labor movement precariously close to Quincy's industrial core—and on former Quincy Mining Company property, no less. The positioning of the Kansankoti Hall and Työmies Publishing Company's buildings in Quincy's "front yard" may have been a momentary lapse of corporate reason by the mining company, but there are indications that Quincy knew full well who the Finnish socialist-unionists were and what they represented. In spite of this, the Quincy Mining Company sold an additional lot in Block B to a Finnish immigrant socialist-unionist local known as the *Jousi Seura* (Bow Society), an organization that had strong ties with the Kansankoti Company's real estate enterprise.[32]

In an attempt to monitor events in the FTN in the wake of labor advocacy in Hancock, Quincy attempted to mitigate contingencies created by class-conscious Finnish immigrants with information from labor spies:

No. 5 reports on Friday, August 17, 1906:

> This evening I visited Wm. Antilla's saloon on Tezcuco St. There were 12 or 14 miners in there talking and drinking. They spoke of the strike and the result, and general satisfaction with the settlement seemed to prevail. A number were talking in a foreign tongue which I could not understand but it seemed to be good natured and not excited.[33]

September 4, 1906:

> On August 31st the operative had conversation with two of the trammers, who spoke about meetings in Funkey's hall during the strike. Operative asked them if that was where the Finns met and had their meetings in their own language, to which they replied that it was where they all met together and conducted meetings in the English language. Operative remarked that he thought they had separate meetings in different places, to which they replied that they did also have separate meetings.[34]

No. 5 reports that on September 7, 1906:

> I met different crowds in the saloons on Franklin and Tezcuco Streets . . . when on the street the miners usually congregate on the corner of Quincy and Tezcuco Streets.[35]
>
> On September 14th the operative spent the day visiting various places around town, among them the saloons at 203 Franklin street, 204 Franklin street, 228 Quincy street, 414 Tezcuco street and the one conducted by Jacob Kyltonen.[36]

The 1906 reports from Quincy's labor spies indicate that proletarian sentiment was on the rise at this time within Hancock's Finnish immigrant community. Theorizing that the company sent labor spies into the FTN because it had reason to be concerned with Jousi activity, a person might wonder why the Quincy Mining Company sold land to a group it perceivably knew to be at loggerheads with capitalism. Perhaps Quincy's management thought it had firm control of company operations on its rocky citadel high atop Hancock, using the reliable information from labor spies. Maybe Quincy just wanted to get rid of land in Hancock, perhaps Quincy believed in a hands-off approach regarding Hancock's administration, or maybe they simply underestimated the competency and vigor of Finnish immigrant socialist-unionists. Regardless of the rationale, Hancock was growing in ways that Quincy management could not fathom. The Finnish socialist-unionists, and thus the labor movement, were making a nice little nest for themselves within greater Hancock.

Of the buildings erected on Block B, the Kansankoti Hall–Työmies Publishing Company building on Lot 1, 201–203 Franklin Street, was the most noteworthy in size and consequence. A boarding house existed on the site as early as 1893. By 1900, a more substantial structure existed on-site that housed two saloons.[37] In 1907, Alexander Nieminen (a Finnish immigrant) operated a grocery store at the 203 address, and a saloon operated at the 201 address.[38] In 1910, the structural dynamics of Block B changed drastically. The Nieminen grocery building, which in 1910 had become home of the socialist-unionist Finnish language newspaper *Työmies*, received a major update as the Kansankoti Hall was grafted to the back of the grocery building. The addition of the Kansankoti Hall dwarfed the original building, as the spacious interior of the hall had to have room for a balcony, stage, and scenery area to accommodate the needs of theatrical productions, dances, gymnastics events, and concerts.[39]

The importance of melding the Kansankoti Hall with the Työmies Publishing Company building cannot be understated. The grand edifice was a center for organization, a consolidation of like-minded organizational components, and a showpiece for the Finnish immigrants' socialist-unionist movement. The Kansankoti Hall–Työmies Publishing Company complex was a significant symbol of concerted challenge to Copper Country oligarchy. The complex stood as a representative icon; it was a response to Copper Country monopoly capital, literally stationed in the shadows of Quincy Mining Company's hilltop industrial structures and million-dollar machinery.

In the lot directly adjacent to the newly constructed and refurbished Kansankoti Hall–Työmies Publishing Company structure, Työmies rented a building belonging to Henry Coughlin, owner of several lots and buildings in Hancock.[40] This building at 207 Franklin Street would eventually house the Työmies Publishing Company's offices, a bookstore, and small-job printing equipment. The Kansankoti Hall–Työmies Publishing Company venture probably rented the Coughlin building around the same time they moved to 201–203 Franklin Street in 1910, thus creating a socialist-unionist "campus" that spanned two lots and three addresses comprising more than 18,000 square feet of built space.[41] After the addition of the Kansankoti-Työmies campus in 1910, the FTN's landscape was visually dominated by the large hall and the bustle of the Finnish immigrant press.

Demographic Characteristics of the Finnish Transitional Neighborhood

The FTN contained a base of Finnish cultural organizations well before the consolidation of buildings on the Kansankoti-Työmies campus. While it is apparent that the Kansankoti-Työmies campus was a socialist-unionist base, by 1909 the Hancock Copper Miner's Union (having many Finnish immigrant members), the *Pohjantähti* (North Star) Temperance Society, and the Jousi Society were all operating within the FTN.[42] While the presses of the Työmies Publishing Company were located in the FTN, its staff was not as only six of the publishing company's thirty-five employees lived within the FTN boundaries.[43] This type of arrangement in which workers with more permanent employment lived outside of the FTN was indicative of the greater trend of non-itinerant workers and business owners not living in the FTN. Seventy-nine percent of business owners in the FTN lived outside the neighborhood boundaries. So, who did live in the FTN? The FTN was a transitional working-class neighborhood that catered to short-term residency (of the FTN's 351 persons 127 were living in boarding houses or rooming in hotels) and industrial wageworkers.[44]

This was a neighborhood where a person could roll into Hancock and flop at a hotel or boarding house while looking for work and more permanent digs. The Northwestern Hotel, the International Hotel, the Heikkila Poikatalo (Heikkila Boys House), the Hotel Salo, and the Scott Hotel were the choice of many "short timers" who boarded and worked in this transitional-living community. A line ad in the 1912 Polk's Directory best illustrates the transitional nature of the FTN. A laundry business located at 325 Quincy Street, operated by Albert B. Scott, advertised that his laundry was the "Only first class laundry in the city" and further boasted "Transient Work a Specialty." Unlike most of the neighborhood's business owners, Scott lived in the same building where he worked. Many buildings with first-floor businesses had apartments in upper floors where employees or boarders could lay their head on a pillow after a long day or night of work.[45]

Spatially, the FTN was an intermediary between strictly commercial and typically residential districts, as well as being a spatial divide between the commercial district of Hancock and the Quincy Mining Company's industrial core. The range in ethnicity of business owners was as broad as the cross section of working-class laborers, commercial merchants, and skilled professionals who walked the FTN's streets and sidewalks. There were department stores owned by Jewish businessmen like Jacob Gartner, a sporting-goods store operated by the German Benjamin E. Wieder, a Chinese-operated laundry, and Finnish-run jewelry stores and food buffets. Although there was a significant Italian immigrant population in Hancock, there were very few Italian immigrant businesses or people in the FTN.

Probably the most unlikely and humorous coupling of lot holders within the FTN occurred in the Village of Hancock's Block 3 on Lots 1 and 2. In 1909, the Bosch Brewing Company operated a saloon on the southern half of Lots 1 and 2, while the aforementioned Pohjantähti temperance society operated a gymnasium and social hall on the north half of Lots 1 and 2.[46] (A person could get on or off the wagon within a couple of steps.) This humorous coupling represented the diversity of entertainment and recreational opportunities within the FTN.

The fact that working class entertainment and recreational opportunities abounded in the FTN was likely an overwhelming reason for locating the Kansankoti Hall-Työmies Publishing Company campus in this area of Hancock. As a Quincy labor spy noted in 1906, "When on the street the miners usually congregate on the corner of Quincy and Tezcuco Streets."[47] Placing the Kansankoti-Työmies campus on this corner was perhaps the single most important factor in any plan to organize workers and spread the socialist-unionist message; the FTN was a working-class entertainment district. On a given night, a person could shoot "stick" at Cubs Billiards Parlor at 125 Quincy Street, bowl a game at Mitchell's bowling alley at 226 Quincy Street, see a performance at the Savoy Theatre at 309 Quincy Street, then have a drink at Antilla's Saloon before stopping by the Kansankoti Hall at 201 Franklin Street to hear of the inevitable proletarian revolution against the Copper Country "bosses."[48]

CHAPTER 2

Finnish Immigrant Cultural Organizations and the "Finn Hall"

As throngs of Finnish immigrants entered the United States, they looked for familiar or recognizable social activities to supplement their mundane work lives. While they most often sought a new life in the New World, they also sought to maintain cultural identity, possibly to ease the transition to life in America. Finnish immigrants founded cultural organizations that nurtured and supported their unfamiliar existence in America; thus, organizational societies became very popular and Finnish immigrants became great "joiners." In this chapter, we will look at Finnish immigrant cultural organizations. We will examine how tangible aspects of those organizational societies cultivated a rigorous and effective response to conditions in the industrial setting, with specific analysis of secular Finnish immigrant cultural organizations in the Copper Country.

An important tangible aspect of Finnish immigrant cultural organizations was the highly valued "Finn hall." Finn halls were an important social aspect in the Finnish immigrant's life for many reasons. Combating individual, cultural, and geographic isolation in remote industrial areas, where Lake Superior Finns tended to settle and work in the booming extractive industries, was certainly a large reason for the popularity of Finn halls. Finn halls were often homes or incubators for a unique, concerted response to a new life in America. From these halls, Finnish immigrants responded to their conditions in a proactive manner. Finnish American historian Michael G. Karni hypothesized that Finns were hoping to maintain and disseminate their values in America: "Most Finns were determined not to be passive recipients of American culture. Whether associated with the church, the temperance movement, the cooperative movement or the radical labor movement, they believed they could shape the American environment and shape it into what it was not."[1] Finnish immigrants aimed to challenge, influence, and shape undesirable aspects of American culture using a distinctive response, their cultural organizations.

A Response to Industrial Life in the Lake Superior Region

In the booming mining districts of the Lake Superior region during the late nineteenth and early twentieth centuries, the Finnish immigrants' organizational responses aimed directly at the problems associated with living and working in industrial America. For Finnish immigrants, problems within industrial America around the "big lake" often depended on how the individual viewed their surroundings; thus, joining like-minded groups that addressed the problems of life and work in industrial America varied within different segments of the Finnish immigrant population. Church groups called for piety and adherence to a moral Christian life, temperance groups called for clean living and abstinence from intoxicating liquors, and the socialist-unionist movement called for contemplation of the working class's plight concerning social, economic, and safety issues.

Finnish immigrant churches were the first organizational groups to develop in America. The first secular Finnish immigrant organizational endeavor in America began in the mid-1880s. These "groups" were actually cooperative boarding houses. The cooperative boarding house was a Finnish immigrant discovery in America, as none existed in Finland. As Helen K. Leiviska remembers, the cooperative boarding house operated economically as such:

> Well you see what they did was that they would buy—so many people would join together and they would build an apartment. It wasn't exactly a true cooperative in a sense according to Rochdale's principles. But these people would jointly own the house and they would pay the mortgage monthly—the rent consisted of mortgage payments, the taxes and so forth.[2]

The cooperative boarding house was more than a place to lay a body down. Leaders in the Finnish immigrant community recognized that the young men streaming into American industrial centers lacked moral direction. These young men spent more time in saloons than in wholesome, enlightening activities. Into this debauchery-laden void came the operators of cooperative boarding houses, which provided comfort, familiarity, and education to newly industrialized workers. In these boarding houses, education was a priority; young men began to read various types of literature, but especially sociological and economic explanations of life.[3]

From this embryonic institution, the rise of other prominent secular cultural organizations took shape. Temperance societies, workingmen's groups, cooperatives, women's auxiliaries, gymnastics societies, debate forums, drama groups, and publishing associations took hold within the Finnish immigrant communities. While there were many different groups and institutions within the Finnish immigrant cultural organizations, they all had one major consideration: they needed a place to meet. Immigrant life revolved around its cultural organizations, and as Finnish immigrant institutions grew, they needed specialized buildings to accommodate their activities.

In America, Finn halls became the center of secular cultural organizations and often architecturally represented the individuals and organizations they housed. Rural Finns built practical log or wood-framed one-room halls, while Finns who were more "urbane" constructed buildings that were more ornate. Often the function of the hall dictated its architectural character. If the hall functioned as a meeting facility, little more than one room was necessary. If the hall was home to plays, more space and often ornamentation was necessary to "advertise" the hall as a place of entertainment. If the hall acted as a store or had a restaurant, it had to house consumer goods, clothes, and a kitchen or dining area in addition to having meeting, athletic, and theatrical venues. Such a setup required commercial, meeting, and performance space that could necessitate the building of a rather large, commodious structure.[4]

Before the turn of the twentieth century, Finn halls accommodated and housed various ideological and cultural groups. This harmony between Finnish immigrant groups would not last. For if it can be said that Finnish immigrants were great joiners, in the next breath it must be mentioned that they were also proficient dividers. Finn halls were often the location where disagreements in ideology played out. If the disagreement was terminal, the rebuffed members left the organization. As the disenfranchised left to set up a new organization, they often retained the basic organizational character of the former group. In addition to antagonistic fractioning, amicable fractioning occurred when an organization became too big for its current facility. For religious groups, this meant starting a new church; for social, fraternal, or benevolent organizations, this meant building a new hall or finding another meeting space to rent. Fractioning, amicable or otherwise, happened at a breakneck pace, and by 1915, within approximately a fifteen-mile radius of the Finnish Transitional Neighborhood there were at least thirty temperance, socialist-unionist, or Knights and Ladies of Kaleva organizations.[5]

Two Case Studies in Fractioning: Finn Halls in South Range and Hancock

Not all organizations were lucky or prosperous enough to have their own hall. Consider the secret fraternal society of the Hancock Knights of Kaleva,[6] which had a fluctuating membership and no meeting facilities. After beginning the *Nyyrikki Maja* or Nyyrikki Lodge of the Knights of Kaleva in Hancock around 1899, the group moved to South Range in 1904. The South Range Nyyrikki held their meetings at the Saima Hall, home to the Aurankukka Temperance Society. In 1910, the Nyyrikki Maja moved to a stately Jacobsville sandstone building a few blocks from the Saima Hall after a saloon owner failed to meet his financial obligations to the building. Hancock reorganized another Knights Lodge in 1906, but still did not have an independent hall to call home. They rented hall space on the third floor of the Kauth Block in the FTN.[7] The South

Finnish Immigrant Organizations on the Keweenaw Peninsula, 1890–1915. A map that locates Finnish immigrant Temperance Societies, Finnish Socialist Federation locals, and Kaleva Lodges on the Keweenaw Peninsula, 1890–1915. Key to abbreviations: S = Socialist Local, T = Temperance Society, K = Knights and/or Ladies of Kaleva Lodge. (Gary Kaunonen.)

Range Knights, in contrast, had an exceptionally large and functional hall or "temple."[8]

In 1913, a socialist-unionist hall joined Saima Hall and the Kaleva Temple.[9] The South Range Socialist Hall was an impressive structure constructed in 1913, seemingly just in time for the 1913 strike in Michigan's Copper Country. The Western Federation of Miners South Range Local No. 196 bought the lot for the hall in February 1910 from Mary Longhead and then sold the property to the Finnish Workingmen's Association in September 1910. It took three years for the South Range Finnish Socialist Federation local to build a hall on the property, but when they did in 1913, the hall's accoutrements and facilities rivaled those of several other Lake Superior–region Finnish immigrant halls in urban areas. The two-story South Range Socialist Hall measured 45' by 90', had stage and scenery, stylish architectural details, office space, a Jacobsville sandstone foundation, and blocks of basaltic mine ashlar for the exterior walls.[10] While the building had less square footage than the Hancock socialist-unionist campus, the South Range Hall was an impressive, fortress-like structure.

Matching South Range's accumulation of three Finnish halls was Hancock. By 1910, Hancock had two temperance halls and the aforementioned Kansankoti Hall. Organized in 1890, the *Pohjantähti Raittius Seura* (North Star Temperance Society) first occupied and held their Sunday meetings at a hall perched on the side of Quincy Hill in the Quincy Hillside Second Addition.[11] The Finnish Coronet Band called the Pohjantähti Hall home and no doubt provided music for hall functions. By 1909, the Pohjantähti took over ownership of the former YMCA building at 306 Reservation Street within the FTN.[12] The Pohjantähti's new hall had a lunch counter, gymnasium, and stage. As Mrs. Hugo Klemetti, a member of the Pohjantähti, recalled:

> There was a big hall and café where we served coffee and pies and sandwiches and things like that. It wasn't a restaurant and there was a swimming pool down stairs and there was couple of saunas and bathtubs in sauna and dressing rooms. You had to have a bath before you went swimming, that was the law in those days and a lot of people came those days . . . They used to have that swimming pool downstairs, but the Finns build the saunas there. That was a beautiful building . . . We served coffee and pies, sandwiches, but not any big meal, there was only two of us (that worked in the hall at the time).[13]

The Finnish Immigrant Temperance Movement and Its Halls

Drinking, or excessive amounts of drinking, had long been a problem in Finland. In the early eighteenth century, church sermons railed against the immoderation of drinking. Formal organization to combat the problems of drinking did not start in Finland until 1817. The Finnish encountered American temperance ideals as early as 1833, when Finnish temperance groups received translated American tracts on the benefits of the teetotaling lifestyle. The growth of the

Finnish temperance movement between 1850 and 1900 followed Finnish immigrants to America.

Finnish immigrant temperance societies grew rapidly in America. By 1900, there were 150 temperance societies with approximately 6,550 members in the United States.[14] Thus, in the early years of the twentieth century, temperance halls were the loci of social activity. According to Finnish American labor historian Carl Ross:

> They [halls] were meeting places for congregations without churches, for clubs without buildings, and held officially banned, but tacitly sanctioned dances. They were home to mutual aide societies where accident and burial insurance funds were collected. People flocked to temperance halls and became involved in a fantastic network of activity. There were speakers' clubs for training and practicing public speech, they read, recited and developed their talent for entertainments and festivals. Performers wrote and spoke poetry. There were drama groups in larger urban centers. Temperance halls were the location of lending libraries where local writers entered in annual essay contests.[15]

There was, however, trouble brewing in the Finnish immigrant temperance movement. The trouble existed between the conservative religious elements of the movement and the secular elements. Ideologically, the religious elements saw intemperance as a transgression against good Christian life, while the secular elements saw intemperance as a social and economically derived problem. There were minor divisions over rather mundane things like those who believed dancing was an acceptable form of entertainment and those who thought dancing was devilish. In actuality though, there existed a very significant gulf between younger, more socially and economically conscious temperance folk and older, pious religious temperance members.[16]

Salomon Ilmonen, a pastor in the Finnish immigrants' conservative Suomi Synod Evangelical Lutheran church wrote in 1910 of the Pohjantähti's history:

> A few strange members have come in. The youth were enamored by thespian pursuits. We had resisted the addition of stage and scenery when the hall was enlarged, but now temporary moveable scenery began to appear in the

hall. This was a clear omen of a new dawn, as yet, lacking in clarity, but with advance hues of a red sunrise.

The *Pohjantähti*'s programs have also changed. That is unwholesome. Some speeches can be genuinely serious, dwelling upon temperance, civility and the importance of faith; but others are flippant, caricatures of faith and even uncivil. Some songs are spiritual, others ribald couplets. Likewise, the poems recited were at times quite damaging. Both groups offer programs in keeping with their own world views.

The other temperance society in Hancock, often in contact with the *Pohjantähti*, the "*Valon Säde*" will [soon] cease to exist. The workers' society "*Jousi*" arose to replace it, and to give voice to workers ideals in the same manner as the workers' society had earlier in Helsinki. By editor N. J. Ahlman's strong leadership it gained status. From this direction came the idea of erecting a united Peoples Home [Kansankoti] in Hancock. This aim received support, but finally *Pohjantähti* withdrew. Our society anticipated what was behind this scheme.[17]

The Finnish Socialist Federation

By the late 1890s, workingmen's groups and thespians were in the midst of reexamining their place within the conservative Christian temperance movement. While temperance movements awakened a cultural upwelling and stimulated intensive "dry" organizational campaigns, they often disregarded the tangible causes of intemperance. In industrial communities, working conditions and the industrial setting were seen by many as the root of intemperance. In the estimation of some, the temperance societies commonly did not address this fundamental problem. Workers' clubs took issue with the social, economic, and working conditions of industrial America and began to formulate a material response.[18]

The workers' associations began to flourish within Finnish temperance societies in the early 1900s. The socialist-unionist movement in turn grew from within the workers' associations. A specific aspect of early workers' and temperance societies' cultural organizations, publishing associations, greatly benefited the early Finnish immigrant socialist-unionist movement. Nonaffiliated newspapers hired socialist-unionist writers to boost subscriptions with controversial articles. This was a boon for socialist-unionist cultural organizations because it gave the movement a voice before it had a large following. Using the publishing associations as an organizational tool, a small number of Finnish immigrant socialist-unionists recruited from within the rank-and-file of the liberal press, from workers' enlightenment clubs, and from the temperance societies.[19]

As the socialist-unionists began to infiltrate the temperance societies, they used sheer mass to wrestle ownership of the organizations from their more conservative teetotaling brethren. Helen K. Leiviska remembered:

> You see what happened with a lot of these temperance societies was the majority would be the so called socialists and then they would vote the whole Temperance Society into the Socialist Party. And then the Finns were always the builders of the halls, and when the majority was at the hall, they would vote the hall over to the Socialist Party. And, I don't think that would create very good feelings.[20]

Early Finnish immigrant working-class organizations began as benefit and fraternal societies. These groups advocated working with American industry to elevate the living conditions of workers, and espoused temperance ideals. One such federated body of Finnish immigrants was the Imatra League, founded in 1903. Imatra locals, of whom many were in New England and New York, were benevolent, cultural, and fraternal organizations that attempted to relieve the stress of life in a new world, establish illness and death benefit funds, and provide moral guidance in unfamiliar environs. Another early Finnish immigrant working-class association, founded in 1904 at a meeting in Duluth, Minnesota, was the Finnish American Workers League. In 1904, at the same meeting held in Duluth, Minnesota, and at a later Cleveland, Ohio, gathering, a plan to join the Socialist Party of America (SPA) surfaced. This plan gained traction among the socialist-unionist element, and affiliation with American socialism occurred at the Cleveland meeting. The outcome of the Cleveland meeting was a formal uniting of the fledgling Finnish immigrant workingmen's societies with the Socialist Party of America as foreign-language members of the Party.[21]

Nineteen hundred and six was another important year for Finnish immigrant socialist-unionist locals in America. At a meeting in Hibbing, Minnesota, attending locals voted to create and join a federation of socialist-unionist locals. The newly coined *Suomalainen Sosialistijärjestö* or Finnish Socialist Federation (FSF), a foreign-language section within the Socialist Party of America, began with 53 locals and 2,622 members and functioned as such:

> The organization is conducted by an Executive Committee of five members, who are elected yearly by a referendum vote; a general committee, in which each state is represented according to the number of locals and by a referendum of the membership . . . For agitation and organization purposes the country has been divided into three organization districts, and a steady organizer is kept in the field in each district. All propositions regarding the Finnish organizations only are transacted through the translators office, which also serves the purpose of the central office of the organization, but in compliance with the rules of the Socialist Party all party affairs are conducted systematically by the various county and state offices.[22]

In a nod to the international socialist movement, the newly organized FSF sent a cablegram to their Finnish comrades embroiled in the Viapori Rebellion against the czar's army in Finland. The cablegram read, "Socialist Executive Committee, Helsinki, Finland: The convention of the Finnish Socialists greets its comrades in revolution. May the Red Flag wave for sacred freedom!—Representatives of the Socialists."[23] By 1907, the number of FSF locals climbed to 133, with around 3,000 members. In this period, the ideology behind the movement drastically shifted. Rather benign forms of socialism were out, in favor of more revolutionary forms of socialism espoused by Finnish immigrant Marxists and radical members of the SPA.[24]

In 1908, Hancock's Victor Watia, secretary for the FSF, wrote in a Socialist Party of Michigan newspaper: "Today the movement among the Finnish population in the country is not the same trembling, weak organization that it was a short time ago." This statement alone is interesting, but Watia's position and reason for writing the letter are equally intriguing: he was writing a report to the Michigan Socialist Party as the FSF's Finnish translator. Watia's position as translator was an essential component in the successful transmission of communications between Finnish immigrant socialist-unionists and the Socialist Party of America. Watia described the need for, and work of the Finnish translator as such:

> The activity of the Finnish comrades and the difficulties in the language compelled them to hire someone to do the translating. This was tried in the states of Minnesota, Michigan and Wisconsin, and on this practical knowledge was brought up the idea of establishing a National Finnish Translator's office for the benefit of every Finnish branch in the country, and locating the same at the National Headquarters of the Socialist Party . . . the National Finnish Translator's office was started at the National Headquarters on January 1, 1907 . . . A number of books and leaflets have been distributed through the translator's office, and the party constitution, platforms and all national, state and county matters have been translated from English to Finnish and propositions from the locals for county, state or national offices formed into English.[25]

Not only did the Finnish members of the Socialist Party of America advocate for establishment of a translator for "Finnish" party members, but also for the establishment of translators for other ethnicities and languages as well:

> The necessity of establishing and maintaining a translator's office for every nationality should be apparent to everyone. As far as the Finns are concerned, there is no doubt that both the National and Finnish organizations are greatly benefited by the office, and I think the same result could be reached among other nationalities . . . This kind of work will require not agitators, but organizers who themselves are interested in the propaganda of forming one solid, unbreakable organization, and as long as there is a large number of persons in the party membership who are unable to speak and understand the prevailing language it can not be done without establishing and maintaining national translator's offices.[26]

Although the FSF had been in the Socialist Party of America for less than two years, this act demonstrated that Finnish immigrant socialist-unionists were taking an active role in an American proletarian movement. It also conveyed that while the Finnish immigrant members of the Party were to some extent seeking to retain their ethnic and cultural customs, there was a desire to become a greater actor in an American political organization.

Socialist-Unionist Halls

By 1905, some temperance societies had become socialist societies, and bitter fights ensued over ownership of the revered Finn halls.[27] This did not mean that socialist-unionist Finnish immigrants did not interact with temperance Finns.[28] Quite the opposite was true. Temperance societies were incubators and disseminating platforms that nurtured the upstart socialist-unionist organizations, as 1906 Quincy labor-spy reports indicated:

Reported August 13:

> The operative reports that he had learned that the Temperance Society among the Finns was said to have been organized to prevent the men from indulging in excesses and needless spending of money; also to prevent the men from "scabbing" in the case of a strike.[29]

Operative K:

> Just before the strike one of the Finlanders notified all the others of his nationality who worked at the Quincy mine to come to their hall located on the side of the hill and that no other nationality was allowed to attend; that when they arrived at the hall this fellow got up and made a speech to the crowd in the Finnish language and told them that that was the time to strike in order to win a ten per cent raise; that after finishing his speech he asked all those who were in favor of a strike to raise their hands whereupon every hand was raised. He further said that they were all told that under no circumstances should they mention who it was that had started the trouble and that after that the agitation went on among the different nationalities but that the men who had first started the trouble did not take any further part in the agitation.[30]

> Opr. P. [Operative P]:
>
> After having mailed report on Sept. 15th at 8:00 P.M. the operative went to the Finnish Temperance Society social in the Pohjan Tahti Temperance Society's hall. W. J. Helstein, a socialistic agitator was given an opportunity to talk, which he did for two hours and a half. He said that the social was for the benefit of the strikers of Rockland, Mich., then went on to speak of lawyers, explaining what they do and how they do it. He also spoke of the conditions of the working man at the present time and explained the difference of cost of living between two houses of the same size, one occupied by four or five persons, while the other was occupied by twenty or more, being a boarding house. He next spoke of different matters in connection with the mines in the vicinity and explained how these conditions might be made better, all through socialism.[31]

Socialist-unionist takeover of a hall was not always a given, especially in the case when a temperance hall was on mining-company property. Fred Torma, an early socialist and union organizer, described his experiences on Minnesota's Mesabi Iron Range:

> I always went to the halls whenever I had the opportunity. There were temperance halls in almost every town. At first, we tried to take over these temperance halls for socialist uses. The first place was at Stevenson Mine—a temperance hall. I joined that temperance league. At that time the Finns were very much enslaved by liquor. When the boss went for his morning drink the working men followed. I then joined that temperance league. I began organizing work to get members into that temperance league. I was always somewhat successful at that.
>
> We tried to take over that hall then so that we could also take up working people matters, but the mining company intervened. They sent representatives to say that they had provided the money and materials for the hall and it would not be used for any labor movement purposes.[32]

In Finnish immigrants' cultural organizations, where temperance societies ended and socialist organizations began is difficult to determine. Comprehending the shifting tides of Finnish immigrant groups is difficult. Finnish immigrant organizations had a distinct penchant for fractioning, and they did it well. As landscape historian Arnold Alanen writes in "Corporate Mining Environment," "Thus, mining town residents often resorted to labels when describing their neighbors from *Suomi*. Depending upon the Finns' politics or proclivities toward alcohol, these labels included 'White Finns,' 'Red Finns,' 'Black Finns,' 'Drunken Finns,' 'Swede Finns,' and 'Russian Finns.'"[33] The rigidity of these general labels was certainly oversimplified, and the copious amounts of ideology and emotion contained within these labels were by no means static. Rather, many individuals likely vacillated between groups and ideology at various points within their lives.

As socialist-unionists left the temperance movement, they replicated the organizational template of the temperance societies. This included the preservation of many temperance-themed goals. A 1908 passage detailed the FSF's maintenance of temperance ethics:

> Realizing the intellectual and personal misery of those members of the working class who are using the intoxicating liquors as a beverage and understanding the policy of old parties [Democrat and Republican] in trying to maintain the system of manufacturing and distributing the liquors and using the method as one of the strongest weapons against the awakening of the proletariat, the sympathy among the Finnish comrades generally is favorable to the temperance and prohibition movement.[34]

The fundamental temperance-hall customs became FSF hall culture as well, but if temperance halls were a rage, socialist halls became a phenomenon. In mining regions, they were centers of refuge in an industrial tempest and quickly became the hub of activity in Finnish immigrant enclaves:

> At the club [local socialist hall] they read their literature, discussed their problems, heard lectures, put on plays, sang, danced, flirted, romanced were married, celebrated the birth of children, had parties, became ill, died and began the procession to cemeteries. At the halls, the miner was able, for a while, to forget his backbreaking toil and his problems of loneliness in what seemed to be a

> hostile world. He met with his own people, reminisced about the homeland, spoke of his aspirations, and vented his hostility against a system which he thought prematurely robbed him of his manhood. As more women began to bring a semblance of civilization into the community, the Hall acted as a center for their lives as well. The one room shack, which many of them called home was drab and uninviting; it was a respite for them to get to the Hall to meet with other women, to put a dent into their homesickness and loneliness.[35]

While the socialist-labor movement carried vastly different ideology from the conservative temperance movement, the basic guiding principle behind the cultural organization remained intact. Moral discipline was the mission. As William Hoglund wrote, "Socialist followers paid dues, read party newspapers, attended classes, and if possible, joined trade unions. Then too, they were reminded to attend their socialist hall, even if there was no dancing, there were speakers, actors, singers and poets to instill moral discipline."[36] In addition, Michael Karni wrote, "At the [socialist] hall, he [the Finnish immigrant] could mix with all his countrymen, be entertained regularly, be culturally enlightened, find self-expression through drama, debate, music and athletics and simultaneously feel himself involved in a movement which promised to bring the good life to all through social and political revolution."[37]

Social Activities at Socialist-Unionist Halls

Most importantly, socialist halls became a cultural core for their members. In an undated interview, Aarre Lahti recalled the Palace Finn Hall in Ironwood, Michigan:

> These immigrant laborers, without any assistance from the town's financial institutions, used their own energy and determination to erect this huge hall in a series of work bees . . . The hall, after completion, boasted the best dance floor in the county and a stage with all the necessary scenery, costumes, and mechanical equipment for a first class little theater. And it was the only facility in town with gymnastic and track paraphernalia.

> The hall was always busy. There were band and orchestra practice sessions, and both men and women's choir rehearsals each week. The little theater seemed to be always preparing some production—involving drama or the opera. And of course, political meetings were held in the hall, too.
>
> The athletic sessions were held on Tuesday and Thursday evenings and again on Sunday morning when the hall's auditorium was set up with parallel bars, a high bar, "horses," mats and other gymnastic equipment. The weekday sessions began about five o'clock to accommodate those who were on the night shift.[38]

According to Lahti, the ideological foundations of the Palace Hall seem like an afterthought. From Lahti's recollections, we may infer that activities at socialist-unionist halls were the most important aspect of cultural organization to Finnish immigrant rank-and-filers. Of the entertainments sponsored at socialist-unionist halls, plays were by far the most popular. Often lacking a repertoire of socialist-unionist plays, local halls frequently substituted liberal-bourgeois plays that stressed social reform. Plays by authors such as Ibsen and dramas like *Spartacus* that stressed social awareness and disruption were often popular thematic performances. These non-Marxist plays were less didactic than most revolutionary-themed plays and therefore more lucrative for local halls because they drew in nonaffiliated Finns in addition to their socialist-unionist counterparts.[39]

Because of their popularity, plays were an almost essential economic component of hall life. Thus, when building or renovating a structure for hall use, creating a proper performance venue was paramount, as Fred Torma remembered of the Nashwauk, Minnesota hall:

> It was November maybe October when we bought that hall. Then the question arose—How would we pay for it? Since I had learned the carpenter's trade from my father I said I'd lead. I made drawings as best as I was able. The older ones thought we should merely put planks on top of beer kegs and keep performances on top of that. I said no we won't do that. Alexis Watanen had horses. I said let's take the horses into the forest and bring back the support joists. We'll build a proper and sturdy stage—for plays, performances, speeches, etc.

> So we built the stage. I got others to help—I worked at the mine and didn't have time to be there other than on evenings and Sundays. The others helped and we made a nice, little stage where we could act out plays . . . That's how we got our funds. Then in 1910, it was too small—that stage and hall. And also some of the new arrivals to the community were actors who wanted to continue pursuing this avocation. They began demanding a bigger stage and hall. I drew up plans for a new hall as best I could. I went to Duluth to get an idea of what a theater should be like. I went to the [*unclear proper noun*] Theater several times.[40]

Specifically recalling the plays, Torma remembered:

> We selected committees to order plays and produce them. And we were so economical that even for big plays we ordered no more than two printed copies. The rest were copied by hand . . . the Socialist Party itself had a sort of storehouse of plays from whence the plays could be rented. When the old plays accumulated at the various halls, the plays were sent to the Socialist Party's offices. There was a good supply of plays there. Then later Lauri Lemberg began to rent plays and we ordered from him as well.[41]

The Työmies Publishing Company also had a store of plays, listing more than one hundred titles for sale in the *Työmies*, ranging anywhere between ten cents to a dollar per copy. The plays ranged from the very didactic, such as *Socialism*, *A Slave's Education*, and *Struggle and Profit*, to more amusement-driven plays such as *Sherlock Holmes*, *The Workers' Wife*, and *Moses of Israel*.[42]

In addition to theater, the Nashwauk hall served as a location for other functions as well. The hall was busy all week long, and activities centered around "[practicing] all sorts of agitation from there." Beginning the week, on Monday nights, the Nashwauk local held meetings to organize weekly activities; Monday was also youth night at the hall when children gathered to play group games and dance. Tuesday nights were play-rehearsal nights. On Wednesday nights, there were dances. Thursday nights brought more play rehearsal. Friday nights saw debating, and Saturday nights more dancing. Sundays, generally the only day off from mine work for the men, saw the week's play rehearsals culminate in performances. In addition to the social activities at the hall, the Nashwauk local organized a library for its members:

> At that time everyone had a desire to learn. For example because wages were, at the most, $2.00 for a 12 hour day no one could afford to purchase books. So we established a library. Then at the debate clubs that we had one had to be knowledgeable in order to defend one's point of view. That also was a reason for our library. Our library grew so big that we had up to 500 volumes. It was all socialist literature. Oh, there had to be some novels too, in the collection, so that the women could also read. In the early times the women did not care for scientific literature.[43]

The largest celebrations at socialist-unionist halls were grand openings, and they were gala events. A slew of advertising typically announced a hall's grand-opening festivities. These ceremonies were not just celebrations, but also declarations of intent. In many ways, the socialist and workers' halls were symbols of stability, a showpiece for the success of the Finnish immigrant's socialist-unionist movement. For FSF locals, having an *oma talo,* or your own house, proclaimed that you had "arrived." Grand halls were a way to demonstrate to community members, other ethnicities, antagonistic Finnish immigrant organizations, and perhaps most importantly, the mining companies, that the socialist-unionist movement could vie for the affection, attention, and loyalty of the working class. To accomplish this, socialist-unionist halls had to create unique proletarian imagery through exhibition, pageantry, and testimony. Due to the bold nature of this proclamation, an opening ceremony had to display grandiose proletarian symbolism.

The Negaunee, Michigan, local advertised the opening of their new hall, the *Työn Temppeli* (Labor Temple) as nothing short of a gala affair, which included a multiethnic program featuring three proletarian "guest-stars." An ad in *Työmies* highlighted significant features of the opening: The Negaunee local scheduled the event for Sunday, December 18, 1910. The event was to begin with a singing of "The Internationale" by a mixed choir organized especially for the event. An Italian Brass Band (a local Marquette Iron Range group) was to accompany the chorus. After "The Internationale," Frank Aaltonen of the Negaunee local would give a welcome to those attending the event. The Italian Brass Band was to play another number, and then a guest speaker from Milwaukee would give a speech in English—the scheduled speaker was Milwaukee's socialist mayor Emil Seidel. After Seidel's address, another number by the Italian Brass Band, and then Yrjö Sirola, professor at the Work People's College in Duluth, was to give a speech. The mixed choir would then sing "Proletaarit" and the brass band would play another tune. Next on the program was a speech in Italian from Tom Corra, member of the Western Federation of Miners. The opening ceremony was to end with three musical numbers, the final being "Työväen Marssi," or "The Workers' March."[44]

That evening, the Negaunee local was to present the play *Daniel Hjort*, a drama written by Swede-Finn playwright J. J. Wecksell. The selection of that particular play was likely no accident. *Daniel Hjort* was about a peasant involved in a proletarian revolt in the Ostrobothnian region of Finland. Scheduled to open for the play were the *Suomalainen Orkesteri* (Finnish Orchestra), rune singer Rauha Aaltonen, and the vocal trio of Frank Lindroos and Children. Ticket prices were not, however, devoid of "class" influence. There were five staggered levels of ticket prices, ranging from $1, $2, $3, $5 for general admission to $10.00 for front-row seating. The Negaunee local's *Juhlakomitea*, or Celebration Committee, undersigned the entire event.[45]

Similar in scale to the opening of Negaunee's Labor Temple was Hibbing, Minnesota's Workers *haalilla*. The Hibbing organization decided to overlap their opening with a New Year's Eve (1909) day and night celebration. For the day's affairs, the Hibbing local scheduled a speech by Leo Laukki, professor at the Work People's College; a reading by Finnish immigrant poet Aku Päiviö; and another speech by Hibbing local member Wilho Leikkas. That night, a performance of Gustaf von Nurmer's *Elinan Surma* (Elina's Death) was scheduled. The cast of characters was long and included eighteen actors to cover all the parts. One of the play's characters was *Vappu* or Freedom, played by A. Ahopelto. Hibbing's play was much easier on the pocketbook, as the local was charging only $1.50, $1.00, and $.75 a ticket for that New Year's Eve night at the theater.[46]

Kesäjuhla, or summer celebrations, were an important part of Finnish immigrant "Hall" culture as well. These summer festivals were a very popular event, not only in socialist-unionist groups, but also in other Finnish immigrant cultural organizations. The most important of the summer celebrations was *Juhannusjuhla*, a traditional Finnish celebration that had roots in pagan Finland. Tradition dictated that *Juhannus* occur on the longest day of summer, and that a *kokko*, or bonfire, be lit at dusk. It was a way for northern people to celebrate the light of summer before the long, steady march into darkness of the winter months. Summer celebrations were a time for socialization, athletic competition, lectures—and for socialist-unionist groups, labor, and political organization. At times, the summer cultural activities left little time for anything else:

> Many regards to you. Can you please forgive me for not answering your letter earlier? There have been all kinds of activities during the summer so from day to day I have just postponed writing to you. Hilja, you said that now in the summer time it is quiet and boring there. The activities among the Finns here [Cleveland] are pretty busy, especially now in the summer. There are festivities every Sunday, even three on the same day. You see, the radicals have their events and the temperance association has theirs—just like anywhere else. Each group and political party has got its own.[47]

In 1913, the Virginia FSF local on Minnesota's Mesabi Iron Range advertised that they had one of the largest midsummer celebrations in the Midwest. This midsummer festival was a three-day affair occurring June 22, 23, and 24. The festival was to feature outdoor concerts by socialist-unionist local brass bands and mixed choirs from Virginia and Ely. In addition, there would be a contest held to find the best solo singer from among the festival's participants. Also scheduled for outdoor programming were speeches and lectures by John Korpi, an I.W.W. union organizer and professor at the Work People's College, and Yrjö Sirola, another professor from the Work People's College. The Virginia Workers' Theater was presenting performances of *Kullervo* and *Valapatto* in Virginia's Socialist Opera House. Prizes were to be given to the festival's attendees, and the midsummer celebration was to end with a *Tanssit*, or dance. It would cost women $0.25 to enter the dance, while men had to shell out $0.35 to attend the soiree. Of course, there were also athletic competitions, which were a seminal part of socialist-unionist culture. Men could run a 5-mile race, while women could sprint the 100-yard dash.[48] Summer in the Lake Superior basin was a beehive of activity, as people of all political leanings tried to cram as much activity into June, July, and August as possible.

As previously mentioned, athletics were an important component of hall culture. As independent athletic groups formed, they lacked the facilities to practice physical skills. By the 1920s, the southern Lake Superior basin (Michigan, Minnesota, and Wisconsin) had eighteen athletic clubs in cities such as Ironwood, Marquette, Negaunee, Ishpeming, and Hancock in Michigan; Iron Belt, Montreal, and Superior in Wisconsin; and Cloquet, Duluth, Hibbing, and Virginia in Minnesota. In addition to athletic clubs in these mid-sized urban environments, smaller rural locations had athletic clubs. Halls in general, and specifically large socialist and workers' halls, became a quick solution to the practice and match venue dilemmas. While gymnastics was popular in the winter, and track and field events were its summer counterpart, wrestling was all the rage in the Midwest. In 1911, the sports periodical *Urheilu-Viesti*, published by the Työmies Publishing Company, took the time and effort to criticize Americans for lauding catch-as-catch-can (freestyle) wrestling. The writers of *Urheilu-Viesti* preferred the taxing upper-body Greco-Roman style of wrestling. Not surprisingly, Finnish immigrants' allegiances were torn between the long-established Greco-Roman wrestling and catch-as-catch-can wrestling, with its popular icons, like Karl Lehto.[49]

Women in the Finnish Immigrant Socialist-Unionist Movement

While the Finnish immigrant socialist-unionist movement was not male-dominated, it certainly was male-oriented. To put some statistical meat on the bones of the overall gender disparity within the movement, consider that in 1912 there were almost 10,000 male members of the Finnish Socialist Federation in the United States. There were 4,000 female members in that same year, despite the organization of a women's committee of the federation.[50] In the Upper Great Lakes region, Michigan's Finnish Socialist Federation locals counted 300 women to 915 men. Only the Iron River local tallied more women (87) than men (13), though Detroit's local split almost evenly along gender lines. In the

Copper Country, Hancock counted 74 women and 153 men, while Ahmeek, another mining community, tallied 83 men and 20 women in the organization. Minnesota's Finnish Socialist Federation counted 2,308 men to 576 women, and Wisconsin's locals reported having 148 women to 389 men.[51]

Further scrutiny finds even greater gender disproportion in the early Finnish immigrant socialist-unionist movement's leadership. On a ballot for the 1913 Työmies Publishing Company's board of directors, of 122 people up for election to the board only twelve were women. Of those twelve, five were on the ballot in addition to their husbands. Furthermore, in photographs documenting meetings of regional or national delegations, there was usually a single woman participant included as a representative of all women, often situated in photographs surrounded by a group of men.

While there was significant gender disparity in the movement, one woman in particular was incredibly important to the early success of the burgeoning Finnish Socialist Federation. Her name was Ida Pasanen. From a biography in *Women Who Dared: The History of Finnish American Women*, Pasanen is perhaps best described as a classic overachiever. Born in Asikkala, Finland, in 1872, as the illegitimate child of a brief dalliance between a female Finnish gypsy and a male civil engineer from a "landed" family, Pasanen never knew her father. She went to school and educated herself, joining the workers' movement in Finland in 1896. In 1900, Ida attended the first organizational meeting of Finnish women socialists, but then in 1903 she emigrated to America with her daughter to join her husband, who had left for the United States in 1900.[52]

Once in the United States, she and friends began the *Edistys* (Progress) workers' society, built a hall, and developed a thriving socialist-unionist organization in Cloquet, Minnesota. From this early beginning in the socialist-unionist movement, Ida began to take an increased leadership role. After moving to Two Harbors, Minnesota, in 1907, Pasanen founded the workers' society there and continued to drive the work of that society for at least another decade. Once the Two Harbors' society was established, Ida began lecturing throughout Minnesota and Wisconsin, thus beginning a lifetime devoted to the socialist-unionist movement, women's suffrage, and feminism. In addition to other activities, Ida was one of three women delegates at the 1906 founding convention of the Finnish Socialist Federation; she wrote articles in *Työmies* on the issue of women's suffrage (among other topics) and in 1909 was a convener of a meeting in Duluth, Minnesota, that began a dialogue about Finnish immigrant women in the socialist-unionist movement. Out of this meeting came the initiative to create a women's socialist-unionist newspaper. In 1911, the paper became a reality, under the title *Toveritar* (The Woman Comrade).[53]

Published in Astoria, Oregon, this newspaper was one huge step toward egalitarianism in the Finnish immigrant socialist-unionist movement. If some considered the Finnish Socialist Federation a radical organization devoted to breaking the bonds of working-class chains, *Toveritar* was an explosion of those chains; not only did *Toveritar* champion views about socialist and Marxist theory (along with practically themed discussions of contemporary women's issues), this espousal came directly from women. Women editors, women writers, and women workers at *Toveritar* were laboring on the heels of the last throes of the Victorian Era, when respectable "ladies" simply did not do such things as publish newspapers about revolution, feminism, class structure, free love (not having a man choose you for marriage), suffrage, or direct action. *Toveritar* created a movement within a movement that polished some of the brightest minds and honed some of the most talented activists in the Finnish immigrants' socialist-unionist movement.

While Pasanen helped to harness *Toveritar*'s proverbial horses, other women took the reins. Selma Jokela was one early editor. She was a practical woman who included articles that appealed to a wide female audience, as well as columns about proletarian issues. Maiju Nurmi edited *Toveritar* through tough times in immigrant circles—World War I. She also passionately pursued an editorial policy advocating that "Socialistic doctrine could be disseminated to children, mothers, and all working class women." Nurmi passed the torch to probably the most noteworthy of *Toveritar*'s editors, Helmi Mattson. Mattson was a gifted writer and pushed *Toveritar*'s subscription numbers to a peak in 1921 with over 10,000 readers.[54] Not unpredictably, *Toveritar* did, however, meet its share of opposition, sadly some of which came from men within the Finnish Socialist Federation: "In the 10th Anniversary issue of *Toveritar*, Ida Pasanen wrote about the many difficulties encountered in the early days of the paper. As Elis Sulkanen reported, 'The women still remember the battle against the men who by open and hidden methods opposed the establishment of the paper.'"[55]

This begs the question as to why. Why were there a larger number of men in the movement versus women, and why did some of the men seemingly refuse to interact with women as equals? The Socialist Party of America, which the Finnish Socialist Federation affiliated with in 1906, openly sought women to join their ranks: "The Socialist Party admits women to membership. For we consider women the equal of man morally, lively, and intellectually. Women are among the best workers in our movement, would not you like to become a member [of the Socialist Party of America]?"[56]

In addition to the male-dominated society of that era, I hypothesize that two distinct variables, geography and socioeconomics, within the Finnish immigrant socialist-unionist movement's cultural setting led to gender inequity in a supposedly equality-seeking organization. The early Finnish Socialist Federation in the Midwest focused on the socioeconomic reorganization of society located in isolated, one-industry areas such as secluded mining communities, remote logging camps, and rough-hewn sawmill towns. This was an isolated industrial setting comprised largely of men on both sides of the dialectic, owners and workers. Women and attention to issues that affected them at this time were mutually sparse. Most often, if a woman worked outside the home in these areas, they were not permitted by mine ownership, logging companies, or sawmill operations to work in the industrial core. In isolated industrial regions, women found employment in occupations such as bathhouse attendants, librarians, teachers, store clerks, camp cooks, or domestics, and as we often read of striking men in a copper or iron mine, we seldom hear of maids', clerks', librarians', cooks', or teachers' strikes in workspaces controlled by mining companies or their owners.

Why? I theorize that because male Finnish immigrant laborers in isolated industrial areas had physical contact with the principal economic resources in contention, their struggle for concessions in the workplace and in the greater social sphere of one-industry areas received primary consideration from the Finnish Socialist Federation. For the most part, Finnish immigrant men were working jobs in overwhelmingly male-populated, isolated areas that created the unevenly distributed wealth that socialist-unionist Finnish immigrants targeted for organizational response. The exceptions to this are Finnish Socialist Federation locals in areas that were not isolated, one-industry regions. If we look at Finnish Socialist Federation membership of women in multiple-industry cities with large numbers of Finnish immigrants, such as New York City, Brooklyn, Cleveland, Detroit, and Chicago in 1912, we find gender balance in the composition of membership less-skewed or equal. Quite simply, big multi-industry cities had more opportunities to offer Finnish immigrant women in terms of wage work in factories and mills, personal independence, and thus a larger stake in the Finnish immigrant socialist-unionist movement.[57]

Not fully recognizing the potential contributions of female wageworkers during this period in one-industry regions was, at the very least, a serious financial and organizational mistake on the part of the male-oriented Finnish immigrant socialist-unionist movement. If Finnish Socialist Federation locals in isolated, one-industry areas had adopted and articulated an overt policy that sought to treat women as equals in the movement, there probably would have been increased cultural participation and monetary involvement on the part of women, especially single wage-earning women. Better wages for domestics, clerks, librarians, cooks, or teachers likely would have equaled more money in Finnish Socialist Federation local coffers, and fewer hours at work could have meant more hours participating in federation activities. A good example of the potential for women to excel in the affairs of the Finnish Socialist Federation comes from a 1913 Työmies Publishing Company subscription-sales contest. Of the top twenty salespersons, five were women. Mrs. Ida Kettunen of Minneapolis, Minnesota, was the highest-ranking woman, taking seventh place in the contest.[58]

Though we have highlighted some of the disparity and inequality in the movement, women as a cohort (though in smaller numbers) did contribute to the early successes and achievements within the Finnish immigrant's socialist-unionist movement. Their participation began with the founding of socialist-unionist locals, even before the association of the Finnish Socialist Federation in 1906. In the listing of early organizational efforts, women often appear. According to Sulkanen's review of Finnish American labor history, "In this early time the [Hancock] Jousi's activity centered around meetings that stated resistance to the mining companies," and women were prevalent resisters in the Jousi's original membership, which included wives as well as single women, such as Katri Hiltunen, Hilja Frilund, Aino Knutti, Maria Ollila, Saima Saviniemi, Hilda Syväjärvi, Hilma Syväjärvi, and Sanna Kallio-Kannasto. Aino Knutti was also an early board member of the Työmies Publishing Company.[59]

The Työmies Publishing Company in Hancock employed a number of women in the printing business as well. Some women found work in traditional roles, such as store clerks and office workers, but the publishing company also dedicated mechanical jobs, such as bookbinder's assistant and platen-press operator, to women.[60]

Hall life in particular was a place of conspicuous achievement by women within the movement. While socialist-unionist halls had traditional female activities, such as sewing clubs that held bazaars and cooking bees for benefits that raised money for the cause, halls were also a place where women could break from the then contemporary norm by effusively participating in socialist-unionist activities steeped in instructive ideology. Women were essential parts of educational activities such as lecturing, reading, acting, debating, and proselytizing. In some instances, women served in leadership roles at halls. The Marquette and Negaunee, Michigan, locals were such places where women served in very prominent roles as early directors of the Negaunee Labor Temple's debating committee and the Marquette Liberty Hall's drama society. Ellen Liljeblad, Hilja Frilund, Hilja Sutinen, and Hanna Kivi were all directors of the Marquette local's theatrical productions, which were a very successful part of the hall's activities.[61]

Another area of participatory significance for women was perhaps the most important of all activities for Finnish immigrant socialist-unionists—strikes. Finnish immigrant women were often the most vocal and noticeable part of strike activity, especially when leading strike parades. These women displayed an incredible will and determination when fronting parades, which often had vociferous and at times violent opposition standing mere feet away. This leadership was nothing less than heroic. Rank-and-file women often led these parades, carrying American flags or Socialist Party banners. The 1913–14 Michigan Copper Miners' Strike was one such event where women had a very important role. Frank Aaltonen of Negaunee, Michigan, described the exploits of a group of striking women and girls in a 1913 article titled "The Gallant Women of the Copper Strike":

> One morning a large group of high-spirited girls was arrested in Calumet, most of them 14–18 years of age. They were transported like some evildoers to the same dirty jail where they put thieves, crooks, robbers and murderers

> too. The old moldy prison walls might have felt then that this group differed from the usual ones. Even the grim gates were certainly smiling when song melodies from the young girls' chests, "My country, 'tis of thee, sweet land of liberty" arrived through the narrow jail's gates to the ears of wondering listeners. Listeners smiled quietly. Songs of freedom echo most beautifully where tyrants are nearest. The gallant women of the copper strike were not bothered with fear and idleness. Hundreds hurried there where battle was at its most intense with such a willingness to make sacrifices that there's hardly a comparison in American labor history.[62]

Hilja Fräki was another rank-and-file woman deeply involved in the Finnish immigrant socialist-unionist movement. Born June 20, 1889, Fräki arrived in the United States from Alatornio, Finland on May 18, 1912. She began her American life in Chicago and joined the Chicago Finnish Socialist Federation of the Socialist Party of America two years later, on September 20, 1914. Assessment stamps in Hilja's red Socialist Party of America card indicate that she paid dues to the Finnish Agitation Committee, while also paying dues to the Socialist Party of America national. On the eve of U.S. involvement in World War I, Hilja paid a special "Party Building, Anti-Militarism Assessment" of $0.25.

From 1912 to 1915, Hilja split time between Chicago and Hancock, where she had extended family.[63] A letter from an Upper Peninsula suitor questioned Hilja as to why she was in such constant transit *and* why she never stopped to see the letter's author: "I realized from your letter that you have now left the metropolis of Chicago and moved to the Copper Island. Why didn't you visit this little village [Ramsay, Michigan] on the way there? It would have been fun to get to see you again and shake your warm hand. You said that you would not stay long there either because of the work contracts and low wages."[64]

In 1916, Hilja moved to Detroit, joining the Finnish Socialist Federation local there, but then moved a year later to the west coast of the United States, joining a Finnish Socialist Federation local in San Francisco, moving again to the Pacific Northwest around 1920. With all this roaming, a September 15, 1917, letter from a friend in Detroit to Hilja in San Francisco indicated that one of Hilja's prominent concerns in this time of transition was keeping her membership status up-to-date with the Socialist Party of America. The letter read, "The Aholainens have been to the Hall with your membership card, but they did not meet the person who is responsible for membership matters. So, Rajala took your card and he is going to take care of the matter tomorrow in the meeting of the chapter. You'll get the relocation card, just be patient."[65] Hilja married Matt Thompson in the 1920s. The marriage to Thompson was perhaps a bit of an odd-couple wedding. Thompson served in the United States military aboard the USS *Missouri* during World War I. Knowing that Hilja did not support the war, he wrote on September 29, 1918, "Are you angry with me for buying a fifty dollar Liberty Bond yesterday? I don't think I am wasting my money."[66]

Hilja was a comely young woman who inspired much admiration from the opposite sex. Many letters from suitors before her marriage testify to her attractiveness, but also in these letters, the reader gets the impression that she was a strong, independent woman, able to "talk" proletarian ideology as well as romance. A number of letters queried as to why Hilja never planned to marry, and still other letters implored that respect and equality are essential aspects of romantic relations, almost implying that Hilja would accept nothing less. In some instances, letters closed, "With Comradeship."

Many of the letters include exchange of ideas about class and social conditions. Toil of the proletariat is also a rather common theme, as one dramatic November 1, 1918, letter from Kaarlo in Seattle, Washington, portrayed: "Oh you who have suffered so much, my noble Hilja. Maybe one day we shall see the Red revolution. Our new wonderful ideals would justify the oppression and remove the unjust—oh you, red waving flag—fluttering justice—we could then enjoy life Hilja, the existence of life."[67] Another letter indicated that women and men were egalitarian toilers within the exploitative capitalist system: "It is a fact that it is not easy for a working class person to be anywhere. I guess that working class women share the same destiny as men. Both of them are the slaves of capitalists."[68]

Debate over Didactics

Within the culture of the Finnish immigrants' socialist-unionist movement, we can distinguish three general types of participants. First, there were the hardcore, didactic organizational members. These dyed-in-the-wool adherents drove much of the organizational response and provided the committed actions and rhetoric that sustained the overarching goals of the movement. Second, there were the "Hall Finns." These people may or may not have been card-carrying members of the socialist locals or unions, but did faithfully attend the hall or became a member of the movement simply for the entertainments. Hall Finns delighted in dances, loved to watch plays, perhaps acting in one or two, and joined in efforts to better the organization through participation in the various athletic, social, and fine arts societies. The Hall Finns were not, however, hard-core supporters of the dogma and rhetoric associated with didactic Finnish immigrant socialist-unionists. They may have believed in a little, some, none, or all of what didactic members advocated, but the complete devotion to proletarian mores was just not a top priority.

Lastly, there were the folks who just walked through the doors on dance or play nights. They came to be entertained and for little else, but supported the socialist-unionist movement monetarily through purchase of tickets, refreshments, and/or donations. It was these people, however, that in essence did much to support the socialist-unionist movement as revenue streams. Socialist-unionist theater societies likely designed many performances just for this third group of people. Many of the plays, lectures, and the like were organizational tools. A theatergoer might walk in the door unaffiliated, but come out engaged—at least that was an expectation of many performances.

As socialist-unionist culture, and hall culture specifically, became trendy, didactic members became disenchanted with folks who used the hall purely for entertainment. Obedience to the socialist-unionist cause was essential to hardliners, and they perceived an alarming trend of Hall Finns overlooking rigid adherence to proletarian principles in favor of maintenance and financing of halls and their activities.[69] Theater groups and hall activity, including elaborate dramas, dances, and concerts, became more popular than agitating for the socialist and labor cause. The theater and halls were becoming lucrative entertainment venues and somewhat shallow ideological pools in the eyes of zealous followers.

This conflict, over just how didactic a socialist or workers' hall should be, played out individually among cultural organizations' members, but one hall, the Socialist Opera House, in Virginia, Minnesota, became a focal point of contention in 1913. This was most evident in the building's architecture, inside and out. Historian James A. Roe writes of the Socialist Opera House: "In their success, however, the builders brought together a curiously contradictory assemblage of images and ideals. Even the name 'Socialist Opera'—so boldly displayed on the façade—joins elements from two usually differing worlds; the working class ethic of socialism and the high culture of opera."[70] The opera house was so ornate and skillfully designed, the conservative press in Virginia remarked that the opera house was "one of the most substantial structures on the Range, modern in every detail."[71] In a 1913 *Työmies* article, A. F. Heiskanen wrote of the opera house: "Our new hall . . . is the epitome of the struggle up to this time of the Virginia working class."[72] To some, the hall and the refinement of socialism, which the opera house symbolically represented, was a source of pride and organizational affirmation.

To others, the opera house was the epitome of bourgeois culture, not working-class mores, and was certainly not in line with Marxist principles. Roe writes: "Yet at the same time they built a theater that was hardly classless in its function, for it boasted expensive box seats and emulated a style especially alien to the working class."[73] Unlike most modest, yet functional halls and theaters, the Socialist Opera House's design competed architecturally with American vaudeville theaters. The opera house was a place that dazzled with its excessive ornamentation and visually intended theatergoers to escape their ordinary worlds.[74] This ordinary material world was, however, the world that socialist and labor leaders wanted to tap with organizational efforts. A large number of Finnish immigrant socialist-unionists were Marxists who believed very much in historic materialism. What did a building like the Socialist Opera House declare about the material condition of the Finnish immigrant working class?

As early as 1909, members at a Finnish workers' gathering in Hancock, Michigan, complained that Finnish immigrant socialism was "burled in art." They further protested that agitation and organizational efforts were taking a back seat to drama, brass bands, and dancing. They were correct. When the Finnish Socialist Federation held its 1912 convention, the minutes revealed that local socialist-unionist hall organizations held 4,433 work meetings that discussed Socialist Party of America or Finnish Socialist Federation business; 3,290 entertainments, such as hall parties, dances, plays, and concerts; and

2,160 program meetings discussing formal education, lecture-giving, and speechmaking.[75] Additionally, in Minnesota there were only seventeen agitation committees as opposed to twenty-four dramatic groups and twenty-seven literature committees, several choruses and the occasional brass band.[76] The Finnish immigrant socialist-unionist movement was entering the realm of popular culture. This was an unsavory development for some.

To Daisy Walkama, Virginia's Socialist Opera House was simply a wonderful place to grow up. Though her family lived almost a mile away, Daisy fondly remembers walking on top of huge snowdrifts to get to the opera house. Her stepfather, John Partanen, was heavily involved in the unionist movement, owned stock in a workers' cooperative, and served on the board of directors of the Työmies Publishing Company as early as 1912. Daisy remembers the Socialist Opera House as being very grand, even in the late 1920s and early 1930s. She remembers the opera house having a beautiful multipurpose room on the main floor. The main floor had wood floors with movable wooden folding chairs, so the seating could be moved for gymnastics practice. Daisy recalls that the sides of the main floor had box seating, and that balcony seating hung over the main floor. The basement had a kitchen and a dining room for serving *kavia* and *pulla* (coffee and Finnish bread). The opera house's bathrooms also served as changing rooms for the actors who performed in the opera house's plays and musicals.[77]

Daisy recalled the songs of choral groups and lectures held at the opera house. She was involved in plays and remembered portraying a beautiful butterfly wrapped in a cocoon for one performance. The opera house was the location of socialist-unionist Sunday schools where children of Finnish immigrants studied the *Aapinen* (Finnish alphabet book) and read stories about the old country in addition to socialist-unionist-themed books and literature. Daisy fondly recalled *Joulupukki* (Santa Claus) on the opera house's balcony, which was teeming with gifts of animal crackers and oranges that were brought by parents to distribute collectively among the children.[78]

Most affectionately, Daisy remembers the dances at the opera house. At times, orchestras were brought in to play waltzes or other high-toned tunes. Polkas and schottisches were also popular at dances. According to Daisy, the men would line up on one side of the opera house and women would line up on the other. The men would walk across the floor and ask the women to dance. Daisy remembers being proud of her mother and stepfather's beautiful waltzing. Her stepfather once tried to teach Daisy how to waltz, but when a boy tried to cut in on the lesson, Daisy ran and hid in the opera house's bathroom to avoid dancing with the young suitor. As she remembers, the Socialist Opera House was certainly a "big part of their life."[79]

Whether the dogmatic members liked it or not, the Socialist Opera House, Hall Finns, and socialist-unionist hall "pop" culture represented an innovative direction for the Finnish immigrant socialist-unionists' organizational efforts. The halls, fancy opera house, and dramatic groups stood as motivational symbols and sources of great revenue for the socialist-unionist movement. They also, and more covertly, stood as enticements for nonsocialists to walk through hall doors and hear the proletarian message. This was purposeful for the most part, as the mission of the Virginia Workers' Organization, builders of the opera house, attest: "It was possible to draw audiences unaware of the movement to hear agitators' speeches, poems and songs and such material with which it was possible to elevate their knowledge."[80] The Socialist Opera House opened on April 13, 1913, to eight hundred people with a Goethe drama titled *Clavigo*. Mixed in with subsequent farcical comedies and high-tech bourgeois stage productions were educational and dramatic plays designed to elevate class-consciousness and create proletarian solidarity.[81]

CHAPTER 3

Finnish Immigrant Socialist-Unionists in Hancock

In the quest to disseminate the socialist-unionist message, we can hypothesize that Hancock's Kansankoti Hall, built in 1910 and located in the Finnish Transitional Neighborhood, was on the same course of class-conscious organization as Virginia's Socialist Opera House. It is important to understand that the Finnish immigrants' socialist-unionist movement organized from the ground up, so to speak. For the most part, the Finnish immigrant laborers entering the Copper Country were unfamiliar with the socioeconomic aspects of industrial life. Finnish immigrant socialists and labor activists perceived abuses in the industrial setting and organized a challenge to the Copper Country oligarchy at a very grass-roots level, tapping Finnish immigrants to organize a concerted response to Copper Country capitalists. The Kansankoti Hall was likely located in Hancock's booming Finnish Transitional Neighborhood purposely to attract foot traffic from Hancock's unorganized laboring masses. Chapter 1 examined the history of the Hancock socialist-unionist local's land acquisition and construction efforts in the Finnish Transitional Neighborhood, but how did the socialist-unionist Finn's cultural organizations get a foothold in mining company–dominated Hancock?

The Finnish immigrants' socialist-unionist organizational history in Hancock is complex and interesting. It begins with prominent socialist orator Martin Hendrickson. Hendrickson, born in Kivijärvi, Finland, in 1872, came to the United States in 1889 and settled in Boston, Massachusetts, working for a time in the New England rock quarries.[1] Hendrickson began to "preach" the socialist message and commenced with an itinerant life, touring throughout the northern United States attempting to convert people to socialism. Sometimes his message struck a chord with listeners. One such place where his message took root was in the Copper Country. Hendrickson left New York on January 20, 1900, headed for mining towns in the Upper Peninsula of Michigan. Hancock was one such stop. Hendrickson obtained permission to speak in a local Hancock hall from Mayor Scott. Approximately one hundred people heard Hendrickson speak.[2] With Hendrickson's words ringing in their heads, and wanting to escape the inflexible dogma of pious religious elements in the Pohjantähti Temperance Society, about thirty intrepid individuals set up their own cultural organization, the Hancock *Jousi Seura* (Bow Society).[3] Some of the Jousi's first members were actors from stage productions who previously held meetings in the Germania Hall while renting out the Kerredge Theater for plays.[4] The Jousi began with a temperance-workingmen's ideal, but over time evolved to include various forms of radical socialism and unionism.[5]

Salomon Ilmonen, Suomi Synod Evangelical Lutheran leader in Hancock, unfavorably recounts the march from Christian temperance principles to socialism:

> A new ideal, socialism begins to appear everywhere and its effect is felt clearly even in the Pohjantähti. The workers' society "Jousi" became clearly a socialistic society, as to its world view, and since these workers' society members had belonged for many years to the Pohjantähti it was of little wonder that socialism began to influence the temperance society. This was most evident whenever reference was made to religious concerns or questions. Brothers with socialistic ideals couldn't swallow anything which smacked of religion or its values. Finally the negative emphasis got the majority vote in a regular meeting held on May 19, 1907, the decision was made to remove the prayers for starting meetings and the words, "By God's help," from the recitation of the temperance vow.[6]

As we have already established in the previous chapter, 1904 and 1906 were important years for Finnish immigrant socialist-unionists. Nineteen hundred four saw local Finnish immigrant socialist groups politicking for unification with the Socialist Party of America. This amalgamation took two meetings to congeal. The first meeting in Duluth, Minnesota, explored affiliation with the SPA. Members of the Hancock Jousi and the *Suomi Seura* (Finland Society) of Calumet attended. Representing the Jousi was A. F. Tanner, F. Lundberg, and Alexander Nieminen, the grocer whose store was at 201–203 Franklin Street in the Finnish Transitional Neighborhood. The Suomi Society of Calumet's representative was J. A. Harpet. In October, a second meeting in Cleveland, Ohio, cemented the Finnish immigrant alliance with the Socialist Party of America. Vihtori Kosonen, a dedicated Marxist, and Nieminen of the Jousi attended the Cleveland meeting. After the 1904 meetings in Duluth and Cleveland, the Jousi joined the SPA on December 11, 1904, bringing only 29 members into the Socialist Party, but that figure grew to 49 members by 1906. In 1906, the Hibbing, Minnesota, meeting built a nationwide federation of Finnish immigrant socialist-unionist locals that joined the SPA as a language federation.[7]

In this early period (1904–1906), the ideology behind the Finnish immigrant socialist-unionist movement drastically shifted. Finnish immigrant Marxists began to give up rather benign forms of socialism in favor of more radical precepts.[8] This ideological shift had major reverberations in Hancock's Jousi. While ties were not entirely severed between the Jousi and the Christian temperance movement, a major shift in ideology was apparent even to those outside socialist-unionist circles. Beginning in 1906, changes became evident in the philosophy and material focus of Pohjantähti as socialist-unionist members attempted to compel the group's ideological base to shift. Ilmonen wrote:

> The years 1906 and 1907 may be regarded as the "socialistic period" in *Pohjantähti*'s history . . . A joint planning meeting was convened in the *Työmies*-newspaper office to gather aid for the crofters at Laukka estate . . . When these joint concerns and appeals continued, there simultaneously arose whispers about joining the regular socialistic movement, but even at its warmest phase, this union did not ensue.[9]

Hancock's Jousi was an especially influential part of the FSF. Since 1904, the Hancock local included a potent publishing association, the Työmies Publishing Company. The publishing company's main publication, *Työmies*, became the officially mandated voice of socialist-unionist Finns in the Midwest.[10] As the importance of the Jousi and the Työmies Publishing Company grew, the Finnish immigrant socialist-unionists found they needed space to achieve their socialist and labor goals. This revelation set into motion a shrewd set of well-orchestrated business maneuvers in 1907. Two highly involved people in these business endeavors were Nieminen and Gustav Frilund, a bookbinder employed by the Finnish Lutheran Book Concern. Nieminen and Frilund had dual associations with two important aspects of the Finnish immigrant cultural organizations. They were on the board of the influential Työmies Publishing Company and members of the newly created Kansankoti Real Estate Corporation.[11] The significance of this incorporation between enmeshed proletarian interests, brokered by folks like Nieminen and Frilund, was that the Finnish immigrant socialist-unionist movement now had the ability to finance major construction efforts, for things like halls, and expanded media offerings. The Jousi was laying the financial foundations to build a hall of their own, a long-envisioned home for the people, and increase the readership of socialist-unionist publications.

Relationship Building: Love, Marriage, and Socialism in Hancock

Socialist-unionist buildings and societies were a great place to meet the opposite sex. The halls provided a place where women and men could flaunt their physical attractiveness and passion for the cause. Courtship in various forms took place in the socialist-unionist halls, at times at inappropriate moments. While delivering a speech, socialist orator Martin Hendrickson reprimanded his amorous audience by advising the men and women to find a better place "for continuing the human race."[12] The Hancock Jousi was one such place where love, for at least one couple, co-existed with ideology.

Laina Ollila, the Finnish immigrant who lived and worked at a boarding house with her mother in the Finnish Transitional Neighborhood, was once such person who found courtship and love amid the socialist-unionist cause. Laina became the object of affection of one Evert W. Björklund, who was a type composer for the Työmies Publishing Company. Evert immigrated to the United States between 1902 and 1903 from Hämeenlinna, Finland. He initially located in Worcester, Massachusetts, possibly joining comrades and working at the Työmies Publishing Company while it was in the eastern United States.[13] Evert likely moved to Hancock in early 1904, when Työmies moved from Worcester to Hancock. Once in Hancock, Evert joined *Reipas* (Activity), an athletic club within the Pohjantähti Temperance Society. Evert was an able athlete and became leader of Reipas's thirty-nine members. "Due to his leadership the society won a nice prize of $25 at the Temperance Societies' annual festival, held at Hibbing [Minnesota]."[14] As *Työmies* was a socialist-labor newspaper, Evert gravitated to the local socialist-unionist activities and was an early advocate of the labor-political cause within the Finnish immigrant temperance movement. Laina and her mother, Maria, also became involved in the socialist-unionist cause.

Laina and Evert grew close while exploring themes in the socialist-unionist movement and eventually married between 1907 and 1909, when their first child, Ensio, was born. Evert moved into the boarding house at 237 Wright Street and shared ownership of the house with Maria Ollila.[15] The 1910 census lists Evert as the head of the household, which included his wife Laina, their son Ensio (eleven months old), Maria Ollila, and four boarders.[16] Evert had a steady job at the Työmies Publishing Company, which was only a short walk from the 237 Wright Street boarding house, and Laina likely had help with Ensio from Maria. Laina and Evert were one of many couples who found love and started families among the activities and functions of socialist-unionist cultural organizations.

The Jousi Surges Ahead, 1907–1910

Nineteen hundred seven was overall a busy year for Hancock's Jousi. Affirming that socialism and the labor movement was not all work and no play, the Hancock local boldly decided to test their First Amendment rights in 1907. Earlier in the year, the Jousi paraded in a trade unions' Labor Day parade, carrying a red flag. After that display, the City of Hancock ruled that display of the red flag at public functions was illegal.[17] The Jousi wanted to confirm that the city was serious about the red flag ruling; it turns out they were: in late July, as part of a summer festival and likely a march of solidarity for striking iron-ore workers on Minnesota's Mesabi Iron Range, the Jousi organized and participated in what became known as the "Red Flag Parade." The parade route ran down one of Hancock's primary thoroughfares in the Finnish Transitional Neighborhood, Quincy Street.

The Red Flag Parade, organized to take place on Sunday, July 28, was a brazen test of resolve for the Finnish immigrant socialist-unionists. Apparently, the Saturday night before the parade, Hancock's Police Chief Andrews went to the Jousi's meeting in Germania Hall and notified the members there that if they were to march with the red flag, it meant sure arrest. Andrews left the meeting after saying his piece, but seemingly anticipated that his words would have little effect. The next morning, he swore in ten additional deputies, who were supplied with "stout billys" in case of trouble. The fortified Hancock police department then went to the Copper Range Railroad's depot to wait for an anticipated fifty or so parade participants coming by train from neighboring South Range. By nine o'clock Sunday morning, there was a palpable energy in the air as people started filling Quincy Street in anticipation of extracurricular activities accompanying the parade. The folks lining Quincy Street would not be disappointed.[18]

As an article in Hancock's *Evening Journal* recounted the events:

> At 10 o'clock the members [Finnish Socialist Federation] started to form their procession in front of the Scott Hotel. A handsome American flag was carried at the head of the line and was greeted by much applause by the by-standers. The South Range City Band came next and was followed by about thirty members of the society. These members all wore small red badges in the shape of flags and some wore red sashes around their waists or over their shoulders.
>
> Then the remaining members of the society bearing ten red flags came out of the hall and formed in line. They raised their flags high in the air so they could be plainly seen. They were large red flags of different shapes, some of them being silk and with gold lettering and two being plain red ones. The inscription borne on most of these was the word "Socialism."

> As soon as the flags were raised Chief Andrews and the police force marched up and pulled down the first few flags, placing the standard bearers under arrest. As soon as this happened a large number of citizens who had gathered along the sides of the street pulled down the remaining flags and seizing them, they smashed the standards into splinters and tore the flags into shreds, leaving only one banner intact and that one is now in possession of the chief of police.[19]

The police arrested thirteen in all, twelve men and one woman, while the rest of the parade continued to the Hancock fairgrounds to begin the day's festivities. For the most part, it was reported that the arrested went peaceably, but in two or three cases, "it was necessary for the officers to use their clubs." The arrested came from a wide cross section of Finnish immigrants in the Upper Peninsula: Fahle Burman was a clerk from Negaunee; Louis E. Henderson was a cigar maker from Calumet; Toivo Hiltunen was a Työmies Publishing Company printer from Hancock; Albert Mainio was a baker from Hancock; Charles Ahonen was a miner from Crystal Falls; John Juntikka was a miner from Mohawk; Fannie Maki was a domestic from Calumet; Paavo Sirvio was a manager of Työmies Publishing Company in Hancock; Leo Laukki was an editor at Työmies Publishing Company in Hancock; Charles Waali was a trammer from Trimountain; Nikoli Tietavainen was a tailor from Hancock; Fred Helander was a baker from South Range; and Frank Aaltonen a clerk from Negaunee. City officials held the arrested in Hancock's City Hall, then placed the offenders on a streetcar that took them to county jail in Houghton. Unknown to the police, before the parade, the FSF gathered a fund to pay bond for those arrested, and the Red Flag 13 were out of jail later that afternoon.[20]

The real problem with the red flags was not, of course, that they were red per se, but rather what the color red symbolized to many in Hancock, the State of Michigan, and the entire United States, for that matter. To many, the red flag was the representation of anarchy and nothing else—not socialism, not a symbol of bloodshed by the working class or even passion for the proletarian cause. Many viewed the red flag as literal anarchy, and to the City of Hancock, that was an arrestable offense. But it seemed the members of the FSF expected some type of seizure by officials. Therefore, in essence, the parade was more of an assertion of rights, liberty, and freedom. Whatever the case, on that same weekend in the highly publicized murder trial of William "Big Bill" Haywood, IWW founder and staunch syndicalist, a jury of his peers found him not guilty of murdering former Idaho Governor Steunenberg. The two articles, the Red Flag Parade story and Haywood's trial outcome, were side by side in Monday's Hancock *Evening Journal*. It was indeed a momentous couple of days for organized labor, both on the national level and in local Copper Country circles.[21]

The euphoria of the Red Flag Parade perceptibly wore off by August 2nd, when the Red Flag 13 went to trial. They lost—despite fiery representation by progressive Calumet lawyer P. H. O'Brien. As his first order of business, O'Brien set the context for the trial by declaring that his defendants were fighting an uphill battle because the court was trying the case in a "hostile atmosphere." According to the *Evening Journal*:

> He [O'Brien] explained the difference between anarchism and socialism, stating that the socialist wishes to better civilization. They believe in government ownership for the benefit of all the people; they believe in the abolition of the wage system of industry; they believe in the republican form of government, but not as it is conducted at present; they believe in peace, not war. "The red flag is the universal flag of the down-trodden and oppressed people, the international flag of an international people. They will fight for the right of carrying their emblems."[22]

The *Evening Journal* went on to write that "[O'Brien] said the citizens were anarchists last Sunday when they destroyed the red flag of the Socialists. The latter were not disorderly he said; the people began the riot."[23] That was bold talk, but then O'Brien outdid himself when he declared that "The police of Hancock were the trespassers and should be punished for it."[24]

On the prosecution side of the aisle was Hancock city attorney Swaby L. Lawton, brother of Quincy Mining Company superintendent Charles L. Lawton. After O'Brien spoke, Swaby called a gaggle of witnesses to the stand who testified that the red flag meant only anarchy. The prosecution called upon a bevy of Hancock's "upstanding" citizens to testify. Everyone from Hancock mayor A. J. Scott to city night watchman Arvid Naaska to Suomi Synod pastor and Suomi College president J. K. Nikander testified that red equaled anarchy. In fact, Mayor Scott went so far as to say "he considered it but one step from the carrying of red flags to the throwing of bombs," and Naaska "thought the red flag was the flag of anarchy; that the socialists did not believe in God, in the church, or in marriage." This act, the Red Flag Parade, cemented the Jousi's disposition as a radical socialist-unionist organization to many in Hancock, and to be quite candid, there were probably a couple of anarchist-minded folks mixed in among the Red Flag Parade's participants. Even so, as O'Brien argued when Swaby Lawton queried whether the red flag stood for anarchy, it did not matter if a socialist or anarchist waved the flag—it should be legal to brandish a symbol of your beliefs.[25] Hancock's Justice of the Peace Oliver found the Red Flag 13 guilty of violating the flag ordinance and disturbing the peace anyway. A district court affirmed this ruling, but the case later faded away when appealed to the Michigan State Supreme Court.[26]

In the aftermath of the parade, the final bonds of the tenuous union between the Jousi and Pohjantähti finally broke. Ilmonen, who remained true to the Pohjantähti's Christian temperance ideals, disdainfully wrote about the period:

> We were all still working together during the so-called "red flag" affair, but that ended all joint activity. Since that red flag mess, the *Pohjantähti* no longer extended support, especially no financial aid. As a result, in 1907, the socialists withdrew from the *Pohjantähti* membership, which then had 400 members, thereafter leaving 160 members [in the Pohjantähti]. The giant *Pohjantähti* was again a small society, but unity and peace were restored, thus resulting in power again.[27]

As the Jousi left the confines of the temperance movement, they found themselves sans a physical home. Planning for a new *Kansankoti*, or People's Home, began in earnest.

To place the Jousi's visions for a new home on paper, the Hancock local chose a Calumet, Michigan, architect by the name of J. K. Hakolahti, who designed a grand edifice for the Jousi in July 1907. Little is known about Hakolahti, but it appears as if he trained professionally as a *rakenmestari*, which translates into "building master" or architect. As evidenced by the architect's

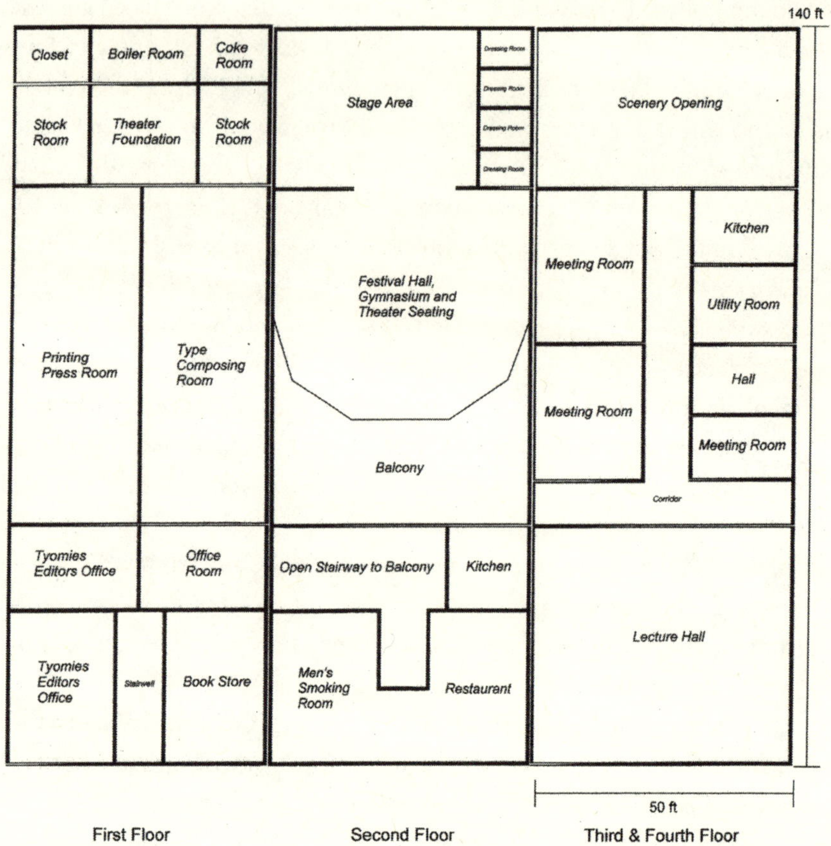

Hakolahti Building, English Translation. An architectural drawing (not to scale) and translation of the interior building design and spatial usage from the original 1907 Hakolahti watercolor. (Drawing and translation by Gary Kaunonen.)

watercolors, Hakolahti's design for the building was rather extravagant. Its architectural character had a rather eclectic design, which included one large center turret and two smaller side turrets constructed of red brick, finials set atop the turrets' roofs, belt coursing at various levels on the building, and patterned stained-glass window arches. From the watercolors, it is difficult to determine if the red stone exterior is rough-cut material, but Hakolahti could have possibly planned to use Jacobsville sandstone, a locally quarried abundant and handsome building material.

The proposed use of interior space in the Hakolahti building seems consistent with later-built large Finnish immigrant socialist-unionist halls in the Lake Superior region. Stage and scenery, a restaurant, kitchens, hall space for performance seating and gymnasium use, lecture halls, and meeting rooms provided space for essential elements of Finnish immigrant proletarian culture. Additionally, the unique spatial needs of the Hancock Jousi dictated that any complex for this FSF local needed to include room for the printing and publishing machinery of the Työmies Publishing Company. The Hakolahti watercolors indicated that the Työmies Publishing Company's quarters would utilize an entire floor. In this first floor, there was space for the publishing company's machinery, offices, and printing supplies. Therefore, in these watercolors we see an early conception of the aspiration to combine the operations of the Hancock Jousi into one central building or campus. It would take three more years to consolidate the physical operations of Hancock's Jousi in the Finnish Transitional Neighborhood, but within that time, important changes took place within the Jousi and FSF's ideological composition.

At the 1909 FSF convention, held in Hancock, all seemed to be going well for the Finnish immigrant socialist-unionists. The Hancock local was as feisty as ever, arguing that the Hancock police caused the commotion at the Red Flag Parade and not vice versa. The number of locals in the FSF had grown to 160, with 5,384 members and the Työmies Publishing Company along with other socialist-unionist publications were steadily increasing both the scope and number of subscriptions to party publications.[28] FSF secretary Victor Watia reported that the federation's coffers held $26,358.11. There were plans to improve organization of the FSF by dividing locals into districts, with each district having its own regional officers and organizers. On the surface, the FSF seemed fighting fit. Underneath it all, there were major ideological differences percolating within the FSF.[29]

As early as 1905, the Finnish immigrant socialist-unionists were looking for direction. Early rancor ensued over association with the American socialist movement's Marxism. The demure socioeconomic principles of Matti Kurikka's utopian communes and bourgeois workingmen's benevolent societies, such as Imatra and the Finnish American Workers' League, promoted by early *Työmies* newspaper editor N. J. Ahlman and writer-poet Moses Hall, came into direct confrontation with a growing Marxist outlook. Through the years 1905 to 1909, this radical sentiment increased within the Finnish immigrant movement. An increasing ideological gulf existed between eastern United States Finnish socialists, described as Yellow Finns, and midwestern and western United States radical Finns, which included an increasing majority of the Jousi's members and the Työmies Publishing Company staff. Organizationally on the national level, this meant a majority of eastern Yellow Finns advocated parliamentary socialism. Radical Finns of the Midwest and West favored a revolutionary track, and some advocated an alliance with the Industrial Workers of the World.[30] The debate raged in the coming years and often played itself out in the Finnish socialist-unionist's cultural organizations, and specifically in the pages of the Finnish socialist-unionist press.

With an increasing sense of radical purpose, the Jousi spearheaded construction of a hall in 1910. The Kansankoti that became a reality was not, however, the Kansankoti Hall of Hakolahti's grandiose architectural vision. Nevertheless, the Jousi likely required a "home" posthaste if they were duplicating the success of the FSF, which in 1910 had grown to 173 locals with 7,767 members.[31] In the Finnish immigrant population, socialism and unionism were spreading like wildfire through a tinder dry jack-pine forest. The need for social facilities was paramount.

At this point, the incorporation of the Kansankoti Real Estate venture paid off. Nieminen's grocery store could serve as a home for the Työmies Publishing Company, while a new hall would provide space for the cultural activities that sustained the Finnish immigrant socialist-unionist movement.[32] The mission to create a new "People's Home" was of course a collective enterprise. According to Hancock resident Mrs. Klemetti, "Even before they started to build the Kansankoti Hall people bought shares in it."[33] These shares funded the construction of a building that became a regional center. The building of the Kansankoti Hall was a communal effort that promised big organizational returns for the Jousi and FSF.

On May 10, 1910, the Kansankoti Real Estate Corporation ran this ad in the Hancock *Evening Copper Journal*:

> Contractors Wanted: To give estimates on rebuilding Kansankoti Company's building, located at the corner of Tezcuco and Franklin Streets. Plans can be seen at Alexander Nieminen's Store, 215 Quincy Street, Hancock. Bids must not be later than Saturday May 14, 12 o'clock noon. Rights reserved to reject any or all bids.

After completion of the hall's construction, which totaled around $30,000 (around $500,000 in today's dollars), in the spring of 1911 the corner of Franklin and Tezcuco was abuzz with activity.[34] As Mrs. Klemetti remembers, "the Kansankoti Hall was right in the corner of Franklin Street and that was the big place there were a lot of doings there, there were all kinds of doings . . . that was beautiful big hall and everything there was dancing and the restaurant downstairs had very good business . . . and there was that newspaper in one part of that building, Työmies . . . it was beautiful big hall and a lot of room, big down stairs where the kitchens were and restaurant."[35] Mrs. Klemetti was correct; the hall was large, at over 10,000 square feet, and included a balcony for extra seating and a large main floor area that most likely had removable chairs, which could be taken out after performances to make way for dances and gymnastic events. Dances were a big attraction, as Nick Hendrickson and John Palosaari, two Hancock residents, remembered:

> *Henrickson:* The Kansankoti Hall in Hancock used to be a dance place years ago.
>
> *Palosaari:* Oh, I went over there, but I never danced. I tried to learn to dance, but the lady I was with said that I was all the time stepping on her toes. So, I never learned to dance. But, I used to like to watch them when they danced. They played with the accordion and stuff like that.[36]

The Kansankoti Hall as built ended up having many of the amenities of the early Hakolahti drawing, but the deviation from Hakolahti's grand vision for the building might have indicated that the Jousi and Kansankoti Real Estate venture did not have the cash on hand to follow Hakolahti's ornate building plans to a tee. On the other hand, perhaps by 1910 the Hakolahti plans were too small to house the rapidly growing Työmies Publishing Company and therefore needed modification. It is clear, however, that the Kansankoti-Työmies complex housed all the necessary facilities to make the Finnish Transitional Neighborhood and Hancock a working-class citadel among the Copper Island's industrially controlled milieu.

Hancock as Proletarian Nexus

The erection of the Kansankoti Hall addition and renovation of the Nieminen grocery building had great impact on the Finnish immigrants' socialist-labor movement in the Midwest. On one lot, the Hancock local assembled: a large Finn hall with balcony, stage, and scenery that also served as a gymnasium, a highly influential working-class newspaper that had subscribers across the Midwest, a proletarian eatery named the Kansankoti Café, and a cooperative bank. The Työmies Publishing Company also quartered offices, a bookstore, and presses within the Coughlin building in an adjacent lot.[37]

From the skillful choreography in the Kansankoti Real Estate venture, it is evident that the Jousi was very well organized and shrewd in their business endeavors. For a group with a purportedly large number of Marxists, the members of Hancock's local played the capitalist game very well. The Jousi's deft business maneuvers made the Finnish Transitional Neighborhood the center for all socialist-unionist cultural activity in the Copper Country and possibly the entire Midwest. This idea of permanence and solidity did not escape the Hancock local's rhetoric, as evidenced in a 1910 article in *Työmiehen Joulu* (Workingmen's Christmas): "Behind the business location of *Työmies*, Kansankoti Company is building a big hall whose foundation and walls of the ground floor are already done. Next spring the hall will be finished. When that building is ready, socialism will be rooted in the hard ground of Copper Island. The shore areas of Michigan and Minnesota will have a fortress for its future operation."[38]

The history of Finnish socialist-unionist cultural organizations is rife with complex interaction and factionalism. Hancock's FSF local was no exception, but its objectives and cultural activity were not unlike those of the early Finnish temperance societies. The Hancock Jousi finally incorporated "as an association not for pecuniary benefit" on May 15, 1918, and held its meetings in the Kansankoti Hall on Mondays.[39] Echoing the purposes of the early temperance societies, the Jousi's organizational goals were "to promote learning, knowledge and enlightenment of its members and educating them in various branches of art, science, literature, history, sociology, drama, gymnastics and music, both instrumental and vocal by hiring teachers and lecturers, subscribing newspapers and maintaining bands, singing societies, study and debating clubs, Sunday schools and libraries and by holding dances, socials and entertainments for the purpose of acquiring funds in order to carry on the aims aforesaid."[40]

While the cultural organizations of the temperance movement were responding to the abuse of alcohol in industrialized immigrant communities, we can infer from the above quote that the Jousi had many of the same goals in response to the social and labor conditions in the Copper Country. The objectives of temperance groups and the socialist-unionist movement were similar: to organize, educate, and elevate the living conditions of their members, but their responses to the challenges perceived in industrial society differed greatly. For a time, the Jousi would win out in the minds of immigrant Copper Country Finns.

Dual Successes in the American Movement and Finnish Immigrant Population

Immigrant socialist-unionist Finns, like those in Hancock, wore their political and organized labor convictions like a badge—and they could literally wear a Socialist Party of America badge that proclaimed for all to see the wearer's affiliation with an American political party. The association with the American socialist movement was prominent in many of the Finnish immigrant socialist-unionists' most important interactions. On Christmas cards sent by individuals to others, "*Iloista Joulua 1911, Onnellista Uutta Vuotta 1912*," the traditional Merry Christmas and Happy New Year greeting in Finnish, is often right next to the interlocking hands of the Socialist Party of America logo and the slogan "Workers of the World Unite."[41] Additionally, a yearly publication by the Työmies Publishing Company, *Köyhälistiön Nuija* (Proletarian Hammer), often featured greetings from Eugene V. Debs, Socialist Party of America presidential candidate.[42]

As we have noted, while Finnish immigrant socialist-unionists sought to maintain a sense of ethnic identity, they also made a strident effort to be a part of the greater American working-class movement by joining the Socialist Party of America and industrial unions such as the Western Federation of Miners and the Industrial Workers of the World. Building the foundations for joining the American proletariat, which meant learning the language and becoming an American citizen, was of preeminent concern. In Michigan, the FSF locals held two English-language courses that were attended by 45 people, counted 194 American union members in the ranks, and saw 158 members take out their first citizenship papers, while 111 members became full citizens in 1912.[43]

The move toward proletarian assimilation paid dividends for the Finnish immigrant socialist-unionist movement. In 1914, of the six highest-level positions in the Socialist Party of Michigan, Finnish immigrants held half. Both Severi Alanne (of Hancock) and Matti Tenhunen were on the board of directors, and Frank Aaltonen (of Negaunee) was the national committeeman. In addition, by 1914, the Finnish Federation of Michigan's Socialist Party was the largest dues-paying entity, contributing roughly a quarter of all Party dues in the state of Michigan.[44] Especially influential within the Socialist Party of Michigan, by 1912, were the Hancock and Negaunee locals of the Federation. Hancock had the publishing company, large hall, and rising membership, while Negaunee had an especially extravagant hall, good regional membership numbers, and an energized local. It was a time of great enthusiasm, leading Matti Tenhunen to state about the Negaunee Labor Temple: "It is a building which the bourgeoisie and their stooges hardly can look at without sweat on their brow, but honest workers can step into it like into their home. It is cursed by the bourgeoisie, loved by the workers—a home for future fights, future victories, sorrows and joys."[45]

This proletarian dynamism was a fragile union between competing ideological entities, but for a time it was a guiding force for the Socialist Party in Michigan. Finnish immigrant socialist-unionists had very adeptly joined and in essence thrived within the early American socialist movement. There was perceivably a good deal of pride associated with being part of a group, both "Finn" and American, that sought to elevate the class consciousness and living conditions of the working class. This devotion to the cause led membership numbers in the FSF to rise quickly at the local, state, and national levels.

By 1912, the Hancock Jousi and the FSF in general were on a decidedly upward swing. The FSF had 13,667 members in 217 locals. Michigan was home to twenty-five locals with approximately 2,000 to 2,500 members.[46] In this same year, the Hancock Jousi had 227 members. In 1912, of Michigan's twenty-five locals, the Jousi was the second largest local (of locals that submitted statistics) in Michigan, following only Marquette, which had 268 members. Cultural activities in the Michigan FSF locals were abundant. In 1912, Michigan locals held 373 workers' meetings, 205 daytime programs, and 202 evening programs, as well as four lecture courses that counted 260 participants, and one summer school with 20 participants. Additionally, there were twelve sewing societies, ten literature societies, nine theater groups, three choral groups, three gymnastics societies, and two agitation committees hosted by Michigan locals.[47] The 1912 figures were decidedly up from levels just six years earlier. In 1906, the FSF claimed 2,622 members and Michigan had only nine locals, with 270 members. None of the FSF locals had their own hall, and only two Michigan locals had lending libraries.[48] There was great momentum in the Finnish immigrant socialist-unionist movement.

The Finnish language socialist-unionist immigrant press stoked this momentum. Almost from the beginning, membership in the FSF also meant a subscription to one of four regional socialist-unionist newspapers. Finnish immigrant socialist-unionist readers subscribed to *Raivaaja* (The Pioneer) in the eastern United States; in Canada, it was *Työkansa* (The Workers Home); in the western United States, it was *Toveri* (Comrade); and in the midwestern United States, it was *Työmies*. The pool of eligible readers was large. In 1912, the FSF estimated that Michigan alone had an estimated 16,874 readers of the Finnish language.[49] *Työmies* was the officially sanctioned socialist-unionist newspaper of "Finns" in the Midwest, and the Jousi was likely very proud that this proletarian newspaper called Hancock its laboring home. *Työmies*'s printed word was an essential component of Finnish immigrant proletarian culture because it spread the socialist-unionist message past the confines of the Finnish Transitional Neighborhood to those who could not walk directly through the Kansankoti Hall's doors. The power and importance of *Työmies* as a companion piece to socialist-unionist cultural activities cannot be overstated. The Hancock Jousi relied on the Työmies Publishing Company to trumpet their challenge to capitalism in America and to call Copper Country workers into action against the perceived abuses of the mining-industry oligarchy.

CHAPTER 4

The Early Existence of the Työmies Publishing Company, 1904–1909

AS AN ASPECT OF FINNISH IMMIGRANT CULTURAL ORGANIZATIONS, PUBLISHING associations played a major role in transmitting ideology and disseminating information to members via the printed word. Socialist-unionist newspapers spread the political and organized labor message to those who could not physically walk through the doors of socialist and workers' halls or attend party and union meetings; newspapers linked distant members to an ideological movement spanning virtually all spatial divides and distances. The Työmies Publishing Company's (TPC) newspaper, known simply as *Työmies* (Workingman), was a powerful early voice for the socialist-unionist Finnish immigrant in the midwestern United States and eventually became an official organ of the Socialist Party of America. The TPC's publications disseminated their message using a tried-and-true formula. Hardcore ideology was interspersed with occasional tongue-in-cheek references and sometimes caustic satire. Quite bluntly, some TPC publications and articles could get downright "smart-assish." This proletarian mixture rubbed some the wrong way, but also endeared the TPC's publications to many for a lifetime. The rancor toward TPC publications could be so great that often the TPC's columnists, reporters, and writers passed on using their own names for fear of retribution, litigation, or incarceration. Instead, many contributors to TPC publications used initials or creative pseudonyms, such as "Tolle Kaivola" to brand their work.

In this chapter, we will examine the growth of the Työmies Publishing Company from 1904 to 1909. The evolution of the paper from small, localized rag to a regional organ of the Socialist Party of America represents the tangible growth of socialism in the Finnish immigrant population. The publishing company's English-language publications also signify the attempt by Finnish immigrant socialist-unionists to engage the overall American labor-political movement. The evolution of the publishing company from an isolated ethnic operation into a regional organ of the Socialist Party of America correlated with the growth of the publishing company's facilities and printing machinery. With surprisingly advanced technology, the TPC's publications, and especially *Työmies*, grew at a rapid rate, successfully challenging and faithfully portraying the Finnish immigrant's confrontation with elements of industrial America.

In the examination of the Työmies Publishing Company, this chapter will highlight some of the key figures that brought the technical knowledge, revolutionary spirit, and working-class ethic to the TPC's publications. An understanding of the people who worked at the TPC will afford a more complete understanding of the ideological intricacies within the publishing company's walls. This chapter will also portray the growth of the publishing company as a type of barometer that measured successive levels of preparation, both economically and rhetorically, in an incremental march toward a showdown with Copper Country capitalists.

Early Development of the TPC

The *Amerikan Suomalainen Työmies* (*AST*) (Finnish American Workingman), printed in Worcester, Massachusetts, began publication in July 1903 with the purpose of spreading socialism and maintaining a flexible attitude toward religion. Finnish Lutheranism had been at loggerheads with the international workers' movement, but the *AST* took an inclusive stance on the religious question. This flexible stance lasted a month. In August 1903, Vihtori Kosonen took over as editor of the *AST.* Kosonen, an avowed Marxist, took a more critical stance on religion.[1]

Kosonen, along with fellow Marxists Taavi Tainio and Kappo Murros, advocated a move of the *AST* to Hancock in hopes of finding fertile ideological fields for a proposed *AST*–Socialist Party of America alignment. In the summer of 1904, the *AST* moved to Hancock and renamed the paper *Työmies.*[2] From Worcester, the Finnish Cooperative Publishing Company brought $990.00 in assets to Hancock. The newly formed Työmies Publishing Company incorporated in Hancock on August 10, 1904. The TPC's purpose of corporation was to "publish a newspaper or newspapers and all kinds of books and job printing and publishing and the manufacture of books and of printed stationary and other business incident to the printing and publishing business."[3] The Työmies Publishing Company arrived in Hancock with $5,000 of capital stock in the corporation coffers.[4]

The TPC's editors, staff, and shareholders did not know it, but they left Worcester and arrived in Hancock unwittingly entangled in a clandestine fight with Copper Country mining companies for the hearts, minds, and subscriptions of Finnish immigrant readers. English-language newspapers such as Hancock's *Evening Journal* and Houghton's *Mining Gazette* had a decidedly pro–mining company stance. Larry Lankton, Copper Country historian, writes that the *Mining Gazette* "never met a union organizer, striker, or socialist that it liked."[5] The *Mining Gazette*'s publisher, E. G. Rice, once stated to James MacNaughton, superintendent of the powerful Calumet and Hecla Mining Company, "the idea of the [*Gazette*] organizers was to have a paper which would be devoted to the interests of the mining companies in the Copper Country."[6] These publications had little overt impact on influencing the burgeoning Finnish immigrant population, because few Finnish immigrants could read English.

The mining companies did attempt to infiltrate the Finnish immigrant community in the Finnish-language press as early as 1902. At this time, Rice attempted to purchase N. J. Ahlman's *Päivälehti* (Daily Journal) and its semiweekly publication *Amerikan Uutiset* (American News), which rivaled the *Mining Gazette*'s circulation of 5,000. Rice's attempt failed, but just two years later, a plot to purchase stock shares of *Päivälehti* resurfaced. In 1904, *Päivälehti*'s circulation was approximately 2,500. Possibly looking to expand the paper, the Päivälehti Publishing Company offered up $3,000 of stock for sale. O. J. Larson, Houghton County's prosecuting attorney and prominent bourgeois Finn, sought to snatch up interests in *Päivälehti*. Larson sought the secret financial backing of several area mining companies including the Calumet and Hecla Mining Company. Superintendent of Calumet and Hecla, James MacNaughton, loved the premise of clandestine ownership in a Finnish-language newspaper,[7] as a May 23, 1904, letter to Calumet and Hecla president Alexander Agassiz reveals:

> Mr. Larson is one of the prominent Finlanders of this County and is heavily interested in a Finnish daily newspaper in Red Jacket. They have about 2,500 subscribers in and about this place and inasmuch as all Finlanders can read, this daily naturally yields a great deal of influence. It has been enlarged from time to time recently but at present they find themselves short of working capital. They want to raise a total of 3,000. I find that Mr. Paine of the Copper Range and Mr. Stanton of the Atlantic and Baltic are stockholders and Larson's visit to me was with the object in view of getting us to become stockholders in the enterprise.
>
> The stock secured by Stanton, Gay, and Paine appears on the stock list in the name of O. J. Larson but has been endorsed over to their names. No one knows nor would anyone know that the mining companies are interested in the paper, which I think is a much better plan than that adopted by the Mining Gazette which is looked upon as a mine paper, and which naturally cannot wield the same amount of influence as if it were independent of the mines.
>
> We have a large number of Finlanders in our employ and this Daily is practically the only Daily they get. I am told that the paper aims to advise them along the proper lines regarding labor agitators and labor organizations, and think if we were to put any money into a newspaper it would result more advantageously to us by putting it in this way than having it known we were directly interested.[8]

The playing field for Finnish immigrant readers and subscriptions was hardly level, but the stakes for readership were certainly high. Calumet and Hecla, the Quincy Mining Company, and the rest of Copperdom were million-dollar companies; Työmies was a small corporation with a handful of shareholders, a little over $900 in assets, and $5,000 in the corporation coffers. At risk for the Copper Country mining companies was a way of life; at risk for *Työmies* was existence. English-language newspapers propagandized the merits of the Copper Country's paternalistic system, but because of language barriers, these English-language papers did not hold sway in the Finnish immigrant community. As Finnish immigrants were the largest ethnic population in many Copper Country locales, propagandizing the status quo arrangement that maintained the mine-dominated way of life was essential to the Copper Country oligarchy.

The first edition of *Työmies* came out into this dialectically charged atmosphere on August 16, 1904.[9] Around the same time, *Työmies* sent editor Kosonen and stockholder Nieminen to the Cleveland, Ohio, meeting that officially united socialist-unionist Finnish immigrant cultural organizations with the Socialist Party of America. This merger assured the Finnish immigrant socialist-unionist movement a degree of representation and exposure in the greater American labor and political dialogue.[10] Thus, the Hancock Jousi and the TPC became stakeholders in American politics and unions.

The TPC's First Building in Hancock

In 1904, at this early stage of its existence, the TPC housed its printing presses in the basement of a building at 741 Franklin Street, and *Työmies* was a weekly publication.[11] The publishing company also began production of *Työmiehen Joulu* (Workingmen's Christmas), a year-end review of newsworthy proletarian events published in time for fireside Christmas reading.[12] The initial scope of the TPC's publications was small, as the building at 741 Franklin Street was only 1,040 square feet in size and not conducive to a large printing operation.[13] From its earliest days, the TPC's history in Hancock was one of marked disputes between staff members. This wrangling began with arguments beginning in the first year of publication. The quarrels were probably indicative of a company—and more so, a fledgling cultural organization—looking for direction and an identity.

An unlikely person who was essential to the early development of *Työmies* was newspaperman N. J. Ahlman. Ahlman began his print career with the

Amerikan Suometar (Finnish American) as its editor in 1899.[14] The *Suometar* was not a socialist labor publication; rather, it was an appendage of the conservative Finnish Evangelical Lutheran Suomi Synod in Hancock. Ahlman decided to start his own publishing company, the *Kansan Kuvalehti* (People's Illustrated Journal) in Hancock around 1901 or 1902, while remaining the editor of *Amerikan Suometar.* At this time, Ahlman boarded with the Reverend J. K. Nikander of Suomi Theological Seminary, but then he moved sometime between 1901 and 1902. What precipitated this move, such as a possible split in ideology because of Ahlman's burgeoning socialist beliefs, is not apparent.[15] Around 1904, Ahlman quit his job as editor of the *Amerikan Suometar* to work solely on his publication, the *Kansan Kuvalehti,* and he also edited the Finnish daily *Päivälehti* in Calumet.[16]

In 1904, Ahlman, then editor of the *Päivälehti,* took over the managerial duties of the TPC. Kosonen, editor-in-chief of *Työmies,* did not get along with Ahlman. Kosonen was an uncompromising Marxist whose actions complemented his ideology. In a letter, Kosonen once wrote: "I was imprisoned yesterday in Ely [Minnesota] as an anarchist. Some Finns had informed the police. I was finally released when Dr. Tanner took personal responsibility for me. In Virginia [Minnesota] I was yelled 'down and out.' I'm glad God has blessed me with a happy disposition and long legs."[17] For his part, Ahlman was likely more concerned with printing professional-quality publications and less worried with revolutionary ideals. The result of the dispute was Ahlman's forced resignation.[18] Ahlman left Hancock for Calumet in 1905 or 1906 and continued publication of *Päivälehti* from a building at 409–411 Pine Street.[19] Ahlman was not the only person moving at this time. His ideological adversary Kosonen lost his editor-in-chief status in 1905 to Kappo Murros while Kosonen was away on a labor agitating tour.[20]

Somewhat remarkably, as *Työmies* went through this revolving array of editorial leadership, it continued to grow and add publications. This early growth was perhaps due to one of the most popular features of the newspaper, the *paikkakuntakirjeet,* or local correspondents' columns. News from local correspondents was not a *Työmies* innovation—many newspapers included news sections from remote reporters—but for working-class readers who depended on mobility in search of work, the local reporter played an important role in unification of the readership. Taisto T. Holm, longtime *Työmies-Eteenpäin* contributor and subscriber, wrote of local correspondents:

> Through local news columns, readers kept track of localities and areas where economic upturns and downturns were occurring and thus of places where job opportunities existed . . . and these local correspondents kept readers abreast of union organizing activity through which workers sought to improve work and workplace conditions.
>
> The columns of our papers were a training ground for the local correspondents wherein they acquired literary skills. They honed and disciplined their reporting, their writing and their editing skills. The correspondence also enabled them to develop analytical and interpretive skills.[21]

By late 1904 and into 1905, *Työmies* was a weekly publication with approximately 1,000 subscribers.[22] Beginning in 1905, the TPC began printing the periodicals *Soihtu* (Torch), *Vappu* (May Day) and the *Työväen Kalentari* (Workers' Calendar).[23] *Soihtu* was the TPC's first attempt at a monthly journal–type publication, which apparently did not go over well, as the publication of *Soihtu* ceased after a second year in 1906. *Vappu* was the TPC's second title offered as an annual, published for distribution on or around May Day, an international proletarian holiday. *Vappu*, which had a long run, examined proletarian issues, including articles and poetry from around the world. A 1912 edition of *Vappu* included articles about the proletarian struggles in "Mexiko" and a summary of the Industrial Workers of the World's Lawrence, Massachusetts, textile-mill strike. Darwin and discussion of evolution also found copy in the 1914 edition of *Vappu*'s pages. The Workers' Calendar contained local Finnish Socialist Federation news and translated the Socialist Party of America's English-language news into the Finnish language. The calendar reaffirmed the Finnish Socialist Federation's intentions to join American politics as an organ of the Socialist Party by publishing photos and commentary about Party presidential candidate Eugene V. Debs.

Työmies's Second Home: The Michigan Street Building

In 1905, likely while Murros was editor, the TPC was looking for bigger digs. The TPC moved to a building in West Hancock built by painter Matt Fredd at 421 Michigan Street. This building was substantially larger than the building at 741 Franklin Street, containing approximately 3,000 square feet.[24] Murros relinquished editorship sometime in 1905 after receiving a $3,000 fine for libelous statements about a Finnish physician made in *Työmies*. Murros retreated to Finland rather than stand trial. Toivo Hiltunen, who was born in Oulu, Finland, in 1880, immigrated to the United States in 1901, then came to the TPC from the socialist-unionist publication *Toveri* (Comrade), based in Astoria, Oregon. Also arriving to work at the TPC around the same time as Hiltunen was a pharmacist named W. W. Korhonen, "known as the Pill Peddler by his enemies." Hiltunen and Korhonen took over as primary editors after Murros left.[25]

In addition to the above-mentioned socialists, two dedicated radicals, Aku Rissanen and Leo Laukki, joined *Työmies*'s editorial staff and became influential members of the TPC. Both Rissanen and Laukki left Finland after participation in the Finnish General Strike and the Viapori Rebellion against the czarist government. Rissanen, born in Viapori, Finland, in 1881, came to the United States in 1907 and was familiar with proletarian newspaper work from his exploits in Finland. He took over as editor-in-chief of *Työmies* after Hiltunen and Korhonen's tenures. Laukki, a former lieutenant in the Russian Imperial Army, also joined *Työmies*'s editorial staff at roughly the same time.[26]

Rissanen left *Työmies* to edit *Toveri* in Astoria, and Laukki became an instructor at the Work People's College in Duluth, Minnesota. Laukki was a fire-and-brimstone radical and gained a reputation as a brilliant, but very polarizing, orator. According to Edith A. Koivisto, who took classes at the Work People's College, "Laukki was a good teacher and knew his stuff, but I did not like him personally. Being among the Finns who knew nothing, according to him and many others, I suppose he thought he knew it all." Douglas Ollila, the Finnish American historian who conducted the interview, added, "I've been reading some of the records of the *Työväen Opisto* (Workers' College), and also many of the newspapers that he wrote into, and read about his activity in organizations, and I found out that Laukki tended to be very '*itse päinen*,' very, very independent and a little bull-headed."[27]

Ollila asked Koivisto to reveal more information on Laukki:

> *Ollila:* I'd be interested in any other impressions of Laukki that you had. He was such an important leader among Finnish Americans, and of course he later became the leader of the IWW faction within the Industrial Liito group.
>
> *Koivisto:* He was a brilliant speaker, he could move audiences, I remember one time he spoke for six hours and people didn't want to leave, but his voice got so hoarse he had to stop, and he promised to continue. I don't remember, I was so young, what he spoke about . . . He spoke very plainly so that you could understand him, he spoke a people's language, not a high language.[28]

After Rissanen and Laukki left the editor-in-chief position sometime in 1907, Severi Alanne took over as head editor of *Työmies*. Alanne, born in Hämeenlinna in 1879, was a chemical engineer in Finland. In Finland, he joined the Social Democratic Party in 1905, but emigrated to Canada in 1907. Alanne worked for a short time in Port Arthur (Thunder Bay), Canada, on the staff of *Työkansa* (Workers Home), but then left for the United States to join the TPC. Alanne was a competent editor and endeavored to raise the standards of *Työmies* by settling the endless quibbling between staff. He soon lost favor with didactic Marxists who saw bourgeois influences in his work. It is perhaps apparent from Alanne's removal as editor-in-chief that didactic, Marxist elements were in control of the publishing company at various times in its early history. Even with Alanne's middle-class influences, he proved to be so competent that his political leanings were set aside in favor of his competency; he returned as editor-in-chief several times throughout *Työmies*'s history in Hancock.[29]

At this early stage of existence in 1906, the TPC engaged the American socialist-unionist movement as an officially sanctioned organ of the Socialist Party of America's Finnish Socialist Federation. Perhaps because of this association, the publishing company received some unwanted attention in the process. Quincy Mining Company spies were monitoring the upstart publishing company even at this early date:

Reported August 31:

> Under the date of August 29th the operative reports that he has been told that the leader of the Finnish miners is not employed in the mines and is a proprietor of a stationary store in Hancock.[30]

Operative P reported on September 16 that

> the other [Jousi meeting was held] in the Tyomies Building, which is the Finn socialistic headquarters and the name "Tyomies" that of the paper published, meaning the workman.
>
> W. J. Helstein [V. S. Holmsten] was one of the editors of this paper, he being evidently a man of considerable ability. Operative learned during the evening that one of the leaders in strikes had been Alex Halonen, a leading socialist agitator, lecturer and organizer, who is constantly traveling over the country and was not at this time in Hancock.[31]

Operative P reported on September 19:

> The operative reports that he has been putting in most of the time around town with the miners and also visited the office of the Tyomies (the workmen) Printing and Publishing Company, the Socialistic publication, but had heard nothing said relative to any strike except the one at Rockland, Michigan, nor did he hear any complaints made as to present conditions among the Quincy miners.[32]

In 1907, Aro Nurmi of Milwaukee, Wisconsin, was president of the TPC; Nieminen was the TPC's vice president; Frilund was the TPC's secretary; Fred its treasurer; and Paavo Sirvio the TPC's manager. *Työmies* was now a triweekly, issued on Tuesdays, Thursdays, and Saturdays. A yearly subscription cost $2.50. The TPC even had a telephone at this time, and dialing 310 connected a person to the TPC's offices.[33] In a June 1907 special meeting of its seven-member board of directors and stockholders, the TPC voted to increase its numbers of shares to 1,500 valued at $10.00 a share, thus increasing the TPC's capital stock from $5,000 to $15,000.[34] The specific reason for the increase in stock is unclear. The increase may have been to finance the growth of *Työmies* to a triweekly,[35] or it may have been done in anticipation of having to cover court-ordered restitution and lawyer's fees to P. H. O'Brien. S. Juntilla, a venture capitalist, sued the TPC (naming August Beck) for libel to the unhappy tune of $10,000. Juntilla sued the TPC for printing a letter accusing him of stock fraud in a Nevada gold-mining venture. A judge ordered the TPC to pay $175 and $81.70 in court costs.[36]

It is also possible that the stock increase was to expand the TPC's publications list. In 1907, the TPC began to publish *Köyhälistön Nuija* (Proletarian Hammer), a yearly look at the working class from a national and international viewpoint. The 1907 edition included articles and poems, as well as essays on Gorky and Liebnecht. A curious poem in 1910's *Köyhälistön Nuija*, written partly in English and partly in Finnish, demonstrated a certain type of acerbic wit that permeated many of the TPC's publications and likely did not endear the Finnish-language press to gentrified, patriotic American society. The poem, titled "American National Hymn: An Adaptation," read:

My country 'tis of thee
land full of rascality,
Of thee I sing;
Land where dollars procure
most humble servants,
the scepter has been wielded:
Great Silver King!

My native country thee
land full of criminality
thy name is known;
Land where dollars,
trample the just
and people in poverty are oppressed
Freedom's unknown.

Let music swell the breeze
and heed the devil's enticing call,

all rascality;
Great bandits tumble out,
Like parasites at night
—dawn will bring great freedom and Liberty![37]

Nineteen hundred seven also saw the TPC publish its first *Työväen Laulukirja* (Workers Songbook) for socialist local meetings and gatherings. The first song in the pocket-sized book was "Työväen Marssi" (Workers March). The ever-broadening list of the TPC's publications was in addition to "jobbing work" for the public, which included printing business cards, fliers, and postings.

Early Printing Machinery at the TPC

Next to its staff and readers, typesetting and printing machines were the most important part of the TPC's business. The TPC's machines were important for obvious reasons—without them there would be no publications, no consumable message for the public—but looking at the machinery of the printing company also affords one a look at the TPC's achievements and economic success. In short, the more presses and the better the technology, the more publications the TPC could put out. More publications meant more readers, and more readers increased subscriptions, thus confirming that the Finnish immigrants' socialist-unionist message was bearing fruit. By extrapolating the technological capabilities and commercial value of the TPC's printing technology, the technology used by the TPC can be seen as an economic barometer for success of the Finnish immigrant socialist-unionist movement.

While at 741 Franklin Street, perhaps due to spatial considerations, the TPC likely had one large jobbing-newspaper press and possibly one or more manually operated jobbing platen presses. The TPC's large press, from 1904 to 1908, was a Cottrell drum-cylinder flatbed press. The basic principle of the drum-cylinder press dates back to the 1830s. It was not until the 1850s, however, that manufacture of the cylinder press shifted on a large scale to the United States. At this time, the cylinder press became important as a news and job press to small "country" printing companies.[38]

The TPC also relied heavily on its one linotype machine.[39] Linotype machines mechanically set text and characters for use in the TPC's presses. Linotype machines were an important advancement in typesetting methods versus hand setting type. The main benefit of mechanical typesetting was an increase in the speed of a publication's character composition. Ottmar Mergenthaler was the first to develop a modern, practically priced linotype machine to mechanically typeset characters for printing. Once made affordable to a wide range of printing companies, automated typesetting became a lucrative business, and many manufacturing companies illegally copied, innovated, and manufactured a wide range of linotype machines.[40]

The *Wage Slave* and a New Press

Nineteen hundred eight brought two significant changes to the TPC. First, the TPC expanded its list of publications with an English-language publication called the *Wage Slave*. A resolution printed in the *Wage Slave* indicated that the paper would be Michigan's Socialist Party mouthpiece, trumpeting all things Socialist Party of America:

> Inasmuch as the Wage-Slave is a Michigan paper and edited by a man of known worth in the movement, a man who has stood first, last, and always for the organized movement, we deem it wise to call upon our party members to assist the Wage-Slave in every possible manner. Through this medium the State secretary may easily reach the members of our party and the growth of the paper will undoubtedly mean the growth of the organization and the progress of our movement.[41]

The *Wage Slave* became a committed advocate of the Socialist Party of America, sponsoring ads that read, "Have you organized a socialist local yet in your town? Write to the Wage Slave for information."[42] The acerbically titled *Wage Slave* was a semimonthly publication, and a subscription cost $0.50 in the United States or $1.00 in Canada; but a reader could subscribe jointly to the *Wage Slave* and another socialist themed paper, the *Vanguard*,[43] for $0.75 a year. The pairing of the *Wage Slave* with another English-language newspaper was a further sign of progress made by the TPC in engaging with American proletarian media.

A May 1908 article in the *Wage Slave* announced the second change. Due to a growing readership, the TPC made a substantial $4,000 investment. According to the article "Our New Press," the TPC put in an Optimus Printing Press because the old Cottrell Press could not meet the demands of the TPC's 2,300 subscribers.[44] Babcock's Optimus press, first manufactured circa 1895, was a two-revolution, hand-fed machine. The two-revolution press was an upgrade from the single-revolution press in speed and quality. While the single-revolution drum-cylinder press could make approximately 1,000 impressions an hour, the two-revolution press reportedly could register 2,500 impressions an hour. The two-revolution press had a continuously rotating gear that accelerated the type bed into printing position much faster than single-revolution presses. This innovation increased speed and reduced press vibration and other maintenance problems,[45] which increased the TPC's ability to "crank out" the proletarian message.

In the same May 1, 1908, article that announced the Optimus Press, the TPC outlined a predicted bright future for the English-language *Wage Slave*, while reminding readers that the Finnish-language triweekly *Työmies* was the main paper of the publishing company:

> Our readers understand of course that the Finnish paper is the big paper in this establishment, a large, seven column paper, eight pages issued three times a week. *The Wage Slave* does not publish *Työmies*. Työmies Pub. Co. publishes *The Wage Slave*.
>
> What we want now is to make *The Wage Slave* in every sense the counterpart of the *Työmies*, and at the rate of which our subscription list has grown since we began it can certainly be done . . . we have now however, a subscription list of 2,300 and after he [A. M. Stirton] is through with his May dates, advertised in this issue, the Editor intends to limit his lecturing, practically to Sundays in point of time and the Upper Peninsula of Michigan as territory and attend more strictly to his Editorial duties making *The Wage Slave* a better paper than ever before.

> The comrades should enable him to do this by doing two things: first keep pushing the subscription list, and secondly, every Local should subscribe for at least one $10.00 share of stock in Työmies Pub. Co. We have the artillery here, boys, if you will only furnish the gunpowder.[46]

The articles, resolutions, and general publication of the *Wage Slave* signaled a new dawn for the TPC and indicated an attempt to give direction to "non-Finns" in the *American* working-class struggle. The *Wage Slave*'s multiethnic nature was certainly evident in articles, but also in its staff, as a "Finn" named John Nummivuori managed the paper, while the aforementioned "Irishman" A. M. Stirton edited the paper.[47] The Irish influence overtly appeared in another edition of the *Wage Slave* when an article proudly proclaimed "*Cead Mille Failte*" and described the events of an Irish parade through downtown Hancock.[48] This was certainly a step in the right direction for "race" relations between the oft-described irascible Finns and "fighting" Irish. As Alanen wrote of the Finnish-Irish divide, "When considering the various ethnic and nationality groups which populated the Calumet area in 1879, a Finnish correspondent claimed that harmony prevailed among Finns and other people, although there was one noticeable exception: the Irish."[49] Some of the ethnic discourse bordered on deadly serious: "Altercations between the Finns and Irish were quite common, primarily in the saloons and dance halls of Red Jacket, Michigan. The Finns were especially renowned for their use of knives in barroom brawls whenever they sought to 'carve the necks of some Irishmen.'"[50]

As ethnic fighting began to take a back seat to working-class solidarity, the *Wage Slave*'s articles and the TPC's support of its publication confirmed that the *Wage Slave* was an important radical, multiethnic mouthpiece for the Copper Country labor movement, Michigan socialists, and the Socialist Party of America. With an air of class confidence, the *Wage Slave* announced itself as a "Working-Class Weekly," stating, "This paper will tell the Workingman's side of the story in case of a Strike."[51] Banner headlines on the *Wage Slave*'s front page proclaimed, "The Worst under Socialism Will Be Better Than the Best under Capitalism," "Labor Produces All Wealth; Wealth Belongs to the Producers There Of," and "A Vote for Capitalism is an Endorsement of Its Every Crime." An editorial even pondered "The Limitations of Political Action" giving print to the non-political, direct actionists in the Socialist Party at this time.[52] Along with publishing Party news and views, the *Wage Slave* printed schedules of notable socialist events and lecture tours that were happening locally, regionally, and nationally: "Lecture in Ishpeming [Michigan]: The Editor will lecture in the Miners Union Hall 115 Cleveland Ave., Ishpeming, Thursday Eve. April 23d. 7.30 P.M. Subject, 'Jesus of Nazareth.' Admission Free. Everybody Welcome."

The *Wage Slave* was very much abreast of national events, including strikes and the rhetoric of 1908's presidential candidates. That election year pitted Republican William Taft, Democrat William Jennings Bryant, and dark horse SPA candidate Eugene V. Debs against each other.[53] The *Wage Slave* wholly supported the candidacy of Debs, assuring its readers that "a vote for socialism will not be thrown away,"[54] and warned that "Papa is in jail for stealing a loaf of bread to feed his hungry children, while the man Papa voted for is in Congress for stealing a railroad." The same edition stated under a Trades Union Label logo:

> All trade unionists know that the above is an illustration of the union label. All trade unionists ought to know that a union working man on Election Day with union made shoes on his feet, a union made hat on his head, a union made coat on his back, a union made cigar in his mouth, and a scab ticket in his hand is a donkey.[55]

As Michigan was the broader intended audience, news and advertising from around the state made it into the *Wage Slave*'s pages. A regular column titled "Ishpeming Sparks" and the likely collaboration of Marquette, Michigan's Socialist Party of America offices, (peopled by H. E. Quarters at 410 N. Front Street), relayed news from the Marquette Iron Range. This attention to the Marquette Range led to a good volume of newspaper sales in that area: "Local Negaunee orders 500 copies of this week's Wage Slave. Local Ishpeming orders 250 copies of this week's Wage Slave."[56] News and information from "downstate" also made copy. Arthur G. Baker, from Albion, Michigan, ran this puzzling capitalist-driven ad: "Socialists who can afford $15 to invest or more write to me. This is a big dividend payer. Investigate."[57]

Locally, in the Copper Country, the *Wage Slave* occasionally harangued area mining companies and provided advertising space for local merchants of different ethnicities. Finnish immigrants were the most frequent advertisers. The TPC, of course, ran an ad in the *Wage Slave* stating, "We print books, circulars, bill heads, handbills, letterheads, statements, envelopes, business and visiting cards." Underneath their ad, the TPC displayed the Houghton Typographical Trades Union's label next to the words "No Scabs."[58] Nieminen advertised his "domestic and foreign groceries at 203 Franklin Street" selling "fresh and salted meat," and Frilund advertised his "first class workmanship in book binding."[59] The *Wage Slave* was for sale in some unexpected local places of business in Hancock—for example, this ad in its pages declared: "Henceforth the Wage-Slave will always be on sale at the Candy store of W. M. Washburn, 616 Quincy St., Hancock, Mich."[60]

A biting type of sarcasm enhanced the TPC's publications, and the *Wage Slave* was no exception. Sprinkled amid the hardcore ideological content and organizational schedules, the *Wage Slave* found time to ruffle feathers. One bit of folk logic questioned the lack of collective action by the working class: "When food is scarce the wolves go in packs—Is the human less intelligent than the wolf?"[61] A rather caustic get-well-soon wish to frequent adversary and Hancock mayor A. J. Scott demonstrated the *Wage Slave*'s "sharp-tongue":

> The Wage Slave hears with great regret of the illness of Mayor Scott of Hancock, who, we understand, has departed temporarily for the Hot Springs, Arkansas. We have no personal vindictiveness toward the man, A. J. Scott in his personal capacity. We are very dissatisfied with him as Mayor of Hancock in his official capacity. We hope that he will benefit from his trip to Hot Springs and return in improved health. In which case we will go after him again.[62]

In addition to acerbic well-wishing, the *Wage Slave* printed uniquely proletarian humor, as a joke entitled "Johnny the Socialist" illustrates:

> *Father* (going to work): Now John, let's see that you drown those kittens today.
> *Johnny* (philosophizing): Well now, this seems to be a roundabout way of doing things, every few months I am called upon to drown a bunch of kittens. I guess I'll make a good job of it this time.
> *Father* (returning from work): Well John, did you drown those kittens today?

Johnny: Yes Father, and in order to use my time to a better advantage in the future, I have made a good job of it this time.

Father: Why how do you mean John?

Johnny: Well, I drowned the old cat too this time.

Moral: Capitalism is the cat that is the cause of our troubles.[63]

With their new Optimus press and the establishment of an SPA-sanctioned English-language newspaper, the TPC had new access and technical ability to meet the demands of a broad, regional, multiethnic audience. The English-language newspaper and direct ties to an established American proletarian organization gave the publishing company an immediate legitimacy in American working-class circles. The ensuing proletarian assault on the conditions of industrial America consumed the pages of *Työmies*, the *Wage Slave*, and the TPC's ancillary publications.

Energized, in 1908 the TPC added two journal-like offerings: *Vallankumous* (Revolution) and *Punainen Juhannus* (Red Midsummer).[64] *Vallankumous* was an annual publication geared toward examining the struggles of socialism on a nationwide scope. Articles, poetry, and translated English pieces appeared in *Vallankumous*. The 1909 edition contained a translated article written by labor lawyer Clarence Darrow. The articles and works in *Vallankumous* demonstrated the TPC's desire to engage greater American socioeconomic conditions with direct action and declaration of physical class struggle against capitalist exploitation.

For many Finnish immigrants, without the TPC's translations of English-authored essays, articles, poems, plays, and books, the Finnish immigrant would not have been aware of the greater socialist-unionist movement in the United States. If *Vallankumous* demonstrated an attempt to bring American news to Finnish immigrant readers, *Punainen Juhannus*, a short-lived two-year annual publication, likely expressed maintenance of tradition. "Juhannus" was an Old World custom, and the TPC's politicization of the event was perhaps an attempt to bond Finnish immigrants with time-honored customs in new ways, using proletarian imagery and writing.

In 1909, the TPC added a sports magazine titled *Urheilu-Viesti* (Athletic News), but this was a short-term venture as publication ceased in 1911.[65] Nineteen hundred nine was also the first year the TPC published in the satirical-journal genre. The endeavor to publish a Finnish-language satirical "comic" was perhaps a natural outgrowth of the TPC's general brand of sarcastic journalism that often found print in its newspapers and annual publications. The name of the new Finnish-language journal was *Amerikan Matti*, and the publishers boldly stated about the journal: "Greatest Finnish comic magazine in United States, published on the 10th of every month at Hancock, Mich."[66] John Salminen and the mysterious Pipokiven Aisakki (likely a pseudonym) were the publisher and editor respectively. *Matti*'s staff was small and possibly located away from the TPC's quarters. However, it appears as if *Matti* was closely linked with the TPC as *Matti*'s printing occurred on the Työmies Publishing Company's premises, *Työmies* advertised in *Matti*, and *Amerikan Matti*'s publisher, Salminen, was a regular fixture in TPC circles.

Amerikan Matti focused on lampooning national Finnish immigrant happenings, the Finnish Evangelical Lutheran Suomi Synod, regional news, and local issues, with comics of varying quality from American and Finnish immigrant artists, mocking textual narratives, jokes, information, and poetry. A sample of *Matti*'s locally focused, sarcastic industrial-themed poetry:

CALUMET MINERS

I'd like to sing a little bit
About those miners of Calumet
With a cigar in their mouth
And collars 'round their neck

They come out of the saloons,
But do not get drunk from beer
They get drunk from liquor
They talk about comets
And wrestle like champions
They go to church to sleep,
And eat confession bread,
They call other people
Only if they are Kaleva-knights . . .
The masters ride them

Like if they were cattle
And pay little salaries
With ten dollar bills

And those boys about their jobs
They do not care at all,
If a rock just happens to kill
It is just the "wish of the Lord" . . .
Oh, you saint and blessed
Oh you big Calumet—The destiny of Sodom would fall
For lack of sense and reason there.[67]

Amerikan Matti also displayed a curious racially motivated hypocrisy. While the Työmies Publishing Company espoused working-class solidarity as a tool for success in proletarian struggle, a particular cartoon image in *Matti* very negatively stereotyped another working-class group, African Americans. Underneath all the TPC's early rhetoric about working-class solidarity, there was perhaps a latent and episodic racism regarding African Americans. Such a portrayal of African Americans could have been endemic of the eugenics-driven era, but for a group that had once been the butt of many stereotypical slanders and vitriol, a person would think the TPC and Finnish immigrants in general, should have known better than to print such bigoted imagery.

It is difficult to understand this type of racist depiction in publications that espoused the equality of the working class. In a time that called for absolute solidarity, a sad sense of hypocrisy permeated copies of *Amerikan Matti* featuring this caricature. It seems as if the last group to stereotype others should be Finnish immigrants or the oft referred-to "Jack-pine Savages." It was a decidedly counterproductive tactic for Finnish immigrant workers, who were familiar with ethnically/racially based discrimination in Copper Country mines, to pass along discrimination to another largely disenfranchised, stereotyped group of American workers. *Amerikan Matti* had a short life. By 1910, the publication of the journal ended.[68]

Despite the unfortunate portrayal of African Americans, the years 1907 through 1909 were ones of foundation building for the TPC. In this time of building for the future, the TPC's staff included not only experienced newspapermen and skillful office managers but also men straight from mineshafts with little professional knowledge. To the Finnish-language publication *Päivälehti*—the Calumet, Michigan, based newspaper that sought the surreptitious financial backing of the mining companies—the TPC's mixture of experience was the subject of humor and ridicule. *Päivälehti* termed the TPC *jatkastaapi*, or hobo headquarters. Later, the TPC turned this moniker into a badge of honor, developing a tramp-like character to laud their hobo status.[69]

However, the moniker of *jatkastaapi* did likely bother the staff at TPC—at least a little. In 1909, the TPC devoted an article in *Köyhälistön Nuija* (Proletarian Hammer) dedicated to *Päivälehti* that detailed the education and experience of the TPC's staff and contributors. While many of the TPC's staff had worked industrial or labor-intensive jobs in the Old Country, and even more so in America, the publishing experience and education of the TPC's staff and contributors was impressive. Of the thirty-seven entries with identified educational background in the article, twenty-five of the TPC's staff and contributors had some formal education in Finland or the United States. Of these people with formal education, fifteen had attended some type of post-primary education such as college courses, lyceum, labor education classes, or vocational schools.[70] Under the guidance of this rather well-educated staff (especially for the era), with a good assemblage of printing machinery and a wide swath of publications in both Finnish and English, the TPC grew by leaps and bounds over the next three years.

From 1910 to 1913, the TPC became the leading Finnish socialist-unionist newspaper in the United States, with over 12,000 subscribers. In this role, the TPC became the consummate mouthpiece not only for the Finnish immigrant socialist-unionists, but also for the Socialist Party of America. The TPC's growth and purpose-driven publishing would require the move to larger quarters that had more square footage for business operations as well as dedicated space for specialized offerings that contributed to the assault on the Copper Country oligarchy and American capitalism.

CHAPTER 5

The Työmies Publishing Company Reaches Maturity, 1910–1913

To the benefit of the TPC, even with the occasional "hobo" running operations, the constant growth in subscriptions from 1905 onward necessitated another move to a larger publishing facility in 1910. In 1910, the Polk's Directory for Hancock listed two locations for the TPC: at the Michigan Street address, and after May 10, at 203 Franklin Street. The Franklin Street location encompassed three distinct buildings on two lots. The Työmies Publishing Company's move to Franklin Street was an indication of prosperity and a proclamation of intended permanence regarding the stability of the Työmies Publishing Company, the Hancock Jousi, and the socialist-unionist Finnish immigrants' message.

Presiding over the move was Nieminen, who served double duty as TPC president and Kansankoti Real Estate board member; Evert Björklund, TPC secretary; and John D. Nummivuori, TPC general manager. *Työmies*, still a triweekly, claimed a guaranteed circulation of 8,500 and charged $2.75 for a yearly subscription.[1] The TPC's new publishing buildings at 201–207 Franklin Street comprised roughly 8,153 square feet, a huge jump in operational space from 741 Franklin Street's 1,040 square feet and 421 Michigan Street's 3,000 square feet.[2] The larger publishing space suited the TPC, as *Työmies*'s readership climbed to nearly 10,000 as a daily by decade's end, which was an incredible jump from *Työmies*'s 1904 readership, consisting of 1,000 as a weekly.[3]

Descriptions of the new location and move appear in a 1910 edition of *Työmiehen Joulu*:

> Last July, in the eventful, but only seven-year history of the Työmies Publishing Company, there was a turning point because we moved to a renovated building owned by the Kansankoti Company . . . where we will be located for a long time.
>
> The building has three floors, 50 by 50 feet in area. On the ground floor is printing space where we are publishing a paper with a big, new printing machine. Also on this floor we have two cylinder machines and two smaller printing machines for print jobbing work. This is also where *Työmies* is mailed, has paper stored and the metal needed for the typesetting machine. There is no extra space, but when everything is practically arranged, it is much more spacious compared with the former buildings . . . on the first floor there is the composing room, book store and offices, of which the composing room takes up half making it quite narrow . . . the bookkeeper has a little room on this floor.
>
> The erection of these buildings is not all that we have to do in order to wake up the hundreds of thousands of workers to carry out the practical goals of unionism and socialism in these big centers of the copper and iron industry. No! Still our equipment and weapons are like children's toys compared with those weapons which our enemy [bourgeois newspapers] has at its disposal. We have to equip our fortress much more strongly.[4]

It is clear from the article that even though the publishing company was in a larger building, their quarters were still too small. If the TPC believed it was involved in a war of words with Copper Country capitalists, it wanted to be both well "armed" and in a well-fortified and amply spaced structure.[5] This revelation likely necessitated the decision to rent the aforementioned adjacent building from Coughlin, though exactly when this building came into the TPC's use is not known. After rental of the Coughlin Building at 207 Franklin Street, the TPC likely housed its offices, a bookstore,[6] a flatbed press, and linotype machine in this building. The press,[7] linotype machine, and a correspondent and composing room were likely on the first floor, while TPC offices, subsidiary publications' offices, and a bookstore were on the second floor.[8]

The TPC and its bookstore served as an important liaison between the proletarian Finnish immigrant and the American and international working class. The publishing company had identified, as early as 1908, the need for translations in their work publishing books: "Tyomies Pub. Co: is now better prepared than ever to publish books. Heretofore our book publishing has been entirely in Finnish, but we intend soon to go into the business of publishing books in English pretty freely."[9] With this mandate, the TPC's bookstore was home to a unique assemblage of books. From its earliest days, the TPC printed books that explored varied aspects of socialism, unionism, science, and revolutionary thought; they translated Marx and Engel's *Kommunistinen Manifesti* (Communist Manifesto), a number of titles by Maxim Gorky, and Alexander A. Bogdanov's *Lyhyt Taloustihteen Oppikirja* (Course of the Political Economy Textbook) as introductions to scientific socialism. An ad in a 1914 edition of *Työmies* listed over 171 titles for purchase. The bookstore sold everything from a publishing of Clarence Darrow's closing arguments in Bill Haywood's Idaho trial, to adventure books about the Himalayas, to books of poetry, Finnish history, and even *Marie Antoinette* by Clara Tschudi. The long list of titles included Finnish, Finnish immigrant, and a number of English-language authors translated by TPC staff.[10]

The TPC translations of American authors served a critical function because these English-language publications were likely the first or only exposure that Finnish immigrants had to American proletarian culture. Professionally translated books and treatises by Darrow, politico James H. Brower, agnostic Robert Ingersol, adventure novelist and socialist Jack London, and industrial unionists "Big" Bill Haywood and Charles H. Moyer introduced the Finnish immigrant to an American viewpoint on social, cultural, and political issues. Of course, the TPC also published books by Finnish immigrant writers in America. Work People's College professor and syndicalist Leo Laukki, writer and lecturer Frank Aaltonen, and poet Aku Päivio, among others, had their work handsomely bound and disseminated nationwide to advance the cause of socialism and unionism.

The original Nieminen grocery building, at 201–203 Franklin Street, was likely home to the TPC's new Duplex press, two or three larger presses, several linotype machines, a jobbing platen, and related materials necessary to the TPC's printing business. The first floor of the building probably housed two or three large presses along with equipment and materials needed to run the presses. The first floor presses were likely the eldest Cottrell single-revolution drum-cylinder press, the Babcock two-revolution cylinder press, and the TPC's newest press, the rather technologically advanced Duplex reel-fed press. The second floor of the former Nieminen grocery building likely housed the composing room with a typesetting and character-selection workstation, proof press area, linotype room with at least three linotype linecasting machines, and an office manager's space.

The TPC was so proud of their new Duplex press they devoted a front-page article in *Työmies* to announce its arrival. The Duplex printing press was state of the art for a small newspaper publishing company. Newspaper printing was the reel-fed Duplex's specialty. This was a significant difference from the TPC's other presses because "the reel-fed flatbed perfecting press was the answer to the requirements of the smaller newspaper, and as far as can be judged the first of its kind was the *Duplex*, invented by Paul Cox in 1889 and built by the Duplex Printing Press Company, of Battle Creek, Michigan." In addition to being the perfect fit for the small newspaper, the reel-fed Duplex required only a single press operator to run the press, thus freeing another press operator for the TPC's other operations. In 1903, under serious competitive pressure, Duplex redesigned its press, adding a third type bed of four pages. This meant that companies like the TPC could now print a twelve-page paper as well as an eight-page paper with a few simple modifications.[11]

Spotlight on Comrades: Leo Laukki and John Välimäki

Beginning in 1910, *Vallankumous* began featuring annual pictures of Duluth, Minnesota's Work People's College. The photos captured the students, faculty, and buildings of the Work People's College. Although some two hundred miles separated them, one gets the sense that the TPC was extremely proud of the Work People's College, and there were many close ties between the college and the TPC. Leo Laukki was one such close tie. Laukki was born in Helsinki, Finland, in 1880 with the surname Lindqvist. In Finland, Laukki attended university and became involved in proletarian newspaper ventures such as the *Kansan Lehti*. Laukki also participated in the Finnish General Strike, and after involvement in the Viapori Rebellion he emigrated to America in 1907.[12] Laukki hit the ground running in the States. In 1907, he participated in the Hancock Red Flag Parade and was one of the arrested Red Flag 13. He became an ardent industrial unionist, syndicalist, and IWW member. He was also a member of the group that wrested the Work People's College away from its original owners, the Finnish National Evangelical Lutheran Church in America, better known as the *Kansalliskirkko* or People's Church.

In 1907, socialist-unionist elements bought out stock from the Church contingent and turned the college into a socialist-unionist educational institution espousing various forms of radical economic and social direct-action ideology. Laukki continued to work as an editor at the TPC, but split time between the publishing company and his favored Work People's College. As aforementioned, Laukki was a charismatic and popular educator. His ideological predispositions, which favored association with the IWW, became popular among Work People's College students.[13] This had significant reverberations within the TPC. As its editor-in-chief, Laukki wrote articles in *Työmies* calling for sabotage and other direct-action measures to challenge capitalism. Laukki and the IWW contingent seemed to control the TPC for a time, to the dismay of those who supported parliamentary socialism, revolutionary or otherwise.[14]

Around 1910, *Työmies* added another important member to its staff. Unlike professional newspapermen such as N. J. Ahlman, and didactic, enigmatic administrators like Laukki, John Välimäki *was* a prototypical "hobo," beginning his newspaper career after a stint in the iron mines of northern Minnesota. Välimäki, born to an out-of-wedlock mother in Lapua, Vaasa province, in 1884, emigrated to the United States in 1901. Välimäki became a "triple-threat" socialist-unionist. In 1906, he joined the Finnish Socialist Federation's Hibbing, Minnesota, local. He then became an organizer for the Western Federation of Miners in 1907, working in the field during the 1907 Mesabi Iron Ore Miners' Strike.[15]

After exploits on the Mesabi Iron Range during the 1907 WFM strike, Välimäki gained respect as a talented union organizer and newspaper editor.

In the following years, Välimäki acted as editor of the Finnish socialist-unionist newspapers *Työkansa* and *Raivaaja* and acted as the editor-in-chief of *Toveri*.[16] Well-schooled in Marxist ideology during his travels, Välimäki used his working-class perspective in the Copper Country, turning up in the copper district around 1910 as an editor at the TPC. By 1912, Välimäki was the TPC's secretary, and a district organizer for the WFM.[17] While Välimäki traded mine labor for a desk job with the TPC, there is graphic and textual evidence of Välimäki's "hoboness." As caricatures often accentuate a person's subtle qualities, a caricature of Välimäki in *Työmies 10 Vuotias* corroborates his roots in manual labor. The noticeable stubble on Välimäki's face in the caricature possibly relates a life less oriented to deskwork and more comfortable with manual labor.

The TPC and Its Unions

When it came to union organization, the TPC practiced what it preached. A document dated September 18, 1911, relates the publishing company's contract with the Hancock Local No. 229 of the International Printing Pressmen and Assistants' Union, headquartered in Rogersville, Tennessee. This contract stated that the terms of the contract were to last one year, and that "hereinafter set forth to the end that fruitless controversy shall be avoided and good feeling and harmonious relations be maintained, and that the regularly and orderly prosecution of the business to which the parties to this agreement have a community of interest will be assured beyond the possibility of interruption."[18]

The contract further stipulated the scale, workweek, hours of a workday, and holiday/overtime wages for Työmies Publishing Company's journeymen press operators and apprentices. Pressmen operating a newspaper perfecting press received the highest wage at $22.00 a week for six days' work. Foremen in charge of presses made $20.00 per week for six day's work. At the low end of the wage scale were platen-press operators who earned $15.00 per week for six days' work. The apprentice scale was staggered to relate wages with experience. A first-year apprentice working on a cylinder or Cox-Duplex press received "not less than $9.00 per week; second year, not less than $12.00 per week; third year, not less than $14.00 per week; fourth year, not less than

$16.00 per week." Platen-press apprentices received less, starting at $6.00 per week in the first year and ending at $14.00 per week in the fourth year. Apprentices could not operate a press at the publishing company unless at least one journeyman was working in the same room. After the fourth year of service to the company, apprentices became journeymen and received the journeyman's wage scale.

The third section of the contract related overtime and holiday pay, something almost unknown to the rest of the Copper Country's laboring masses:

> Pressmen working overtime shall receive time and one-half from the regular quitting time to midnight and from midnight up to the regular hour set for those working the day shift.
>
> Pressmen working on Sunday, New Year's, Fourth of July, Thanksgiving and Christmas, shall be paid for at the rate of price and one-half, work performed after the regular quitting time shall be paid for at the rate of double time. Pressman working on Labor Day shall be paid at the rate of double time.[19]

Additionally, no. 10 of the section "Rules Governing the Scale of Wages" gave the TPC employees something that had been desired by Copper Country mine workers for many years, "Eight hours per day shall constitute the regular day's work. All work performed outside the regular eight hours shall be rated and charged as overtime."[20]

The final section of the contract outlined the "Prevention of Strike and Arbitration Provisions." This section specifically denies the press operators the ability to strike, but also denies the TPC lockout measures. This portion also outlines the process of arbitration between the two parties, stating that arbitrators in a dispute will be a joint committee of the two parties at hand, the Työmies Publishing Company and the Pressmen. If these two groups were unable to come to a decision, then the matter would be sent to a three-member board of arbitration. This three-member board would include one member from each party and a third board member mutually agreed upon by both parties. Their findings would be the be-all and end-all in labor disputes.[21] Was this contract a symbolic pact to show Copper Country capitalists how a wage system should read, or was it a contract of necessity that addressed labor problems at the TPC?

It is unclear if there was labor unrest in the TPC, but we can only imagine the very palatable irony of a workers' strike at *the* workers' publishing company.

The TPC was a two union, trades union shop, as the type composers, linotype operators, writers, and mailers belonged to the International Typographical Union. The TPC's employees belonged to the Houghton Typographical Union No. 596, along with the employees of other Houghton Country newspapers, including the mining company–influenced *Daily Mining Gazette, Evening Copper Journal, Calumet News,* Keweenaw Printing Company, and the Scott and Roberts Job Printing Company. Union local meetings were likely an interesting affair as the workers of *the* socialist newspaper sat down to wax upon union ideals with the "mining company" newspapers. However, there was apparently a sense of solidarity between these newspaper workers, as a *Työmies* ad proclaimed: "Mr. Businessman. When you support us, we support you. [Names of above newspapers.] Demand this stamp [Trades Union Logo]. Publishers, printers and newspapers of the Copper Territory will carry this logo on printed products. Who will be the first retailer to support this logo by advertising in these journals?"[22]

The Birth of *Lapatossu*

In late 1911, a second attempt at creating a satirical journal commenced. This publication had "legs" and grew to be a very popular offering. This monthly journal's success was in large part due to the increased space at the TPC's new publishing campus, the addition of new technological capability, and the hiring of competent artistic staff and writers. The TPC christened the new journal *Lapatossu* (Shoepack), whose title character was the illustrated symbolism of the TPC's "hobo-ness." *Lapatossu* lampooned conditions in American industry with biting satire and well-drawn comics. The subjects of *Lapatossu*'s comical wrath were usually national figures such as presidents and robber barons, but occasionally regional and local happenings landed in its pages. *Lapatossu* had its own staff and editors' offices on the TPC's campus.

Lapatossu became a reality only after a talented socialist Finnish immigrant satirist and cartoonist joined the TPC's staff in 1911. Kalle Aleksanteri Suvanto, born March 16, 1887, was somewhat typical of the motivated, preordained southern

Finnish socialist immigrant who arrived primed for a response to industrial America in the first part of the twentieth century. Suvanto began cartooning as a boy in Finland for the satirical magazine *Tuulihattu*. He gravitated to the Social Democratic Party in response to abuses by the Russian czarist ruling class as early as 1905, after the Finnish General Strike of the same year. Suvanto worked for another socialist publication, the *Kansan Tähto*, until he left to experience life outside Finland, working for a time at a shipyard in St. Petersburg, Russia.[23]

Between 1910 and 1911, Suvanto relocated to America and after a short time with the TPC, Suvanto created the hobo "Tossu," in response to the aforementioned jabs by the Copper Country's conservative Finnish-language press. Of Tossu and *Lapatossu*, Suvanto remembered:

> We decided to give the new magazine the name *Lapatossu*, because it will be based on the traditional humor, satire, and critique that prevails among workers.
>
> My pencil began to create the figure of *Lapatossu* on my drawing table this way: Mouth in a wide grin, surrounded by stubble, with an American corn-cob pipe hanging down from one corner. A small nose, the right eye far-reaching, round and bright. The left eye closed. On his head a worn bowler hat, pulled down to the ears. In the hat-band a little flower, as a symbol of idealism. In the picture Lapatossu comes from afar, walking along the railroad tracks like hundreds of immigrant boys have had to do in this wide land as they've searched for work . . . Tossu is a cheerful worker who lives on the borders of society. The name has been given by other workers. He is always ready to trade word for word with his fellow workers as well as his employers.[24]

Suvanto was a professional, with clearly held beliefs in the power of satirical journalism, once stating, "The highest level of culture in journalism is represented by satirical publications, which speak the truth with words and pictures, while other papers are bogged down in their own seriousness." Suvanto left the TPC and *Lapatossu* to edit the Canadian satirical *Väkäleuka* shortly after Tossu's creation. After a short stint with the Canadian satirical, Suvanto returned to the TPC and his Tossu.[25]

The TPC Reaches Maturity

The early part of the decade 1910–1920 was a defining moment for the publishing company. This period saw the TPC push toward critical mass, meaning that the growth of the company began to meet the expectations of its ideology. According to Marxist theory, socialism is an inevitable force that grows out of a corrupt capitalist system. The rather meteoric growth of the TPC probably seemed to indicate to its staff that the hour of inevitability was at hand, and the TPC began organizing its considerable assets to confront the Copper Country's capitalist system.

The 1912 financial report indicated a large increase in TPC's assets from its meager Hancock beginnings in 1904. The TPC's assets in 1904 were $990.00; in the fiscal year 1911–1912, the TPC's assets were $49,006.14 (over $1,000,000 in contemporary finances). Of those assets, the TPC owned $21,096.25 in printing-related machinery and $4,459.08 in office furnishings. The TPC's largest expense by far was the wages it paid to workers, which cost $34,962.12. Curiously, with all the money flowing in and out of the publishing company, the company managed to pull exactly even, as 1911–12 profits matched the year's losses. This was likely an indication that the TPC operated on Rochdale cooperative principles, distributing money back to shareholders or investing in educational programs.[26]

In 1912, the TPC added two dynamic publications to its press offerings. The first of these offerings was a *Suomalais-Englantilainen Sanakirja* (Finnish-English Dictionary), edited by V. S. Alanne. At over nine hundred pages, this was the first truly comprehensive Finnish-English dictionary. A benchmark linguistic work, the dictionary punctuated the move to join American culture through understanding and use of English. The other new publication targeted the nonindustrial, rural working-class element. The title selected for this journal was *Pelto ja Koti* (Farm and Home). It began as a monthly, but changed to a semi-monthly publication in 1913. *Pelto ja Koti*'s editor was William Martilla, who was born in Simo, Oulu province. He emigrated to the United States in 1900.[27] Martilla was likely more of an agrarian than a revolutionary, and this ideological paucity was reflected in *Pelto ja Koti*'s pages. Class-conscious ideology

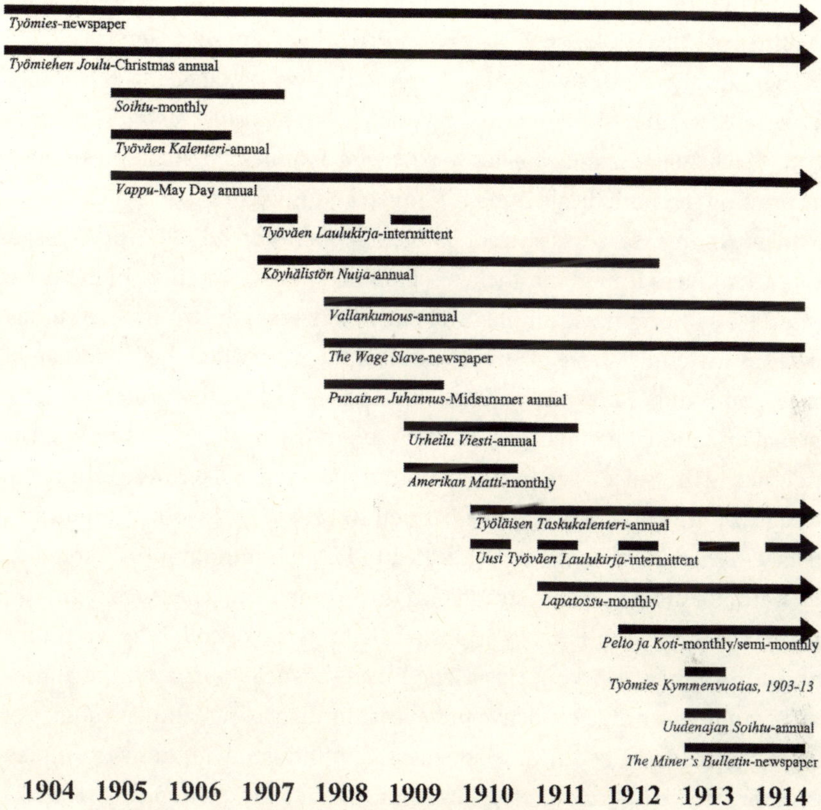

Työmies Publishing Company Publications, 1904–1914. Työmies Publishing Company periodicals, 1904–1914. (Gary Kaunonen.)

and revolutionary socialism were not a large part of *Pelto ja Koti*. Instead, barn plans, crop recommendations, and contemporary fashions for the rural family were highlighted in this publication.

The year 1912 was an apex or coming of age for the TPC's publishing endeavors. In the last two years, the publishing company moved to larger digs, signed a benchmark labor contract, and established two noteworthy monthly journals, *Lapatossu* and *Pelto ja Koti*. There was also an expansion of ancillary publications during this time. By 1912, the TPC was publishing an updated songbook, *Uusi Työväen Laulukirja* (New Workers Songbook) which now featured the "Internationale" as its first song and another attempt at a proletarian almanac titled *Työläisen Taskukalenteri* (Workers' Pocket Calendar). These new periodical offerings were in addition to the two newspapers *Työmies* and *The Wage Slave*, and aforementioned periodicals *Työmiehen Joulu*, *Köyhälistön Nuija*, *Vallankumous*, and *Vappu*. By 1912, the Työmies Publishing Company was printing ten periodicals in both Finnish and English.[28]

While the articles, essays, floor plans, and poems of the TPC's broad list of publications were important, the iconographic images contained in the pages of the TPC's offerings sometimes stole fury from textual narratives. At times, the TPC's cartoonists/artists Suvanto and Sallinen provided the iconographic images, but syndicated work of English-language publications often depicted regional or national happenings that were unknown to those at the TPC. The syndicated progressive cartoonists Art Young and Ryan Walker were featured in the pages of the TPC's publications frequently. Perhaps the work by syndicated artists with non-Finnish names indicated to Finnish immigrant workers that they were not alone in their struggle against capitalism. These iconographic images created by non-Finnish artists created a sense of solidarity within the Finnish immigrant working class. The images visually portrayed the abuses against, and power of, a collective proletariat by displaying familiar themes of struggle, awakening, social consciousness, and industrial gluttony to Finnish immigrant socialist-unionists. These images displayed the plight of those exploited by capitalism, and solicited an emotional response to the inequality surrounding fellow workers of all ethnicities.

While solidarity with fellow workers was a major theme of the TPC's publications, a unique characteristic of these publications was that they were a discourse on current events and the socialist-unionist interpretation of these events. The TPC had a distinct bias as to its spectrum of publications—they were all pro-socialist-unionist—but they were fully open to debating the proper course of socialism and/or the merits of anarcho-syndicalist tactics. There always seemed to be room for a debate on the issues. This consistently open dialogue in America drew the ire of Old Country socialists:

> Nowhere in the world are newspaper columns filled with such torrents of official, semi-official, and unofficial resolutions, proclamations, statements

> and records of the local chapters, committees, boards, individuals and groups in perpetual conflict with one another . . . nagging, splitting hairs, bickering, arguing, and ending where they began in extricable confusion.[29]

For the great amount of internal strife and debating at the TPC, or perhaps because of it, readership of the TPC's publications ultimately soared. In 1912, as a daily, *Työmies* claimed a guaranteed circulation of 12,000 readers and charged $3.75 for a yearly subscription. At this time, Richard Backman was president of the TPC, the union organizer Välimäki was secretary, and Nummivuori remained general manager. The Finnish Socialist Federation's membership also reached an all-time high with 11,536 members in 248 locals,[30] and the TPC employed an all-time high with sixty-three workers. Wage records relate the steady increase of employees at the publishing company. In 1909–10, the TPC paid $16,841.00 in wages to its employees. In 1910–11, TPC paid its workers $23,640.00; in 1911–12, $34,962.00 was paid; and in 1912–13, the TPC paid $49,776.17 in wages.[31] The following table lists the occupations and number of workers employed by the TPC in 1912 and 1913:

1	Business Manager
8	Editors on the *Työmies* editorial board
1	Editor of art/drawing/comics
1	Editor for *Lapatossu*
1	Editor for *Pelto ja Koti*
1	Editor for the Finnish-English Dictionary
8	Librarians and office aides
1	Proofreader
13	Type composers
2	Composer's apprentices
2	Printers
3	Printer's apprentices
3	Shipping and handling clerks
1	Book binder
3	Book binder's assistant (females)
1	Janitor

1	Errand boy
3	Branch attendants at offices in Ishpeming, Mich.; Duluth, Minn.; and Virginia, Minn.
4	Branch office aides
5	Regular sales agents[32]

Altogether, the TPC was riding an upswing in financial terms between 1912 and 1913. The TPC increased their assets from roughly $49,000 in 1911–12 to $126,085.51 in 1912–13.[33] By 1912–13, the TPC owned $24,123.81 worth of printing machinery, $5,989.37 in office furnishings, and $13,112.67 in printing supplies. The Hancock bookstore was sitting on $18,279.18 in overstock. Wages and credit payments were the largest debts paid out, at $49,632.73 and $36,939.98 respectively. While it is clear that the TPC was thriving in this time of prosperity, controversy was also a regular obstacle. Of the TPC's expenditures at this time, incidentals amounted to $758.97 and one of those incidentals was $194.49 used in a legal fund;[34] it seems the TPC, and specifically *Lapatossu*, had a run-in with the federal government in 1912. The conflict centered on the mailing of two 1912 *Lapatossu* issues. The TPC, business manager John Nummivuori, and editor John Salminen were charged with three counts of sending obscene literature through the mail. According to Count 1, the TPC, Nummivuori, and Salminen:

> deposited and caused to be deposited in the Post Office of the United States, to-wit; certain non-mailable matter, to-wit; 3000 copies of a certain obscene, lewd, lascivious and filthy paper and publication of an indecent character, then there addressed to diverse persons, receptively, which said paper and publication is printed in the Finnish language and bears upon its cover and title page, the name, "Lapatossu," the same being a semi-monthly publication bearing date of April 24th, 1912 and each then and there, containing matters of print, so obscene, lewd, lascivious, filthy and indecent in character that the same would be offensive to the Court here, and improper to be placed upon the records thereof, wherefore, the Grand Jurors aforesaid do not set forth the same in this indictment.[35]

The first and second counts in the federal indictment before the grand jury dealt with the same issue, published on April 24, 1912. The second count translated the dialogue of the cartoon under scrutiny. The dialogue read, "Hey, Jakko; why did you dirty teacher's chair? Careful, my man, everything comes to be blamed on the socialists." The cartoon graphically portrays a man pulling up his drawers after defecating on a chair. According to the indictment, the cartoon was "contrary to the form of the statute in such case made and provided, and against the peace and dignity of the United States of America."[36] One has to wonder if the teeth of the indictment were not aimed at other cartoons, such as the one on the preceding page of that month's *Lapatossu.* That religious-themed cartoon derisively portrayed a clergymen posing on Lady Liberty's pedestal, using Christ and Satan as a measure of counterbalance.

The third count of the indictment charged the same malfeasance, but for a different cartoon. This cartoon, published in the December 10, 1912, issue of *Lapatossu,* portrayed Adam and Eve in conversation about censorship in the Garden of Eden. The heading of the cartoon reads "The Worries of Paradise," and the count transcribed the dialogue between the two characters: "Adam; Eve, won't you loan me your handkerchief for a little while. [The handkerchief of which Adam speaks of is covering Eve's pubic area.] Eve; I dare not my dear Adam. If I did the publication of 'Lapatossu' would be stopped."[37] The grand jury found there was enough evidence for a trial, and in time, the three defendants were found guilty on most of the original charges.[38]

The TPC's legal problems did not affect subscription numbers. The TPC was enjoying success and unprecedented growth in the Finnish-language publishing business. That meant successful delivery of the socialist-unionist message. It is unclear what effect the indictments and trial against the TPC had inside the walls and offices of the publishing company. There was already enough tension in the room so to speak as disputes and very substantial differences between the political and IWW factions were becoming increasingly obvious in the TPC's staff, but perhaps the growth in *Työmies*'s readership was because disagreement and not cohesion drove the publishing company's success. For many, participation in the immigrant Finns' socialist-unionist movement meant knowing, reading, writing, and debating the issues. The TPC and its members in the Hancock local seemingly fostered an adversarial discourse, and even extolled it by way of printed sanctioning in its publications. Strangely, for a time, this discourse seemed to create a sense of solidarity between Finnish immigrant workers.

With this unique sense of solidarity, the Hancock local and *Työmies* set out to contest a unilateral source of ire, the Copper Country "bosses." These Finnish immigrant workers, who toiled together in the mines of the Copper Country, walked the Finnish Transitional Neighborhood's streets together, went to the Kansankoti Hall together, and read the TPC's broad range of publications together, formulated a challenge to the Copper Country oligarchy and responded to the mine bosses together. The reply to Copperdom's abuses became a district-wide strike, which at times escalated into open class warfare. The Hancock Finnish Socialist Federation local, Kansankoti Hall, and the TPC played a central role in this proletarian awakening.

CHAPTER 6

The 1913–14 Copper Country Strike

THE 1913–14 STRIKE WAS THE CULMINATION OF ALL PREVIOUS SOCIALIST-unionist Finnish immigrant activities, and in a way Finnish immigrant socialist-unionists were spoiling for a confrontation with the mining companies. While the strike became a district-wide action throughout the Copper Country, strike organizers focused attempts on confronting the paternalism and oligarchy of the Calumet and Hecla Mining Company (C&H) and to a lesser extent the Quincy and Copper Range mining companies. The strike was at times open class warfare and as in any such conflict, the strike had its casualties. The strike also dramatically polarized the Copper Country. The Western Federation of Miners (WFM) printed its own newspaper from the Työmies Publishing Company building while copper companies printed their version of events in newspapers ostensibly controlled by the mining oligarchy. Not surprisingly, the two sides of the dialectic often had their own interpretations of strike events.

Rhetoric came fast and furious from both sides, but in the following two chapters, we will look particularly at the strike from the perspective of organized labor, and specifically from the viewpoint of striking Finnish immigrant socialist-unionists. This specific perspective, the socialist-unionist Finnish immigrants', has thus far eluded books that deal solely with events from the 1913–14 Copper Strike. Original primary research on Finnish immigrant socialist-unionist organizations in the Copper Country and *Työmies* are scant in Arthur Thurner's work and completely lacking in recent research on the Italian Hall by author Steve Lehto; neither author even lists *Työmies* in their bibliography even though *Työmies* published a number of English language articles about strike events. The oversights in primary research of the Finnish proletarian perspective by Lehto and Thurner are regrettable because Finnish immigrants played a major role in this, the most significant of all conflicts between labor and capital in the Copper Country. This gap in original primary research leads to incomplete analysis of significant events (such as the Italian Hall tragedy), and in some instances, inaccuracy and neglect in examination of the complete historic record.

In the next two chapters, we will outline early labor activities in the Copper Country via historiography and then examine the contribution of Finnish immigrant socialist-unionists in the effort to organize Copper Country workers before and during the calamitous 1913–14 Michigan Copper Strike. We will evaluate many of the strike's events in two unique ways. First, we will use the writing of Työmies Publishing Company editor Antti O. Sarell to interpret the actions of striking workers from the perspective of a Työmies Publishing Company staff member.[1] Sarell's viewpoint will afford us the chance to view the strike through a unique lens, that of the Finnish immigrant socialist-unionists. Secondly, we will use banner headlines and articles from *Työmies* and its English-language counterpart, the *Miners' Bulletin*, to give a chronological sequence to the strike's major occurrences. In essence, these chapters are a look at the strike through the lens of the Finnish immigrant socialist-unionists and the WFM. We will also use primary and secondary sources and oral histories to give context and complete the story of the 1913–14 Michigan Copper Miners' Strike.

Early Labor Unrest

The 1913–14 Copper Country Strike was a monumental showdown between monopoly capital and labor (represented by the WFM), but this strike certainly was not the first labor grievance issued by Copper Country mineworkers.

Though some have portrayed the Copper Country as a peaceful backwater of labor-management relations, it was not such a serene setting. Localized histories such as mining-company historian C. Harry Benedict's *Red Metal: The Calumet and Hecla Story*, travel-writer Angus Murdoch's *Boom Copper: The Story of the First U.S. Mining Boom*, and even one-time history professor, at DePaul University, Arthur Thurner's *Rebels on the Range: The Michigan Copper Miners' Strike of 1913–1914* have either neglected or blatantly refused to address the Copper Country's working class on its own terms, in essence embezzling labor's ownership of its own history on the Keweenaw Peninsula.

While Benedict and Murdoch rarely bring labor into the industrial equation of the Copper Country's labor-management calculus, throughout his writing Thurner downplays the early efforts of labor organizers in the Copper Country and attributes strike efforts almost exclusively to outside forces. Thurner goes so far as to write in *Rebels on the Range*, "But opposition of operators does not sufficiently explain the lack of a sustained union movement among Michigan Copper workers before the early twentieth century."[2] Despite Thurner's assertions, early wildcat strikes, walkouts, and officially organized labor activities in the Copper Country indicate otherwise.

Labor unrest fomented by the Marxist International Workingmen's Association spurred a Copper Country strike as early as 1872. Thurner downplays the magnitude of organized labor's actions during 1872, writing: "Michigan copper mine owners first expressed their adamant opposition to trade unionism in 1872 when they crushed a strike which followed some local activity by the International Workingmen's Association. Soldiers were first summoned to the district because of labor turbulence at Calumet during this strike, but they arrived as the rebellion was quieting, encamped for a short time, and departed as the men went back to work."[3]

In contrast to Thurner's rather sanguine account of the 1872 strike, Arthur Puotinen, a Finnish American historian, wrote about the same event: "Organizers from the International Workingmen's Association had circulated among the employees and gained support for such demands as higher wages, an eight-hour working day, and improved safety conditions in the mines."[4] Puotinen went on to write that conditions worsened so for C&H during the strike that mine superintendent R. J. Wood wrote to Governor H. P. Baldwin asking for troops to "control strikers who reputedly threatened the lives of officers, threw stones at non-striking workers and generally disrupted mining operations."[5] Conditions got so bad that Houghton County sheriff Bartholomew Shea wrote Governor Baldwin that "Rioters have rescued prisoners from me and taken arms from my men. Want troops very badly. The situation is very alarming. My posse has failed in arresting ringleaders."[6]

In fact, this 1872 strike was a watershed event in Copper Country labor relations, as Copper Country historian Larry Lankton points out in his book *Cradle to Grave*. Alexander Agassiz, president of C&H at this time, initially took a conciliatory attitude toward the striking workers. Agassiz commissioned Superintendent Wood to write a "My Friends" letter that outlined employee benefit programs placed on the bargaining table to workers. The workers rejected the paternalistic plans, and as Lankton writes, "The letter however did not dissuade the men from striking. Violence erupted as strikers confronted loyal employees and the Houghton County Sheriff and his men."[7] Agassiz presumably perceived the strikers' denials of conciliatory gestures as a betrayal to C&H, and this event shaped Agassiz's malcontent relations with organized labor for the rest of his life.[8]

Two years later, in 1874, Finnish and Swedish trammers led a walkout at the C&H mines, putting Agassiz's newfound resolve to a test. Thurner makes no mention of this labor action, but both Lankton and Puotinen grasp its impact on Copper Country labor relations. This small-scale walkout by Finns and Swedes was met with contempt, and a "My Friends" letter was not forthcoming from Agassiz. Instead, he dictated a strongly worded letter to newly appointed superintendent James North Wright:

> We cannot be dictated to by anyone. The mine must stop if it stays closed forever . . . I have attempted formerly to try and get their good will by offering them a share of the profits . . . Wages will be raised whenever we see fit and at no other time (if they don't like it they must go and get employment elsewhere . . .).[9]

There was a period of relative labor peace between the mid-1870s and the mid-1880s, but a series of suspicious fires at C&H beginning in 1887 rekindled animosity between labor and the mining oligarchy. Lankton relates that most mining authorities believed the fires were an industrial accident, but C&H officials believed otherwise. Sure that the fires were some sort of industrial sabotage or acts of a disgruntled employee, C&H offered a $10,000 reward for information leading to specific details about the fires, but found no takers.[10] These suspicious fires were literally a flashpoint that signaled a quarter-century era of labor unrest in the Copper Country.

In 1890, workers walked out at the Tamarack Mine, located slightly to the northwest of C&H's main copper lode. Other small-scale strikes occurred at the Atlantic Mine and at C&H in 1892, when almost eighty workers walked off the job "amidst signs of violence."[11] In 1893, this upheaval continued as workers struck C&H's stamp mill on Portage Lake, and then a more serious dust-up occurred later in 1893 when trammers struck the company. This violent clash pitted unskilled laborers versus skilled labor and found strikers in possession of a C&H engine house for a brief moment. C&H blacklisted the strikers and used the county sheriff to run off holdout strikers.[12]

More walkouts and strikes occurred in the following years. As Puotinen writes: "The Tamarack mine again in 1894, the Quincy mine in 1896, and the Atlantic mine again in 1897. While not indicative of a widespread shutdown in the copper industry, these incidents refute C. Harry Benedict's generalization that before 1900 good times existed in the Copper Country in regards to labor unrest."[13] It further refutes Thurner's assertion that there was no sustained labor movement before the 1900s. It is clear that the Knights of Labor worked to organize, or at the very least influence and shape, Copper Country workers' responses to monopoly capital beginning in 1879. The Knights were ostensibly gone from the Copper Country by the late 1890s,[14] but perhaps left a mining district ripe with unionist sentiment. From the aforementioned labor initiatives, it is apparent that there were some local, regional, and/or national organizational efforts driving labor ideology and consciousness during the late nineteenth and early twentieth centuries in the Copper Country.

Where the Knights of Labor left off in regards to organized labor, a more radical union came to nest in the Copper Country, and Finnish immigrant socialist-unionists nurtured and in some instances helped to build the house of organized labor in the Copper Country. As early as 1903–04, workers in Michigan's Copper Country requested help from the Western Federation of

Miners (WFM). The call for help from the WFM by Copper Country workers coincided with the move of the Työmies Publishing Company to Hancock from Worcester, Massachusetts, in late 1903 and early 1904. In its early stages in the Copper Country, the WFM established locals in Laurium, Hancock, Painesdale, Allouez, a smelterman's local in Lake Linden, and a district local also sited in Lake Linden. Strikes at the Quincy Mine followed in 1904 and 1905.[15]

The WFM's burgeoning foothold in the Copper Country was short-lived, and the Copper Country locals collapsed within a year or two. In 1905, while the WFM sputtered nationally in the wake of costly strikes in the American West, they joined and became the largest section of the Industrial Workers of the World (IWW). This union of unions did not last long, and after two years, the WFM left the IWW haggling about direction, tactics, and members. During this time, the Finnish socialists and unionists banded together in a tense solidarity under WFM-IWW dual unionism. Finnish immigrants, many of whom were not citizens and thus devoid of the right to vote, flocked to the IWW's apolitical, all-inclusive platform. Radical Finns especially joined the IWW in large numbers, but maintained a shirttail affiliation with their Finnish socialist locals and thus the Socialist Party of America's preferred miners' union, the WFM.[16]

In 1906, two wildcat strikes began the slow burn to an explosive district-wide labor-management clash in 1913. The strikes occurred at relatively the same time during the summer of 1906. A strike at the Quincy Mine lasted for three weeks, but was ostensibly a stalemate for Quincy's labor force. Instead of gaining a 10 percent increase, Quincy's workers accepted a 5 percent wage increase.[17]

During this strike, Quincy managers surveyed worker sentiment through labor spies:

> No. 5 Reports:
>
> I spent the forenoon about the Quincy Mines and talked with and listened to the miners' conversation which was principally about the meeting which the miners are to hold this afternoon to decide whether they will go back to work or continue the strike. All those who expressed themselves in my presence appeared to believe the strike would be settled and work resumed Monday.
>
> The meeting was held at 2:30 P.M., in Funkey's Hall on Quincy Street. I was unable to gain admittance to the hall as only miners were allowed to enter

upon presentation of their card. The meeting closed at 4:30 P.M., and the crowd appeared to be excited, as they had come to no settlement. Those most excited were the men of families who wish to go back to work.[18]

Though the Quincy strike placed difficulties on workers and their families, as Operative P wrote, "Operative also met Paabo [Paavo] Pyykkonen, a saloon keeper, who said [conditions were good], but they had had a strike at the Quincy Mines which prevented the men there from drawing pay for two months; that they had returned to work with a slight increase in pay, which amounted to so little that it was scarcely noticeable."[19] The same spy also indicated that "During the day operative was around among the miners as much as possible, but nothing was said in regard to the late strike, the only mention made of anything of that nature being in regard to the Rockland, Mich., strike, which was in effect at this time."[20]

The 1906 Rockland Strike was a much shorter, yet more intense effort that smoldered almost a year before the actual strike. In 1905, a small labor upheaval at the Adventure Mine motivated Ontonagon County Sheriff McFarlane to make a horribly prophetic promise that would come to fruition in Rockland a year later. McFarlane stated at this time that future labor activity would result in gunfire on the sheriff's part.[21]

On July 4, 1906, a labor organizer for the WFM attended a temperance gathering in Rockland, Michigan, a hamlet close to the Michigan Mine. The organizer asked the *Valko Ruusu Raittiussuera* (White Rose Temperance Society) to speak at this function. The White Rose Society agreed to give the man platform. The man proceeded to speak, imploring the workers gathered at the Independence Day celebration to strike for better wages and industrial democracy. The speech did not immediately take root, but by July 30, the workers of Rockland had had enough and walked off the job. Most of those that struck were Finnish immigrant trammers and likely newly christened members of the labor movement.[22]

Sheriff McFarlane arrived at the Michigan Mine's dry house, prepared to confront the strikers. Accounts vary as to the events of the ensuing battle. According to those partial to McFarlane, as McFarlane peaceably escorted workers from the dry houses to the shaft, a mob of striking trammers jeered and chided those crossing the line. The war of words turned to rock throwing, and then the crudely armed mob rushed the sheriff and his deputies. The armed mob reportedly had clubs, knives, and guns and were the first to shoot, but it was the sheriff and his men who drew first blood. In the melee, two "Finlanders" paid the ultimate price: "Ludvig Ojala's head was shot off at point-blank range."[23] Oscar Ohtonen was shot in his stomach, receiving fatal wounds to his lower intestine, while nine other strikers were wounded, and one hundred were locked up in a makeshift cell as sheriff's deputies searched area homes for weapons. Amazingly, there were no reports of wounded on the sheriff's side of the clash.[24]

The workers involved in the strike had a different version of the events. They recounted that Sheriff McFarlane and his deputies attacked the 280 to 300 striking workers unprovoked. They stated that August Huuskonen was the only person carrying a gun and that he departed the scene as soon as the melee got underway. According to the strikers, nonparticipant bystanders received injuries from the sheriff's efforts in addition to the strikers. Ohtonen was shot and died from his injuries, while Ojala's body lay in the street until the middle of the next day as a warning to other residents that martial law prevailed in Rockland.[25]

As one might imagine, the sensational reports coming out of Rockland from both sides shook the greater Copper Country. The one hundred or so strikers arrested in the activity now had to find legal counsel to fend off charges stemming from the dispute. Support in the way of monetary funds came in from various sympathetic organizations, and the plight of the strikers was headline news in the Finnish-language press. A generous donation of $10,000 from "foreign residents" in Calumet found its way into the legal coffers to defend the Rockland strikers.[26] Hancock's Pohjantähti Temperance Society assisted as "Aid was gathered for the strikers at Rockland by sponsoring evening programs, where large amounts in gifts were given by the society to the strikers' fund."[27]

The strikers chose John Kiiskila of Hancock to represent them over the other well-known Finnish immigrant lawyer, Oscar "O. J." Larson.[28] This was likely a good choice, because Larson was the fellow who solicited James MacNaughton of Calumet and Hecla to buy clandestine stock in a Finnish-language paper to promote the mining companies' interests. The passion and tragedy of the strike wound down into court proceedings and fines. Kiiskila secured the release of many of the strikers for a $23.50 fine, which was not couch change at that time, but thirteen of the strikers had to stand trial for intimidation, assault, and intent to do bodily harm. The judge acquitted the "Rockland Thirteen" of all charges in March 1907.[29]

Copper Country labor organizers attempted to portray the events of the Rockland Strike as a call to action by the working class of Rockland, and those shot, tried, and jailed as martyrs to the proletarian cause. The Copper Country agitators and organizers continued to rail against the mining-company oligarchy:

> On Saturday and Sunday evening the operative attended [a] meeting of the Finn Working Men's Society. Several speeches were made, among them the more prominent speakers being Mr. O. Maki and others. Maki spoke about social democrats and also about the strike in Rockland. He said the men had demanded a little betterment of their condition, namely, one hour less and 25 cents increase in wages; that they had made their request without threats of any kind but that the company had called in the police officers and ill treated the men. He went into a Socialistic discourse about capital and labor and asked the men to unite together and stand up for their rights and they would surely win. The operative states that Macki [*sic*] is a radical agitator.[30]

Nevertheless, as labor organizers in the Copper Country portrayed the Rockland strikers as victims and implored Copper Country mine workers to carry on with the fight, the Quincy men were still languishing from the summer of 1906's unproductive strike. In spite of the 5 percent wage increase, wages remained a sore topic between labor and management. Wages and hours were a prominent concern in 1906, but working conditions in area mines were becoming a major component of workers' grievances, as Quincy labor spy Operative P detailed:

> On Sept. 16 the operative was around town and met a number of miners, among who were Victor Hendrickson and J. Lumptula. Speaking of the mines it was said that they were very bad; that the Quincy mines were very hot, particularly No. 7, which was called "the men's slaughter" for the reason that each week something happened to the men employed there; that there were

> not over twelve gangs and that of each gang every week someone was either killed or injured and for that reason they would not work there at any price.[31]

Another Quincy labor spy reported that the "fight" seemingly had left some Quincy workers in the wake of the stalemated 1906 strike, even as casualties mounted in the Quincy mines:

> On October 3 the operative reports that from conversations with various employees of the Quincy mines he finds it is very evident that they are not satisfied with their present scale of wages, but they are not anxious to go on another strike as they do not think they could gain anything by doing so.
>
> On the previous day, about 4:20 P.M., while the operative was at the Quincy Company's smelter an air blast was heard in the Quincy mine, which shook the ground, streets and houses slightly. A man was also hurt or killed in the mine on the preceding day.[32]

The WFM Achieves Critical Mass

In 1908, Quincy's workers seemed to get a second wind. Perhaps this renewed gusto came from solidarity-evoking events like the publication of the *Wage Slave,* an English-language offering from Työmies Publishing Company, and/or from direct-action measures such as the 1907 Hancock Red-Flag Parade. In the wake of these events, the WFM, with the help of Finnish immigrant socialist-unionist groups, again sent a cadre of organizers into Copper Country mines. From the Finnish immigrant contingent, experienced organizers such as John Välimäki, Frank Aaltonen, John Kolu, Heimer Mikko, Charles E. Hietala, and Axel Kolinen helped to organize a multiethnic effort to unite the workers of Michigan's Upper Peninsula copper mines. Between 1908 and 1910, five locals of the WFM were set up in the Copper Country's largest mines at C&H, Quincy, and Copper Range, and later at Mass City and Ahmeek.[33] The WFM locals were slow to take hold, but gradually they grew in size and number, achieving a membership of over 7,000 by 1910. The Houghton County locals experienced meteoric growth in these few years. As Lankton described, "The South Range local began at 30 and grew to 1,580 members. Hancock's local grew from 363 members to 1,450, and the Calumet local grew from 440 members to 2,048 members."[34]

In 1910, there was one big difference in the WFM's organizational efforts: they cut across ethnic lines and the underground labor hierarchy. The WFM recognized the need to organize a union that transcended ethnic lines and sent in organizers with names like Aaltonen, Hietala, Kolu, and Välimäki (Finnish); Ciagne, Jedda, and Bartalini (Italian); Verbanec and Strizich (Croatian); Arseneault (French-Canadian); Sullivan (Irish); Stodden (Cornish); Oppman (Hungarian); Holovatsky (Polish); and Shaws (Slovenian). Some organizers were from outside the Copper Country, hailing from places like Duluth, Minnesota; Butte, Montana; Chicago and Collinsville, Illinois; Winnipeg, Canada; and Kennett, California; but more often the WFM organizers had Copper Country residences. Of fifteen prominent WFM organizers identified in 1913's edition of *Työmiehen Joulu*, nine had Copper Country addresses.

The addition of multiethnic organizers gave the strike actions a solidarity previously lacking. For many of the previous strikes, Finnish trammers and other unskilled laboring ethnicities went on the offensive alone, without the assistance of their skilled underground brethren. In addition to this multiethnic organizing force, the introduction of the one-man drill, a labor- and cost-cutting device, brought the underground workers together as the skilled Cornish miners came into the fold to protect their way of life.[35]

As related numerically, union activity in the Copper Country began as a whimper, progressed to a mutter, and became a roar. Wages, working conditions, and the recognition of the union as the workers' representative were the major grievances of Copper Country mineworkers. In 1913, while trammers in Copper Country mines were making $2.59 a shift on average,[36] the press operators at Työmies Publishing Company in 1911 were making on average $3.09 a shift.[37] When hourly wages are considered, the *Työmies*'s press operators, who worked a forty-eight hour week, earned $.39 an hour.[38] In 1913, trammers in the Michigan copper mines, who worked on average a fifty-five hour week, earned less than $.29 cents an hour. The *Työmies*'s press operators received a better wage for working shorter hours in much less dangerous conditions, received time-and-a-half pay for overtime and holidays, and double time on Labor Day.[39]

As mentioned, working conditions were another factor in the push for local union representation. While the Copper Country mines were less deadly than their western United States counterparts, death and injury were an all-too-frequent occurrence. In 1911, there were 63 deaths (more than one death a week), 679 serious injuries, and 4,260 slight injuries in Copper Country mines. Sanitary conditions underground were at best crude, at worst deplorable. The most sanitary work areas had quick lime and empty blasting powder or candle boxes to defecate in, which were then hoisted to the surface for disposal. Some mines, like those of the Copper Range Company, provided no sanitary materials, reporting, "There are no sanitary regulations beyond requiring levels to be cleaned up from time to time."[40]

Proper ventilation in the depths of a mine was not even a consideration to the mining companies: "The mine managers seem to consider that the mines are sufficiently ventilated, but the mine workers allege the contrary and complain about the poor air they are compelled to breathe from 10 to 11 hours a day."[41] In addition to the stale air, as the mines went deeper, the temperature got hotter. Many of the shallower mines remained a comfortable 50–60 degrees Fahrenheit, but some of the deeper shafts got down right uninhabitable. The depths of some C&H, Quincy, and Tamarack mines hit a constant 80-plus degrees.[42] The high temperatures and stale air made for deplorable working conditions—a laboring environment that was laced with a bevy of sensory offenses such as the smell of decaying excrement, absence of light, and the deafening noise of industrial rock drills and high-powered explosives.

To stimulate organization, the WFM structured a central core of organizers that rotated around a base at the Kansankoti Hall. "Finns" not only comprised a large number of rank-and-filers in the Copper Country WFM locals, they also occupied positions of influence within the WFM. Charles E. Hietala was secretary of WFM District 16, secretary-treasurer of the Hancock local, and a member of the Työmies Publishing Company, and John Välimäki was a District 16 organizer for the WFM as well as secretary of the Työmies Publishing Company. The concerted efforts of Finnish immigrant socialist-unionists to associate with the greater American labor movement paid off as the Finnish Transitional Neighborhood and the Kansankoti Hall–Työmies Publishing

Company's campus became WFM central. As the Copper Country drifted closer to a strike, the Finnish immigrants' translations of labor tomes from English into Finnish and publication of English-language materials secured their place among WFM leadership and as dynamic, informed members of the WFM rank-and-file.

The March toward a Strike

For many working-class folks, the discrepancy between those with the wealth and those who made the wealth was too much to ignore. While Finnish immigrant trammers pushed thousand-pound cars each day, earning roughly $.29 an hour while often working over fifty-five hours a week, Calumet and Hecla paid $3,347,000 in dividends (equal to over $76,000,000 in contemporary times) to stockholders in 1912 alone. In this same year, Copper Range paid out $788,000 in dividends and Quincy paid out $550,000 in dividends.[43] Inequitable distribution of wealth aside, it was hours, working conditions, and labor-management relations that led to a class-conscious understanding of the "haves and have-nots." Along with other Copper Country mineworkers, Finnish immigrants were taking action, formulating an ultimate response against capitalists who did not seemingly care to understand the material conditions of their own workers or their industrial environment.

Many of the Copper Country mine owners simply did not "get it," when "it" came to the working class. While the mining companies provided things like bathhouses, libraries, and housing at low rental rates, paternalism was an underlying complaint of Copper Country proletarians. Paternalism made mineworkers and their families reliant on the company for a livelihood. Many immigrants, and especially immigrant Finns, left their home countries to escape this sort of dependence on hegemonic landowners. Copper Country mine owners did not understand that in many cases, paternalism created a rift instead of a bridge between the "fathers" and their perceived "dependents."

An oral history interview conducted with William Parsons Todd, board member of the Quincy Mining Company during the decade 1910–1920 and son of then Quincy Mining Company president William Rogers Todd, related the manner in which Copper Country capitalists viewed their laboring class. When asked about labor relations of the era, Todd stated:

> It was up to us to look after them and so that we didn't like unions coming in and trying to tell us that they were going to look after the men. We felt that we'd do a better job . . . in fact we very seldom had any labor disturbance, practically almost never. We always tried to keep a step ahead and increase wages really before the men expected it. So they got the habit of just depending on the company . . . when hard times came and the company went down, we never had any trouble with reducing wages somewhat to keep the company going . . . the men and the companies all worked together as friends and we paid them as much as we could.[44]

When asked about out-migration of labor to Detroit and wages, Todd replied:

> I don't know if they were paying better wages or not; but our men loved the mines. They were satisfied with the mines, but their families were not so well satisfied because they kept hearing about opportunities for their daughters, you know, in the automobile plants.[45]

Todd's attitude toward workers seems to be somewhat disconnected from reality. If the workers were actually satisfied with working conditions and wages, would there have been strikes at all? Did Todd really believe that stockholders and workers were united as one? The two groups certainly did not receive the same financial reward from mining operations. If he truly thought of the workers as equals and part of a family, why did he feel that the workers needed coercing to accept a wage reduction?

Todd further hinted in the interview that his protection of the workers' welfare was conditional and extended only so far. While Todd explicitly stated that the company took care of the men's every need and that the company was the sole protector of their health and well-being, when accidents befell the men underground, it was solely the workers' fault and responsibility. When asked about the cause of accidents, Todd replied:

> Men being careless. We used to lay a fuse and maybe we had a thousand men or more underground altogether, somehow or other we used to lose . . . seemed to lose two men a year. Funny! I remember one year we went up until about the 10th of December . . . we hadn't lost a man and between that and the end of December we lost two men.
>
> And underground almost entirely . . . very seldom was it really anything but the men's own fault.[46]

In a final nod to his disconnect with the working class, Todd opined that the reason for the strike in 1913–14 was that the men were after "the easy life, naturally," and when asked if the men were satisfied with wages, Todd replied: "As far as I know, that wasn't discussed . . . that wasn't to come up."[47] Apparently, the men were not as satisfied with the mining companies as Todd suspected. Tension mounted in the Copper Country. On June 10, 1913, *Työmies* reported that three thousand C&H mine slaves awakened at a public meeting during which Välimäki spoke. The pace of labor agitation quickened, and the Työmies Publishing Company's publications foreshadowed the impending industrial conflict.[48]

There was a sort of concentrated energy in *Työmies*'s pages. Weeks ahead of the strike, the newspaper featured news from other labor actions in the United States and around the world. Nineteen-thirteen was also *Työmies*'s tenth anniversary. The July 15 edition, printed on red paper, featured 10th anniversary greetings from former firebrand editor Vihtori Kosonen and Camille Huysmans, Belgian socialist and labor leader.[49] Laina and Evert Björklund, along with hundreds of others from the Upper Peninsula, were on the 1913–14 Työmies Publishing Company's board of directors ballot at this crossroads in Copper Country history.[50] There was an electricity in the air. Libby Koski-Björklund remembers that her grandmother, Maria Ollila, recalled that before and during the time of the strike, men in the boarding house at 237 Wright Street stashed guns in their quarters. Maria Ollila was not in favor of this, but the tide of proletarian discontent was rising, and many years of working-class frustration were ready to boil over into the Copper Country streets.[51] Presumably, the question of *if* a strike was coming was already answered; the more pertinent question seemed to be: Was this going to be the class war and revolution that people like IWW adherent Leo Laukki had been agitating for? Were the guns hidden in Maria Ollila's boarding house going to be necessary, or would the Finnish immigrant socialist-unionists force the mining companies to the table with non-violent direct action and orderly parliamentary procedure? What course would the Copper Country "revolution" take?

The Strike Consumes the Copper Country

In the run-up to the strike, *Työmies*'s pages seemed to indicate that it was increasingly looking like a labor action was an itch that Finnish immigrant socialist-unionists had to scratch. The Hancock WFM local, the Jousi, and the Työmies Publishing Company agitated in lockstep with Copper Country WFM locals for a confrontation. In mid-July 1913, the WFM locals, "goaded on by the Hancock local, home to a number of socialist Finns,"[52] voted to send a letter to the mining companies to coerce labor negotiations. If the letter failed to get the mining companies to the bargaining table, a strike was the only other option built into the ballot's language. According to WFM officials, 98 percent of nine thousand members of the WFM locals voted "yes" to ratify the referendum to send the letter, and if the letter did not work, they were prepared to strike.[53]

This letter was against the wishes of the WFM's national leadership, but the Copper Country locals sent these harshly worded letters to the superintendents of the major copper companies anyway. At the heart of the WFM locals' wishes was attaining the right to have the union represent workers in labor negotiations, an increase in wages, safer working conditions, and the abandonment of the one-man drill as a labor-saving device in mines. The mining companies did little if nothing to acknowledge the Copper Country locals' request, and Quincy's superintendent, Charles Lawton, was reported to have sent his letter back unopened. With the wheels of the strike already in full motion, the WFM national had no other choice but to call out the workers, and on July 23, 1913, Copper Country mineworkers struck the Michigan copper operators.[54] The red WFM union card took its place as an oppositional symbol to Copper Country oligarchy.

Though the red WFM union card became the symbol of organized response to worker grievances in the Copper Country, there was perhaps a strong undercurrent of rank-and-file IWW ideology driving the actions of the Copper Country workers. After all, it had only been six years since the WFM had left the IWW, and within this time, the WFM had joined the American Federation of Labor or AFL. Many of the Finnish immigrant socialist-unionists despised the AFL's craft unionism because the AFL "groped after bourgeois support" and "opposed class warfare."[55] Many within the Finnish immigrant rank-and-file had no time for the conservative unionism of the AFL and thus the seemingly new course of the WFM.

It definitely seemed that in this opening volley of "belligerence" toward the mining companies, the Copper Country locals trumpeted a decidedly decentralized strike declaration. Motivated by the Hancock WFM local, which as we have already noted was rife with strong IWW sentiment, it appeared as if the Copper Country locals purposefully charged ahead of the WFM bureaucracy. This perhaps indicated that IWW-like decentralization was driving the actions of striking workers. The IWW's so-called "cult of spontaneity,"[56] as oppositional American communists later described it, disliked the overt centralization of strike administration and directives from a distant central body to the rank-and-file. This eschewing of the WFM bureaucracy indicated that the Copper Country locals were not waiting for the consent of a centralized body, much in the same way that the rank-and-file powered previous IWW-led strike actions.

Segments of the IWW, and especially the rank-and-file of Wobblies in the western United States, from its very earliest stages beginning in 1905, promoted the decentralization of labor and clamored for local control. In isolated western mining areas, this likely aided the fluidity of strike actions in that decentralization made union locals highly responsive units with the freedom to act on rank-and-file demand; but in the highly corporative and controlled Copper Country, decentralization made preliminary strike actions sustainable for only so long. Outside help, in monetary and organizational form, had to arrive soon, or highly solvent, not-so-distant eastern U.S. mining companies would rout the still-growing WFM Copper Country locals.

As WFM organizers got their bearings, the union quickly rallied money and personnel to the Copper Country. The WFM had five centers for organization in the Copper Country: In the Calumet area, the Calumet Miners' Union, WFM Local No. 203, set up headquarters on 6th Street in Dunn's Hall.[57] In

Keweenaw County, striking workers were under the banner of the Calumet local, but had offices and held meetings in Ahmeek at Lesh's Hall.[58] For workers of the Copper Range Company (Champion, Baltic, and Trimountain mines), the South Range Miners' Union, WFM Local No. 196, had offices and held its meetings in Kämäräinen's Hall, while using the Saima Finnish Temperance Hall for speeches and other functions.[59] At a yet-to-be-determined time during the strike, a newly constructed Finnish Socialist Federation Hall in South Range began hosting speeches and large gatherings. Farther south, in Mass City, the Mass City Miners' Union, WFM Local No. 215, apparently did not have a dedicated meeting space, but rather listed the name of the local's secretary to gain information about union activities. The Hancock Miners' Union, WFM Local No. 200, held its meetings and had offices in the Kansankoti Hall, and Hancock also had a Ladies Auxiliary, WFM No. 5, which also met at the Kansankoti. Each of the WFM locals announced meeting times and office hours, which *Työmies* and the *Miners' Bulletin* published.[60]

Working in tandem with the WFM locals were the Finnish Socialist Federation locals. The Finnish socialist-unionist locals in Ahmeek, Calumet, Hancock, Mass City, and South Range also had regular advertised meetings during the strike and rallied hard to support the WFM. The Finnish Socialist Federation locals and the WFM locals were so intertwined that in many instances, the Finnish Socialist Federation locals shared meeting spaces with the WFM locals. The Hancock, South Range, and Ahmeek (comprised of Finnish immigrant workers from the copper-mining towns of Mohawk, Allouez, and Ahmeek) locals all shared meeting space with the WFM in their respective halls. While the Mass City local did not list a meeting place, the Calumet Finnish Socialist Federation local, *Voima* (Strength), met in a separate hall from the WFM, as Voima used a rented hall at 813 Portland Street in Red Jacket for meetings.[61] For Finnish immigrant socialist-unionists there seemed to be almost a total immersion in the ideals and activities of the WFM.

Työmies Publishing Company's employees jumped feet-first into the fray. *Työmies* editor Severi Alanne had a significant strike coffer to work with during the labor unrest. According to the Articles of Association, the capital stock of the TPC jumped from $15,000 to $100,000 on August 16, 1913, less than a month after the strike began.[62] With this influx of strike capital and the influence of IWW radicals, such as Laukki, *Työmies* became the most combative media advocate of the strike. At this time, *Työmies* was a daily publication in Finnish, but the Työmies Publishing Company also printed the English-language newspaper the *Miners' Bulletin* to rally multiethnic support for the striking miners. Members of the Jousi rallied money and food for the striking workers. Serving as strike headquarters, the Kansankoti Hall was where the WFM held union meetings, votes, and fundraisers, and started or ended parades.[63] On July 25, *Työmies* reported that at a mass meeting held in the Kansankoti, there were so many attendees that the participants spilled out into the street, but remained peaceable.[64] The Työmies Publishing Company, Jousi, and Kansankoti Hall were throwing everything they had into the fight to organize the Copper Country.

While Quincy, Copper Range, and a host of smaller companies were in the WFM's cross hairs, C&H was the potential big prize. C&H employed the most workers by far, was located in the most populous urban area of the Copper Country, had national prestige, and had the largest sums of money to thwart WFM efforts. If the WFM could force C&H to the bargaining table, it was likely that the other mining companies would fall in line. In fact, many of the Copper Country mining companies looked to C&H for direction, recognizing that C&H's size would lead in this time of tumult.[65] C&H's entrenchment in Calumet was a bit of a geographic wildcard for the WFM because the bulk of the WFM's public-relations resources were in Hancock, located within the Finnish Transitional Neighborhood. The largest WFM-controlled meeting space was the Kansankoti Hall, and the Työmies Publishing Company's presses, which would be a vehicle of strike-news dissemination, were in Hancock as well. Roughly ten miles separated C&H's main offices and the Kansankoti Hall–Työmies Publishing Company's campus. We can speculate as to what this distance meant to the strike-consumed parties.

Perhaps the distance was good for the WFM, Kansankoti, and Työmies, as the miles could provide a buffer between the two heavyweights, of which the WFM fold was the underdog. On the other hand, perhaps the distance detracted more from union efforts. To the staff at the Työmies Publishing Company, it may have seemed like they were on the sidelines of a major clash. Early in the strike, massive workers' parades, takeover of mining-company property, and street agitation were all occurring with much publicity on a daily basis in the Calumet area as the WFM bombarded C&H with all sorts of "direct action."

Ten miles to the south, Hancock's smaller population and the Quincy Mining Company's lesser number of workers did not have the same potential impact and propaganda excitement to offer successful WFM efforts. At this time, Quincy was the third largest employer of workers behind Copper Range, and its consequence to the efforts of organized labor paled in comparison to the prestige of taking the fight to C&H. To better visualize the part the competing structures had to play in the showdown between labor and capital, perhaps we could think of the strike in terms of a dialectical tournament. The Mining Company "bracket" would have C&H as a no. 1 seed, Copper Range a no. 2 seed, Quincy the no. 3 seed, and Ahmeek the no. 4 seed. On the WFM side, comparing local union-controlled facilities: Hancock's Kansankoti–Työmies Publishing Company campus would have been the no. 1 seed, the South Range WFM headquarters and Saima Temperance Hall the no. 2 seed, Dunn's Hall in Calumet the no. 3 seed, and the Ahmeek WFM headquarters the no. 4 seed. Therefore, in essence, the no. 1 WFM facility (Kansankoti-Työmies) was paired with the no. 3 Mining Company squad (Quincy), and the no. 3 WFM facility, Dunn's Hall, was competing against the overwhelming favorite, the no. 1 seed, the mighty Calumet and Hecla Mining Company.

Despite being at a distance from the largest fray in Calumet, *Työmies* ran large front-page headlines about the opening volley of strike events. On July 24, the first edition to come out after the commencement of the strike actions, *Työmies* ran the headline "Michigan Copper Territory Mine Workers Striking." The July 25 headline was "15,000 Mine Workers Strike Copper Territory." On the next day, the newspaper printed "State Army Posted in Copper Island Strike Territory." To combat spatial isolation of union locals and members, the WFM, *Työmies*, and the *Miners' Bulletin* took pains to portray the strike as a district-wide labor action in an effort to generate energy for the strike, promote solidarity between workers of various companies and ethnicities, and prevent the compartmentalization of striking workers in physically separated locations. Good examples of efforts to avoid compartmentalization of strike actions as solely against any one mining company or occurring in any one area came

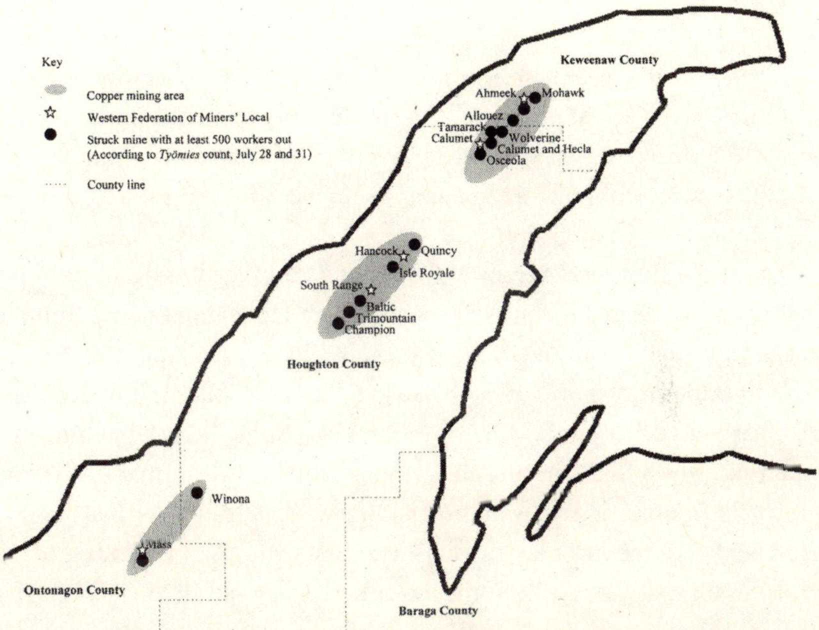

Strike-affected Areas of the Keweenaw Peninsula, July 1913. Areas of the Keweenaw Peninsula effected by the strike actions of the Western Federation of Miners. (Gary Kaunonen.)

from *Työmies*'s headlines, which often heralded strike news from *Kuparialueella* (Copper Territory) or *Lakkoalueele* (Strike Territory).

By defining the boundaries of areas affected by the labor action as one geographic region, *Työmies* made the strike an all-consuming affair for Finnish immigrant socialist-unionists in the Copper Country. For many Finnish immigrant socialist-unionists, this strike was the culmination of their long-exercised response to abuses within the capitalist system. To people like Leo Laukki, John Välimäki, Frank Aaltonen, and Martin Hendrickson, the strike was an ideological and in some cases direct physical confrontation with paternalism, monopoly capital, and in essence, the industrial way of life. To many rank-and-filers, the strike was more about bread-and-butter issues such as putting food on the table and bettering working conditions.

According to A. O. Sarell, the strike began in grand fashion for the WFM:

> When the first big group meeting of the strikers of the farthest corner of Calumet was held, the mighty Palestra building of Laurium was filled to the top with strikers, the majority being that part of the mine workers who had just before the strike shown ignorance towards organizing.[66]

The strike stretched over sixty miles along the jagged Keweenaw copper range from southern Keweenaw County through Houghton County and into eastern Ontonagon County. On July 24, a day after the strike started, *Työmies* proclaimed the swift spread of the strike into far-off Ontonagon County: "The strike has reached all the way down to the Mass Mine, Lake Mine, Algoma, South Lake, North Lake, Indiana and Winona Mines." *Työmies* made their first count of the number of idled workers on July 28. *Työmies* estimated that roughly 15,700 workers were on strike. Two days later, on July 30, *Työmies* made another count, this time specifying the numbers for Keweenaw and Ontonagon County mines: 18,460 workers out. This tally concluded that there were about 15,500 striking Houghton County mineworkers, 1,500 or so from Keweenaw County mines, and around 1,000 idled in Ontonagon County mines. These figures with zeros at the end may indicate some generous rounding up, but the allusion was accurate; workers were walking out of the mines by the thousands, though mining companies claimed only 15 to 20 percent of their workers joined the WFM and struck, which would put the number of striking miners at roughly 3,000. The table below recounts *Työmies*'s count of numbers of workers out on two different dates.[67]

Regardless of actual numbers, mining operations in the Copper Country came to a standstill. The million-dollar machinery of the big three mining companies, C&H, Quincy, and Copper Range, stood silent and still in the midst of the raucous strikers, while Finnish immigrant strikers enthusiastically belted out the "Kuparialueen lakkolaisten marssi" or "Copper Territory Strikers' March." This was a song penned by Jukka S. and printed in editions of *Työmies* specifically for the Michigan Copper Strike. Sung to the tune of "Varsovalainer," the first verse and chorus contained vivid proletarian imagery:

Työmies's Count of Striking Workers

Työmies Strikers Count, July 28		*Työmies* Strikers Count, July 30	
Mine	*Workers Out*	*Mine*	*Workers Out*
C&H Mines		*C&H Mines*	
Calumet & Hecla	5,000	Calumet & Hecla	5,000
Ahmeek	800	Ahmeek	800
Allouez	500	Allouez	500
Centennial	150	Centennial	150
Isle Royale	750	Isle Royale	750
Laurium	50	Laurium	50
LaSalle	50	LaSalle	50
Lake Superior	200	Lake Superior Smelting Co.	200
Osceola	1,300	Osceola	1,300
Superior	250	Superior	250
Tamarack	750	Tamarack	750
Independent Mines		*Independent Mines*	
Copper Range [Mines]	1,800	Copper Range [Mines]: Baltic, Champion, and Trimountain	3,500
Quincy	1,500	Quincy	2,500
Mohawk	1,000	Mohawk	1,000
Wolverine	200	Wolverine	800
Hancock	100	Hancock Consolidated	200
Winona	500	Winona	200
Mass	300	Mass	150
Franklin Jr. (Boston)	300	Lake	150
Kearsarge	200	Wyandot, St. Louis, Indiana, New Arcadian, Oneco, South Lake, North Lake, and New Baltic	160
Total	15,700	**Total**	18,460

Source: Työmies, July 28 and July 30, 1913.

Copper miners have gallantly risen
To fight against oppression and exploitation
From a long dream like a wintry bear
To demand human rights
We have slept enough already and been slaves
Just kissing MacNaughton's whip
Let's rise brothers and throw the chains
Into the dirty oppressors' faces

To the fight for human rights
For our bread
Off, off miners off you go![68]

According to a report by the federal government, the first days of the strike were violent, "After the rioting which occurred on the first two days of the strike, 16 men who tried to go to work were injured by the strikers badly enough for hospital treatment."[69] *Työmies* and Sarell put their own spin on the first day's volley:

> When it was announced on July 23rd that the famously content copper miners of northern Michigan went on strike, it got people wondering throughout all of America, but especially among the residents of the "Copper Island." At first, it seemed almost incredible that these mine slaves, who had toiled in content for decades, would really have the courage to fight for their rights. But it was true!
>
> The strike started so well that it went beyond even the bravest expectations; the wheels of the mines of the whole Copper Country stopped on the aforementioned day as by magic. The cocky bosses of the mines watched with amazement as the group of mine slaves, who before had submitted contently, determinedly rose from the perpetual darkness of the mines to daylight to fight for those relatively small demands to which their whimpers weren't even bothered to be answered.[70]

The receivers of the first day's violence were likely not so enamored with the initial results of the strike. Gabriel Popovich, who was a timberman in Hecla no. 6 shaft, was "attacked and struck over head and left shoulder; scalp wound 1 inch long; contusion of left shoulder; disabled from July 24 to August 7." Kenneth McLeod, watchman at Red Jacket shaft, was "hit by thrown rock while resisting attempt of strikers to gain entrance to the engine house; contusion of right eye; fracture of nose, punctured wound about nose and over right eye; disabled from July 23 to August 26." Of all those injured on July 23, John T. Hand, a miner, seemed to get it the worst, as he was "struck by a piece of gas pipe; contusion of left side of chest with fracture of eleventh rib; still disabled September 11."[71] Unfortunately, these men were in the midst of the euphoria of a proletarian awakening and suffered the scorn of ideology unfurled with rocks and blunt objects.

The chaos of the first day led to a reserved anxiety on the part of the mining companies. William Parsons Todd remembered that after the first days of the strike at Quincy, "Most of the men [those crossing strike lines] had to have their wives take them to work and also come around to take them in the afternoon; had a howling mob. The union men were shouting their heads off . . . sometimes stopped the men going underground and the men had to go through these men. They couldn't get through unless they had their wives with them. They'd let a man go through if he had his wife."[72] C&H's general manager, James MacNaughton, described by Sarell as "the emperor of the Copper Country" and by *Työmies* as the *Tsaari* or czar of the Copper Territory,[73] led the way for the mining companies' united response. He was content to let the strikers beat their way to a less than favorable public opinion, believing that public sentiment would side with the companies after the strikers' violent tactics came to public attention. Counting on public opinion to stem the tide, MacNaughton implored Houghton County's Sheriff Cruise to deputize two hundred C&H employees, but not give them guns. If this became a shooting match, MacNaughton did not want the mining companies to be conspicuously involved.[74]

MacNaughton did, however, secure the C&H dynamite magazines and beseeched the Michigan National Guard's Calumet unit to safeguard its ammunition reserves because he feared the WFM had brought in sharpshooters. After a bit of cajoling from Sheriff Cruse, MacNaughton agreed to invite the Michigan National Guard to the Copper Country.[75] The U.S. Labor Department's report stated that with the arrival of the Guard, things quieted considerably into a relative stalemate between the WFM and the mining companies, who refused to acknowledge that there was any such thing as the WFM.[76]

Työmies's assessment of the situation refuted the government's report and did not see the arrival of the Guard as a benefit to anyone but the mining companies:

> Two or three days after the declaration of the strike, the entire Michigan army arrived to protect "the property and lives" of the mining companies. Calumet, whose name is said to mean peace pipe in the Indian language, resembled the most heavily equipped war camp. The soldiers had settled around the mines with their daggers, their revolvers, their sabers, their rifles, their machine guns and other murder tools. All the roads that had been in common use before were blocked from the public by these strike breakers, the proud "defenders of Michigan's fatherland" dressed in yellow soldiers' uniforms.
>
> Yours truly saw it with his own eyes how these Michigan Cossacks attacked the peaceful strikers and other people in the streets of Calumet, threatening to decapitate them with their sabers and pushing the bayonets of their rifles to the backs of the people waiting for the street car . . . Like the wildest Russian Cossacks, these seemingly drunken cavalry soldiers rode along the sidewalks knocking down a couple of wives and their baby carriages.[77]

The *Miners' Bulletin* published a sworn affidavit accusing the Michigan National Guard soldiers of raping two Calumet teenage girls. This affidavit might have been considered rabid propaganda against the Michigan National Guard, but the accusations came from Calumet night watchman Paul Spehar. An article titled "Soldiers Bestial Conduct" recounted the actions of Guardsmen with one girl:

> At about two o'clock on the morning of August ninth, [Paul Spehar] was on duty as nightwatchman, and he was at Sixth and Oak Streets, when he was approached by one of the Calumet & Hecla watchmen who said to him, "You had better go up and see what the soldiers are doing with these girls up there."
>
> When he got to the east end of Oak Street, he found that there were five or six soldiers with one girl in the alley back of Shea's barn. When he

approached them, the soldiers scrambled from the recumbent positions, and they ran pulling the girl after them until they reached Collier's and Manley's barn, to where the watchmen went and took hold of the girl, taking her into custody.[78]

As August events festered, the Copper Country gained national attention. Famous champions of the working class such as Clarence Darrow and Mother Jones appeared in the Copper Country. Upon her arrival in the Copper Country early in August, Mother Jones sarcastically quipped, "If I were Sheriff Cruse's wife I would give him castor oil twice a day."[79] Mother Jones was an especially welcome figure and received accolades from the Finnish language press:

> The mineworkers' friend, famous throughout the land, Mother Jones arrived to the strike area on August 3rd, welcomed by a group of thousands of strikers in the Calumet railway station. This white-haired 81 years young fighter walked to the union offices through the alley of strikers as they greeted her with cheers. Mother gave fiery speeches to the strikers in different localities of the strike area . . . When Mother really got into describing the wretchedness of the workers' position, the listeners' eyes filled with tears.
>
> Mother criticized and scorned the scabs and the capitalists strongly and the soldiers too got what they deserved. "Don't worry boys," Mother said to the strikers in her speeches, "you can make a man out of MacNaughton as long as you unanimously keep your hands in your pockets and let MacNaughton try if he can run the mines without you." In every speech, Mother told the strikers to use their brains from now on and not just their hands, for the unknowing worker is a donkey for the capitalists to ride anywhere they want. "Be men, my sons, then you will make the mine bosses humble," Mother said, "and remember that you must only trust yourselves because nobody else can improve your condition" . . .
>
> The Copper Country strikers will always remember Mother Jones with love.[80]

Despite the national attention, according to a Quincy Mine labor spy, the WFM was becoming concerned that the strike was losing its luster with Copper Country workers:

> Under the date of August 3rd I have a letter from the Finnish operative who was working for you, in which he says that he has received a letter from his wife who states that the union men are becoming afraid that if the strike lasts for another week they will have to get to work and then there will be no more union in the copper country. He informs me that his wife found out that the union officials had a private meeting one night in Hancock recently, and they are afraid that the Austrians and Finns will soon go back to work if the strike is not settled within a week. Present at this meeting were Vice President C. E. Mahoney, Executive Board Members Lowney and Guy Miller, and John Välimäki and C. E. Hietala of Hancock.[81]

The operative seemed to recognize, like C&H's Jim MacNaughton, that the strike's success hinged on the WFM getting outside financial and moral support:

> This morning I have reports from one of our men in the iron fields in Iron County and he states that the union at Crystal Falls received a circular letter from Hancock signed by the officials of the copper union No. 16, saying that the shut down in the copper country is complete and asking for aid, morally and financially, and requesting that assessments and donations be sent to Ernest Mills, national treasurer at Denver. Also a circular issued by the Denver officials stating that more than seven thousand miners of the copper district of Michigan belonged to the Western Federation of Miners and that the entire copper mining district of Michigan is tied up and all mines closed and stating that an assessment of $2. has been levied by the executive board of the W.F.M. for the month of August and asking that the locals remit this assessment from funds on hand.[82]

The *Miners' Bulletin*

The previously mentioned infusion of $100,000 capital stock into the Työmies Publishing Company on August 16 was most certainly for strike-related affairs, and perhaps the most important piece of WFM "artillery" was the establishment of a device to distribute WFM-sanctioned news to Copper Country workers. On

August 14, 1913, the TPC rolled out an English-language publication appropriately named the *Miners' Bulletin*. As a triweekly two-page (and later a four-page) publication, the *Miners' Bulletin* was a seven-column newspaper that devoted space solely to strike-related news, messages of solidarity from other industrial workers, updates on other strike actions across the United States, lampooning mining-company and local-government officials, and announcements regarding parade and speech gatherings in the Copper Country.

While the *Miners' Bulletin*, like the *Wage Slave*, was somewhat independent of *Työmies* in that it had a mixed-ethnicity staff and a singular subject matter, there were no doubt meshed influences. An example of meshed messages was *Työmies* correspondent A. O. Sarell's moniker for Michigan National Guardsmen. While Sarell referred to them as "Michigan Cossacks," the *Miners' Bulletin* referred to them as *American* Cossacks. There was unity of message, shared facilities, and staff, and continuous collaboration between the two newspapers. After August 23, the *Miners' Bulletin* featured an important difference from *Työmies*; it began publishing in multiple languages on a regular basis. The paper featured both Italian and Croatian news on its back pages in addition to English-language reports throughout the newspaper.

The *Miners' Bulletin* was an essential vehicle for the successful communication among striking workers isolated by physical space. The announcements in its pages were a boon to organizational efforts, creating a sense of purpose regarding the strike activity while bestowing a sense of solidarity among the various striking ethnicities. An August 14 announcement read: "The parade and assembly at the Palestra [in Laurium] Wednesday broke all previous records. Joseph Lesch of Ahmeek, Mrs. Mikko and W. J. Rickard led the parade of fully six-thousand people." Another September 13 announcement read: "A Picnic—The Hancock Local of the Socialist Party will hold a picnic at Anthony's Farm, Sunday September 14. Speaking in all languages, begins at 1.30 P.M. Admission free."[83]

Much like many of the other Työmies Publishing Company offerings, the *Miners' Bulletin* had a very caustic brand of journalism. A September 13 regular column entitled the "Hancock Kind" went so far as to publicly out scabs: "Matt [surname withheld by author]—among the nationality [Finnish] that stands almost solid in their support of the strike, Matt is practically alone in his disgrace . . . Matt is a black mark against the Finnish race, but they are not to be blamed on account of him . . . he is branded for life as a company tool and all around suck." In October, the newspaper began a regular column titled "As Seen by the Search-Lights," no doubt a literary jab at the powerful searchlight known as MacNaughton's Eye, which perched high atop a mine shafthouse in Calumet. One "As Seen by the Search-Lights" read: "On Friday and Saturday of last week. Place: Soldiers quarters at rear of the Armory. Grand Fall style opening, showing the latest and finest in ladies' lingerie." Another article in a fake "Classified Ads" read: "Wanted—to know what profit it is to the Keweenaw scabs to earn a few scabby dollars and sell their honor."[84] The strike was indeed getting nasty.

Top: *A postcard of the Työmies building and Kansankoti Hall, ca. 1915. The stage and scenery area is the highest point of elevation on the building.* (Finlandia University's Finnish American Historical Archive.)
Bottom left: *The Työmies Publishing Company buildings. The building on the right is the former Nieminen grocery building and the building on the left is the Coughlin building.* (Työmies 10 Vuotias.)
Bottom right: *The Tezcuco Street entrances to the Työmies Publishing Company building and the Kansankoti Hall. The sign for the Kansankoti Café hangs over the first ground floor window of the Kansankoti Hall.* (Finlandia University's Finnish American Historical Archive.)

Top: *Negaunee, Michigan's Labor Temple debating committee, ca. 1910.* (Finlandia University's Finnish American Historical Archive.) Middle: *Women at the head of a strike parade on Quincy Hill, Hancock, Michigan, 1913.* (Työmiehen Joulu.) Bottom left: *Finnish immigrant women arrested by Calumet police and lodged in the Red Jacket jail, 1913.* (Työmiehen Joulu.) Bottom right: *Hilja Fräki, ca. 1910.* (Finlandia University's Finnish American Historical Archive, Hilja Fräki and Regan Family Collection.)

Top: *The caption on the back of this photograph reads, "Socialist Picnic," ca. 1905. Evert Björklund is seated in the bottom row, second from left; Laina Björklund is standing in the second row, second from left; and Maria Ollila is also standing in the second row, last person.* (Finlandia University's Finnish American Historical Archive.) Bottom left: *Hancock Socialist local's mixed gymnastics group, ca. 1905. Laina Björklund is seated in the first row, second from left, and Evert Björklund is standing in the back row, last person.* (Finlandia University's Finnish American Historical Archive.) Bottom right: *Laina and Evert Björklund with first child, Ensio, ca. 1908.* (Finlandia University's Finnish American Historical Archive, Libby Koski-Björklund Collection.)

Above: *The Red Flag 13 after release from jail in Houghton, Michigan, 1907.* (Työmiehen Joulu.)

Opposite: *The 1907 watercolors of the proposed Kansankoti building by Calumet, Michigan, architect T. K. Hakolahti:* top: *façade view;* bottom*: cross-section.* (Finlandia University's Finnish American Historical Archive.)

Oikealleko? — Vasemmalle?
Ei, vaan suoraan eteenpäin!

Left: *"To the right, to the left . . . No, we must move forward." This 1905 cartoon advocates the movement of the Finnish American Workers' League (the lunch box character) toward Marxism (the rising sun). According to the artist's imagery, to the right is the ooze-filled pit of the Imatra and Finnish American Workers League's liberal-bourgeois socialism, represented by Moses Hahl and N. J. Ahlman. To the left, the dead end rock wall of utopian socialism, represented by Matti Kurikka, founder of the Sointula Commune in British Columbia, Canada.* (Vappu.)

FASADIPIIRROS KANSANKODIN UUDISRAKEN-
-NUKSEEN HANCOCKIN KAUPUNGISSA MICH.

Above: *Työmies Publishing Company's second home, at 421 Michigan Street in Hancock, Michigan:* Top left*: Exterior view of the TPC building façade, 1907.* (Köyhälistön Nuija.) Top right*: Interior view of TPC's type composing and linotype machine room, 1907.* (Köyhälistön Nuija.) Bottom*: Two workers operating a drum-cylinder press in the basement of the building, 1907.* (Köyhälistön Nuija 1907.)

Opposite: *Työmies Publishing Company's first home, at 741 Franklin Street in Hancock, Michigan:* Top*: TPC staff outside their offices and print shop, 1904.* (Työmies 10 Vuotias.) Middle*: Type composers working inside the TPC building, 1904. Axel Kantola is on the left, Annie Mattila in center, and Evert Bjöklund is working on the right.* (Työmies 10 Vuotias.) Bottom: *J. A. Harpet* (on left) *and Vihtori Kosonen* (to his right) *working in the editors' office of the Työmies Publishing Company, 1904.* (Työmies 10 Vuotias.)

Above: *Masthead of the Työmies Publishing Company's first English-language newspaper,* The Wage Slave, *1908.* (Copper Country Historical Archive.)

Middle*: The masthead from* Amerikan Matti, *drawn by Työmies Publishing Company artist Henry Askeli.* Bottom*: Stereotypical depiction of African American features used in the pages of* Amerikan Matti, *ca. 1909.* (Amerikan Matti, 1909 and 1910.)

Above: *Four interior images of the Työmies Publishing Company's printing complex on Franklin Street, 1913:* top left: *Type composers working at character selection;* top right: *The linotype machine room;* bottom right: *The Työmies Publishing Company's bookstore and staff;* bottom left: *Two operators working the drum-cylinder press.* (Työmies 10 Vuotias.)

Left: *Suvanto's Tossu, the little hobo, carrying a May Day banner.* (Vappu, 1914.)

TYOMIES PUBLISHING CO.
PRINTERS, BOOKBINDERS, STATIONERS
AND PUBLISHERS OF

TYOMIES
(DAILY)

The Leading Socialist Finnish Newspaper of America
Guaranteed Circulation, 12,000
Advertising Rates on Application

201-203 Franklin St., Cor. Tezcuco, HANCOCK, MICHIGAN

Above top: *Työmies Publishing Company staff, including delivery boys, ca. 1913.* (Työmies10 Vuotias.)
Above bottom: *An advertisement that ran on a regular basis in the* Työmies *newspaper claiming a "guaranteed circulation" of over 12,000 subscribers, ca. 1912.* (Työmies.)

Opposite top: *The* Lapatossu *cartoon cited in counts 1 and 2 of the federal indictment, April 1912* (left), *and the* Lapatossu *cartoon cited in the third count of the federal indictment against the TPC, December 1912* (right). (Lapatossu, 1912.)

Opposite bottom: (top left) *Mother Jones, Guy Miller, and others walking in a strike parade through downtown Calumet, Michigan, August 10, 1913.* (Työmiehen Joulu.) (top right) *Gathering of striking workers and their families outside of WFM headquarters in downtown Red Jacket. One person in the group is holding a sign of a small man standing behind his wife with the text reading, "Scab Woman . . . Leading Scab to Work."* (Finlandia University's Finnish American Historical Archive.) (bottom) *Panoramic view of the Michigan National Guard encamped in the C&H industrial core, Calumet, Michigan, ca. 1913.* (Finlandia University's Finnish American Historical Archive.)

JAAKKO HOI! MIKSI SINÄ SOTKIT OPETTAJAN TUOLIN?
HUOLETI MIINUSENI! KAIKKI TULEE SOSIALISTIEN SYYKSI!

Aatami: — Eeva hoi! Elkö lainaisi minulle vähän nenäliinaasi?
Eeva. — En uskalla, rakas Aatu, sillä silloin kiellettäisiin Lapatossu ilmestymäst

STRIKERS PARADE CALUMET MICHIGAN AUG-10-1913
GUY MILLER
MOTHER JONES

SCAB WOMAN
LEADING SCAB TO WORK

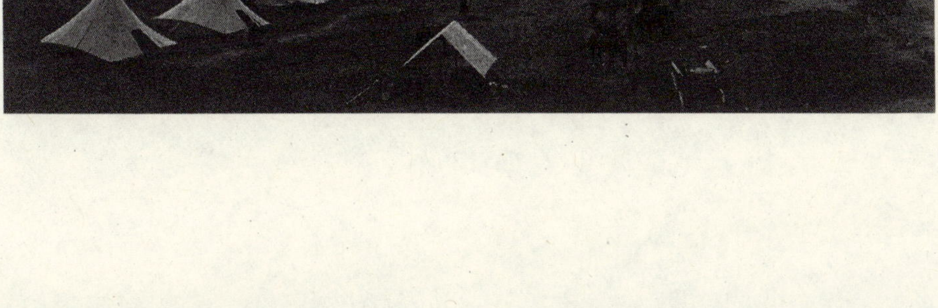

Top: *Strike parade on Quincy Street, downtown Hancock, Michigan, September 13, 1913.* (Finlandia University's Finnish American Historical Archive.) Bottom: *Strikers outside the Työmies Publishing Company-Kansankoti Hall complex as snow falls all around, winter 1913.* (Finlandia University's Finnish American Historical Archive.)

TYÖMIES

AMERIKAN SUOMALAISEN TYÖVÄESTÖN ÄÄNENKANNATTAJA

Tietoja Calumetista

KUOLLEIDEN LUKU 80

Christmas Festivities End in Carnage of Death

TYÖMIES

AMERIKAN SUOMALAISEN TYÖVÄESTÖN ÄÄNENKANNATTAJA

83 MURHATTU!

Calumetin lakkolaisten lasten joulujuhlasta tehtiin julma kapitalismin uhriteurastus

MINERS' • BULLETIN

Published by authority of Western Federation of Miners to tell the truth regarding the strike of copper miners.

December 28th 1913

A HARVEST OF DEATH

Striking Miner's Children In Christmas Joys Are Called By The Angel Of Death

Moyer and Tanner of Federation Deported

Affidavits of Gunmen

Työmies Publishing Company's reactions to events at the Italian Hall. Top masthead*: Special edition of* Työmies *printed on December 25, 1913, that read, "Information about Calumet-Dead Number 80." To the bottom right of the headline a rare English-language article appeared in the newspaper that proclaimed, "Christmas Festivities End in Carnage of Death."* (Työmies.) Middle masthead*: The next day* Työmies *ran another headline that upped the number of dead to 83, but also claimed that those dead were "Murdered." The headline went on to read that, "Calumet Strikers' Children Christmas Celebrations were a Cruel Sacrifice to Capitalism."* (Työmies.) Bottom masthead*: A December 28, 1913,* Miners' Bulletin *headline about a "Harvest of Death."* (Miners' Bulletin.) Bottom left*:* Lapatossu*'s front cover depiction of who they believed were the perpetrators of the tragic events at Italian Hall left little doubt that they blamed the Citizens' Alliance.* (Lapatossu, January 1, 1914.) Bottom right*: A cartoon titled, "The Moral Authority" was another depiction by* Lapatossu*'s staff regarding the lawlessness of events in the Copper territory. The ghoulish figure is the "Copper Trust" and the sword tucked into his belt is identified as the Citizens Alliance. The sash over his chest reads, "Seeberville, Painesdale, Calumet" and the Copper Trust figure is saying, "We cannot accept the WFM because it is a murderous organization."* (Lapatossu, January 15, 1914.)

TYÖMIES

AMERIKAN SUOMALAISEN TYÖVÄESTÖN ÄÄNENKANNATTAJA

MAANANTAINA 13 P. HUHTIK. — APRIL 13, 1914

tuneet
ien asemaan

Kuparialueen lakko on päättynyt

Juutalaissyöjät
toimessaa

Above top*: The strikers' last march was held in downtown Hancock and followed down Quincy Street during what appears to be a heavy, wet snowfall, ca. March 1914.* (Finlandia University's Finnish American Historical Archive.) Bottom: *"Copper Territory Strike is Now Over," this decree issued by* Työmies*, April 13, 1914.* (Työmies.)

Opposite: *A* Lapatossu *cartoon depicting the Negaunee local's fight over control of the Labor Temple as a cockfight with many interested parties watching from all over the United States. At the top of the page, characters watching the fight represent the Canadian Finnish Socialist Federation local in Port Arthur (now Thunder Bay) and their publications* Työkansa *and* Väkäleuka*. To the left are the Hancock local represented by* Työmies *and* Lapatossu*. Just below the Hancock local is the Duluth, Minnesota, local's character who is sitting on a representation of the Work Peoples' College. In the bottom left corner is the Astoria, Oregon, local represented by a man and a woman (*Toveri *and* Toveritar*), and in the bottom right corner is the Fitchburg local and* Raivaaja. (Lapatossu, June 24, 1914.)

TYÖMIES
TOISU
VÄHÄLEUKA
TYÖKANSA
Port. Arthur
Superior järvi
Hancock
Duluth
NEGAUNEE
Astoria
Raivaaja
Fitchburg

Top: *A* Lapatossu *cartoon that depicts Leo Laukki as a horse jumping the fence from the "Socialist Party" to "broader bourgeois pastures" and dragging various people, represented by the tin cans, with him. Some of the people that are being dragged over the fence are Victor Brander, Martin Hendrickson, Edi Solu, John Kolu, and William Risto. Riding on "Laukki" is a monkey, who represents "Great Madness."* (Lapatossu, June 24, 1914.) Bottom: *Another* Lapatossu *cartoon depicting the move of the Työmies Publishing Company from Hancock, Michigan, to Superior, Wisconsin. In the cartoon, the tug-boat is carrying* Työmies, *represented by the man holding the club, Tossu, who is sitting at the back of the tug, and* Pelto ja Koti, *who is being dragged in the small boat behind the tug. The person on shore in Superior is "Proletarian" and is saying to the figures on the tug, "Anchor at this dock." The people on shore in Duluth are supposed to be characters associated with the IWW and its publications and facilities such as the Work Peoples' College. Many of the people portrayed as tin cans in the Laukki cartoon are also portrayed in this cartoon as well.* (Lapatossu, October 1, 1914.)

CHAPTER 7

Gun Hounds, Scabs, and Tragedy

WITH EACH PASSING WEEK, THE STRIKE SEEMED TO MULTIPLY IN INTENSITY. Great fits of passion spilled over from the pages of *Työmies* and the *Miners' Bulletin* into the streets of Copper Country towns, locations, and villages. Tension was palpable on both sides. For every step-up in rhetoric by the WFM, the mining companies counteroffered. For every WFM strike parade, pro-company businesses, the Citizens' Alliance, and the mining companies organized a counterdemonstration. As it became clear that the strike was no short-term affair, the mining companies began to dig into time-tested, steadfast tactics, including the hiring of "peacekeeping" forces and importation of replacement workers. These actions only served to incense and foment a sense of anxiety in striking workers. The copper bosses' attempt to break the strike, and the WFM's determination to fully represent striking workers, was heading toward a tumultuous crescendo. Sadly, in events that will likely always remain a dark mystery, that climax came bearing the loss of life, including the lives of some fifty children. In the wake of these events, the Copper Country, the Finnish immigrants' socialist-unionist movement, and the WFM would never be the same.

Kenraali Waddell's *Pyssyhurtia*

Labor spies were not the only tools the mining companies employed to force the WFM from the Copper Country. As the strike actions endured, mining companies called on the services of supposed "detective agencies." Much like the Pinkerton Agency, the Waddell-Mahon Detective Agency specialized in union-busting and strikebreaking. In an October issue of *Työmies* that featured the headline "The Waddell Menace," the newspaper reprinted excerpts from a circular they claimed to have procured from the Waddell-Mahon Company:

> We point with great pardonable pride to the fact that this corporation has been selected by James A Cruse of Houghton County—the storm center of the strike—to aid him in maintaining the integrity of the law. We are now engaged in "policing" the 1,019 square miles of territory contained in Houghton County. We are safeguarding the property of the mine owners against intrusion and violence. We are also protecting the lives and home of the 80,098 men, women and children of Houghton County against overt acts. The Western Federation of Miners is doomed to inevitable disaster and defeat in the Upper Peninsula of Michigan . . . We are sure of defeating the Western Federation of Miners in this operation because we have met and defeated them before . . . We ask you to watch the progress of the present strike, because we know it will be a triumph for law and order, a triumph for the mine owners and will furnish still another evidence of the success we have always met with in breaking strikes. We ask you to judge us by results.[1]

The Waddell men certainly had an impact, but not the "law and order" impact described in their circular. The Waddell-Mahon Detective Agency's men became especially notorious as hired company thugs known as *pyssyhurtia* in Finnish, or gun hounds in English. *Työmies* indicated that Houghton County's Sheriff Cruse worked with the detective agency, referring to the team as "*Sheriffi Cruse ja pyssyhurttien Kenraali Waddell* (Sheriff Cruse and the Gun Hounds of General Waddell)."[2] Sarell reported about the Waddell tie with Houghton County law and order: "In addition to the soldiers, the officials held on a leash, the mining companies hired Waddell-Mahon's Detective Agency gun hounds to be the so-called 'guardians of order' in the strike area. They were assembled from the major cities' most crooked elements and as far as their fees; Houghton County had to pay and is still paying tens of thousands of dollars monthly as this is being written."[3] In addition to the Waddell men, C&H and the Mohawk Mining Company hired men from the Ascher Detective Agency out of New York City. The Waddell men were disliked, and the Ascher men were received with the same sentiment. The *Miners' Bulletin* wrote this about the Ascher men: "They are as tough a looking bunch of men as have ever applied a sandbag to their victim."[4]

Possibly the most notorious of the Waddell men's exploits occurred in mid-August 1913:

> The character of these bloodhounds dressed as humans revealed itself for the first time on August 14th when they executed one of the most cold blooded massacres known to the history of the American workers' battles in Seeberville location near Painesdale. For absolutely no reason six crooks identified as sheriff's deputies, of which four were Waddell-Mahon's Detective Agency gun hounds, attacked the men of Croatian Joseph Putrich's boarding house, driving the men from the courtyard to the inside of the house and after that shooting in through the house's windows with their revolvers. The consequence was that 18-year-old striker Aloiz Tijan was instantly killed and a striker named Steve Putrich died from gun shot wounds some days later. Two other strikers and the infant who was in the arms of the house's lady suffered gunshot wounds, with a shot of the revolver burning the child's face. After they had committed this cruel deed, the gun hounds went to the road in front of the house where they loaded their revolvers again and jeered amongst themselves "we wonder how many dead bodies there are in the house."[5]

For his part, Sheriff Cruse appeared to do as much as possible to befuddle the case. According to Sarell, "The hounds that had committed the massacre were let to be on the loose for a long time before the sheriff, pressured by public opinion, saw that it was better to take them 'under his surveillance' in the county jail where they weren't treated like other prisoners at all, but were allowed to live like kings."[6] Architectural historian Alison K. Hoagland writes of the company-sponsored shooters: "The governor's representative, Judge Alfred J. Murphy, investigated the incident in August and concluded, 'I questioned four Waddell men involved as to their antecedents. They are scum.'" Hoagland also wrote that another observer from the U.S. Department of Labor quipped, "These Woddell [*sic*] men I have seen are about the toughest looking lot I ever saw."[7] This action severely affected public opinion and tipped the scales of public sentiment toward the WFM. Findings of the U.S. Labor Department reported:

> Anthony Lucas, prosecuting attorney of Houghton County, visited the scene of the shooting, and after an investigation denounced it as wanton murder, and called upon the sheriff, James A. Cruse, to arrest all of the six men. The sheriff, however, allowed them all to escape and for several days, their whereabouts were unknown.[8]

The funeral for the slain strikers occurred August 17. Sarell estimated that there were 12,576 men, women, and children at the funeral.[9] Though *Työmies* probably exaggerated the number of mourners, the funeral was a well-attended, yet incredibly somber event. At a large WFM meeting in the Kansankoti Hall that followed the funeral, Frank Aaltonen politicked for and passed a resolution calling for the dismissal of the Waddell-Mahon men from the area.[10] *Työmies* and the *Miners' Bulletin* combated the Waddell-Mahon men's violence with a barrage of their own, launching a war of words against the "gun hounds and their General." These words must have struck a chord, because:

> According to a Detroit paper, James Waddell, head of the strikebreakers, first assistant to Sheriff Cruse, will bring suit for libel against the Western Federation of Miners and Tyomies, the Finnish paper at Hancock. Sheriff Cruse is also reported as planning a suit against the Federation.
>
> Nothing that could be printed would convey an adequate description of these two men. We call them men for the lack of a better word. Perhaps it would be better to state that they are members of the genus *homo*.
>
> No self-respecting member of the human species would care to be more closely connected with an official who would prostitute his office as Sheriff

> Cruse has done since the strike begun, or touch in the most distant way, a man who follows the profession of strikebreaking and whose aids are such brutal murderers as those who dipped their hands in the blood of Tijan and Putrich at Painesdale.
>
> We are glad to note, that though these individuals may violate an oath of office, and are so careless of human life, they don't like to have the light of publicity thrown upon their actions. Publicity sometimes helps to make men decent when they have no natural inclinations in that direction.[11]

The Seeberville murders were not the only act of wanton, lethal violence against striking men, women, and children by company-sponsored heavies. One of the WFM's most frequently used tactics was the parade, which was an exercise in bravery and fortitude that often resulted in violence against strikers. Armed Michigan Guardsmen—and worse, armed county sheriff's deputies—often shadowed the strikers on their parade route. At times, the parades could become violent, and one time "as a result of a clash between deputy sheriffs and a body of strikers and women, a girl 14 years of age, named Margaret Frazakas, daughter of a widow, was shot in the head at North Kearsarge."[12]

In this case, a group of fifteen deputy sheriffs shot into a parade of marching strikers, women, and children, after the strikers exchanged epithets with the deputy sheriffs. Reportedly, the order to fire on the unarmed strikers came from a deputized mining captain. One of the first shots hit Frazakas and she "was struck above the right ear by a bullet and part of her brains oozed out." Miraculously, she survived the wound. The deputy sheriffs fired over ninety rounds at the strikers and then ran like hell with the strikers in hot pursuit, who only then began to throw rocks at the armed but "ammunitionless" deputy sheriffs.[13]

Skaappi

As voiced by Mother Jones, scabs or imported workers (termed *skaappi* by Finnish immigrant socialist-unionists) were especially detested by strikers. Copper Country proletarian circles were rife with innuendo and speculation about what might happen in connection with the import of new workers to break the strike. Sadly, the latent racism of the Työmies Publishing Company reared its ugly head again during the strike. On August 22, *Työmies* ran a front-page article that stated, "Neekereitä will be appearing in Calumet."[14] The paper indicated that along with the aforementioned Waddell gun hounds, African Americans were sure to come as well. This accusation was no doubt in reference to the previous importation of African American workers by American corporations in past labor disputes. The overt acrimony and suspicion regarding African American scabs was likely the ugly consequence of veiled fear and great uncertainty regarding the outcome of the strike, which displayed the actual fragility and tenuous situation of striking workers.

Despite *Työmies*'s assumption, Copper Country mines did not hire African American workers as scabs, but by September the big three mining companies, C&H, Copper Range, and Quincy, were back in limited production with the help of imported European immigrant workers. Quincy brought in their first scabs on September 19. The company secured favorable terms from a New York labor agent, who supplied the mostly Austro-Hungarian strikebreakers. Quincy was to pay the men $2.50 per nine-hour shift, of which Quincy deducted the cost of the scabs' train tickets from New York, where they contracted the imported workers' services.[15]

In an oral history interview, William Parsons Todd, who helped recruit replacement workers for Quincy Mining Company, recalled the problems with introducing New York strikebreakers into the Copper Country:

> First batch we sent up, we lost the whole batch the third day they got there . . . Well they went, the union got them another job down near Chicago. They got . . . induced them all to leave . . . it taught us a lesson though. We had to know more about what was going on in the car [railway train car] too, you know . . . We hired an entire car (forty or so men) . . . put the food on, took care of them all the way up and we kept them in the car until Monday morning. It scared a few of them once in a while because the car would be going up in Michigan and then they'd cart it [the car] back away because we wanted them to land there Monday morning by six o'clock and we had them underground about an hour after we got them there. Didn't want anybody getting next to them.

> We'd not wanted them to see what the conditions were. Not have anybody scaring them out in advance and along the line there from Houghton south, why there was nothing but a long line of electric lights . . . they stopped . . . cars being mobbed by strikers. Tough days!
>
> Most of the cars got there without any windows in them. Cities . . . Detroit, other cities when the cars were in the stations, had Eastern cars . . . New York Central, Lackawanna, Erie . . . haven't those in Michigan . . . it was known there were strike breakers in them and they'd throw rocks through or stones through. We used to have the men lay on the floor and put the seat cushions on top of them trying to keep what came through the windows away from them. Awful! Any man showed weakness, we gave him a ticket back to New York . . . quick.[16]

The U.S. Department of Labor's findings add to Todd's memories of the first "batch" of strikebreakers that came to the Copper Country: they arrived in Hancock after being locked in a train car for several hours and then were brought to Quincy mine. Upon seeing thousands of strikers in the street, fourteen of the thirty-one men fled the mines and sought out strike organizers to apologize for coming into the Copper Country during a strike. These misinformed replacement workers then went to the Kansankoti Hall, WFM headquarters, in Hancock. Twelve of them signed affidavits stating that Quincy duped them into coming to the Copper Country while a strike was happening, and that they went to the Kansankoti to "get protection against the Quincy Mining Co., as we were in the belief that we would be forced to work in the mines under conditions against our will." Several Waddell Detective Agency men went to the Kansankoti and demanded that the AWOL scabs return at once. The Quincy Company "detectives" raised a ruckus, but arrested only one person, as most of the imported workers had left Hancock, sensing trouble on the way.[17]

This pattern repeated itself in late September. Quincy hired a number of men from a labor agency in Chicago. When the men arrived in Hancock, twenty-four signed affidavits stating that "they swore the agent of the agency informed them that there was no trouble or strike at the place where they were to work, that on arrival at the Quincy mine they were guarded by deputies and soldiers and not permitted to leave the bunk house and boarding house at the mine, and that they were otherwise mistreated."[18] According to Sarell, dispersion of the scabs was a well-orchestrated and planned event:

> At first, the scabs came to the Quincy Mining Company from New York and Chicago, but they proved to be useless to the company, for as soon as the scabs got to know that there was a strike going on they refused to go to work and marched to the union offices at the Kansankoti. The strikers provided the men with food and a place to live until they were able to get jobs for them outside the strike area to where they were then transported by the union. The Quincy Company soon tired of this game.[19]

Fall brought isolated acts of violence and retribution. On September 17, *Työmies* wrote, "Dynamitings occurring in the Copper Territory strikers fight."[20] *Työmies* went on to opine that these were not the acts of striking workers, but the truth of the matter was that, regardless of who did the actual dynamiting, the mining companies and the Citizens' Alliance would pass on the credit to the WFM. There are no reports of deaths from the dynamitings, but the ploy put a scare into the citizenry that further escalated the already tense Copper Country. A late-October event found strikers and gun hounds at particular odds. "Today [October 23, 1913], right before noon, there was a skirmish in the Hancock station where some over-enthusiastic strikers broke the train windows because it carried some tens of scabs who were going to Calumet. One of the gun hounds on the train shot a Finnish striker through the thigh, but the wound doesn't appear to be severe."[21]

The late October shooting followed an earlier October 8 shooting in which "the strikers gave the hounds a taste of their own medicine." Apparently, a Hurontown altercation led to a dead "gun hound" and a deathbed confession that added mystery to an already convoluted account. "According to the dead striker, whose name was Joseph Manerich, gun hound Pollock attacked him and shot him in the stomach after which the gun hound shot himself in the head. According to other rumors, the wounded striker took the revolver from Pollock and shot him dead with it."[22]

The Strike in Winter

As the Copper Country days grew shorter, winter loomed on the gray autumn horizon. Public sentiment, after the shootings by company thugs and the importation of scab workers (who in some cases were held against their will in train cars and boarding houses), was teetering toward the side of the strikers. The mining companies hoped the harsh, snowy Copper Country winter, and deficiency in WFM funding would combine to wear the strikers' resolve down to nil. The WFM promised and delivered strike benefits as early as mid-August, and to the chagrin of the mining companies, there were no signs that funding would run short.

As part of the strike relief, the WFM distributed $3.00 a week for single men, $7.00 a week for family men with five or more children, and $9.00 a week in cases of emergency.[23] John Palosaari, a member of the Hancock WFM local, remembers, "At that time [during the strike] they gave a kind of coupon book—for three dollars a week—to get your food on and they had a union store down there in Hancock. They had tickets from $.10, $.05 and $.25, and $.50—something like that. You had to bring coupons to get your food at the union store."[24] In addition to the Hancock store, there were three other union stores opened in the strike district, as an article in the *Miners' Bulletin* noted: "The WFM has established stores at Calumet, Hancock, Ahmeek and South Range with John L. Hennessy as general manager and purchasing agent. Each store is managed by a competent and able set of clerks. These stores have been opened within the last week and the business being done is phenomenal."[25] The material support provided by WFM stores was in addition to locally owned stores and companies sympathetic to the strikers' cause. One such store was the Finnish Workmen's Co-operative Company in Kearsarge. The cooperators of Kearsarge ran this ad in the *Miners' Bulletin*:

> Boys we have stood with you from the start and will continue to do so. Our store is a co-operative store made up of workingmen. Our business rests upon workingmen, your cause is our cause. We fully appreciate all you men have

> done for our success in the past and will appreciate everything you can do in the future.[26]

With strike benefits available and public opposition to the acts of violence committed by company thugs and importation of workers, the resolve of strikers increased as national labor organizations such as the American Federation of Labor and the United Mine Workers offered assistance to the Copper Country strikers and their families:

> The Illinois State Coalminer's Association (Illinois District of the United Mine Workers of America) was the first to offer help, sending the strikers $100,000. The quick aid was of course due to the fact that their former President, J. H. Walker, who was elected as the Worker's Union President for the same state, was here almost from the beginning of the strike giving powerful speeches at strike meetings. At around the same time, the Beer Brewers' Association sent strike aid of $25,000.
>
> In addition to this the Socialist Party of America is planning to collect a strike aid for the Copper Country strikers. The local divisions of the Finnish Socialist Federation have already sent strike aid and will continue to do so.
>
> Even though the Copper Country's winter is hard, the fact that America's organized workers have taken on an aid collecting of such a wide scope makes the position a more hopeful one. The farmers in the area have for their part substantially aided the strikers by donating potatoes and other products of their land.[27]

Sarell's article about the strike's events ends in late October. Not surprisingly, as a reporter for the Työmies Publishing Company, his predictions for the future of the strike leaned heavily on the efforts of people at the corner of Franklin and Tezcuco Streets:

> The Copper Country Finns have to this day fought so gallantly in the strike that they have become especially hated among the mine bosses, but at the same time they have earned the respect of the entire organized labor of America.

> The other nationalities as well have stood gallantly in the battlefront, except for the "Cousin Jacks."
>
> The future of the strike depends entirely on whether the strikers will get enough aid from the outside, do they have enough will to stand unanimously behind their demands.
>
> If you have ever read *Työmies* in the Copper Country, then its been during this strike. Even hours before the arrival of the newspaper, the workers have been waiting for it. "Miners Bulletin," which has had writing in the Italian language too alongside the English language, has been distributed three times a week (now only two times a week) freely to all people in the strike area and its class conscious writings have been most carefully read. The reading of these papers and the speeches that have been held for example in the Kansankoti in Hancock every morning after the strike watch procession have surely had their influence on the striker's view of the world.[28]

Morale of the striking workers was good, the WFM was keeping them clothed and fed, support was coming from other sectors of organized labor, and a general solidarity permeated much of the organizational activity. Announcements in the *Miners' Bulletin* heralded the direct action of resolute striking workers: "A parade headed by the Finnish band took place in Hancock during the afternoon. 3,000 men, women and children marched in the lines for many miles in the slush and cold of a November day."[29] While all seemed to be going well, the great equalizer was on the horizon—a Copper Country winter.

A Long Agonizing December

December was a powder-keg month, literally. The first day of December set an ominous tone. A "Wanted" poster produced by the Quincy Mining Company relayed the building anxiety, "$250, Reward, EACH, will be paid by the Quincy Mining Company for information leading to the arrest and conviction of any or all persons implicated in the dynamiting of House No. 63, Hardscrabble location, during the night of December 1, 1913."[30]

In December, the WFM appeared to go on the offensive, even though the pendulum of public opinion had swung toward the strikers due to the tacitly sanctioned acts of violence by mining company "gun hounds." On December 7, 1913, WFM members were accused of making what seemed like a huge mistake that swung the pendulum back to the mining companies. In the dark hours of a December night, John Huhta, a "Finnish" recording secretary of the South Range local; Nick Verbanac, a WFM organizer; and Hjalmer Jallonen and John Juntunen, both "Finnish" WFM men, reportedly fired a volley of shots into the house of Thomas Dalley, a Cornish miner. The Jane brothers, Arthur and Harry, who were boarders at the Dalley house, died immediately from the gunshot wounds. Worse yet, a thirteen-year-old girl who lived next door was hit by one of the stray gunmen's bullets. Many knew that the Jane brothers came back to the Copper Country to resume work in the mines, making them scabs. It did not take long for people to conclude that the shooters were probably WFM men trying to scare off scab workers.[31]

Shortly after the shooting, which the WFM contended was a frame-up, the Citizens' Alliance, a staunchly pro-company group, advocated for vigilante-style justice, and a number of antisocialist Finns agreed. Citizens' Alliance groups were frequently in opposition to early-twentieth-century efforts to organize wageworkers. The *Miners' Bulletin* pegged Citizens' Alliance members as villainous vigilantes who were "stooped down as low as possible, to do so any lower than that, they would need a ladder to get into the office of Satan."[32] Antisocialist Finns, of course, welcomed the influence of a group such as the Citizens' Alliance in the fight to rebuke their wayward socialist countrymen and women. For antisocialist Finns, it could have been a reactionary retort to the Jane shootings or just an overwhelming difference in ideology, but their resentment against *Työmies* and the Finnish Socialist Federation's Hancock Jousi had found an English-language partner. Finnish immigrant merchants, conservative churchgoers, and pro-company laborers joined antisocialist leagues that portrayed the strikers as half-wits, loafers controlled and duped by outside agitators. As antisocialist Finns joined ranks with the Citizens' Alliance, they mounted a formidable and well-organized campaign to rid the Copper Country of its unwanted "agitators."

Throughout the strike, mining-company officials and their English-language newspaper organs, like the *Mining Gazette*, painted the WFM officials and Finnish immigrant organizers as outside agitators and anarchists, something less than a desirable element that was bent on pulling the Copper Country into the abyss. The Citizens' Alliance decried a resolution condemning the strikers and claimed that the Jane shooting was a "repetition of the numerous outrages that have been perpetrated at the instance of the non-resident agitators of the Western Federation of Miners." A headline in the *Gazette* the next day read, "Foreign Agitators Must Be Driven from District At Once."[33] A type of xenophobia aimed at working-class ethnic groups was gripping the Copper Country.

In reality, the strike was an organic movement comprised of many Copper Country ethnicities, with "Finns" having a strong effect due to a majority ethnic representation in the Copper Country's communities and proletarian organizations. Sarell wrote that the grassroots effort to start a union was a way to empower the local working class: "The strike was simply the consequence of unbearable exploitation that the mining companies practiced here on their workers."[34] Heimer Mikko, one of the WFM's "foreign agitators," was in actuality born in the Copper Country. His 1982 eulogy read:

> Heimer W. Mikko was born in Allouez, Michigan, on January 4, 1884. He was very active in the Michigan copper mines where they were trying to start a union to improve working conditions and benefits for the miners. There was a lot of antagonism against him even by a Finnish group because of the unpopularity of unions, and at one time he was picketed with a sign that said, "40,000 Finns demand that Mikko must go." He was arrested and jailed eight times, but his supporters always bailed him out.[35]

A small number of the Finnish immigrant strike leaders were perhaps outside agitators, but the majority of the Finnish immigrant leaders and rank-and-file were persons involved in the local socialist-unionist movement, the Laestadian movement, general laborers and nonsocialists alike. Moreover, of course many were originally from outside the Keweenaw, the simple reason being that many had emigrated from Finland to the Copper Country. Most were even welcomed by the copper mining companies until they began to question status quo worker-company relations. Collectively, these local immigrant Finns agitated for, voted for, and supported the strike. The strike was such a grassroots effort that even the WFM national had little say in the beginning of strike actions. The WFM national wanted to hold off on a strike, but the Copper Country locals, spurred by Finnish immigrant socialist-unionists, pushed for the confrontation. An article in the *Miners' Bulletin* confirmed this: "You men of the copper country rebelled against unbearable conditions and brought about a strike of your own volition without the sanction of the official head of your organization."[36]

From previous labor actions described by Lankton and Puotinen, it is evident that the origins of organized labor took root in the Copper Country well before the 1913–14 Strike, and to some extent before Finnish immigrants came to the area en masse. It was, perhaps, the influx of Finnish immigrant workers and the rise of the Finnish Socialist Federation and Työmies Publishing Company in Michigan that created a critical mass in the area that could organize, agitate for, and commence a strike of such ambitious proportions. The 1913–14 Strike was a grass-roots organizational effort started by and nurtured in the Copper Country by disaffected, disenfranchised workers. It is true that some of the "agitators" came from outside, but the organizational groundwork, the vote to send the ultimatum letter to the mining companies and the vote to strike, was cast by large numbers of people inside the Copper Country and not by the handful of outside agitators.

Once empowered against the mining companies, there was no turning back for many union members—as another ill-fated event in South Range evidenced. On a December night in 1913, Sheriff Cruse "heard" that trouble was brewing in South Range in the form of armed strikers who were assembling in South Range's WFM office headquarters on 1st Street. Cruse determined that the South Range WFM offices were in need of a good old-fashioned siege. On December 10, Cruse quickly deputized one hundred men, many members of the Citizens' Alliance, and headed by train for South Range. Once in South Range, the armed posse surrounded the WFM offices, as they did not have a warrant to enter. The deputies initially arrested twelve armed men who were outside the offices, but at this time in Copper Country history, there were probably many people on both sides of the strike walking around with guns. John Välimäki, Työmies Publishing Company editor and WFM organizer, was one of those arrested. Cruise cordoned off the building and sent for reinforcements. Three hundred or so men responded from Houghton.[37]

The standoff lasted until three in the morning, when the portly (reportedly over 300 pounds) Deputy John Chellow knocked on the door, deceivingly announced that he had a search warrant, and threatened to bust down the door. A female's sobbing was heard, and then a male voice from behind the door replied, "Why don't you come around in daylight?" That type of insolence apparently negated the need for a warrant and the deputy tried to smash in the door. The person associated with the voice from behind the door promptly shot Chellow in a nonfatal area, and the armed posse of three to four hundred turned back.[38]

The posse waited until daybreak and raided the building again. They found three men in the union offices, unarmed but sitting on a weapons cache of around six rifles without ammunition. According to the company affiliated press, a search of the building revealed about thirty other people, thirty guns in the WFM offices, red flags, red dominoes, red jackets, and "red" literature. The posse arrested forty in all. Charges on those arrested were later dropped, with the exception of the shooter, Henry Koski, who was the secretary of the South Range WFM local.[39]

Työmies described the South Range raid as an unlawful break-in, and rumors of roving bands of armed WFM strikers looking to shoot up the South Range area were later dismissed as a fabrication used by the Citizens' Alliance as ammunition for the raid on the South Range offices. The South Range raid set in motion other raids across the Copper Country.[40] On December 11, *Työmies* reported: "Kansankoti and Työmies menaced by law and order." On that night in Hancock, automobiles sped up to the corner of Quincy and Tezcuco, and out popped five or six "gun hounds," who promptly raided the hall and publishing company in the middle of the night.[41]

In an added effort to dissuade any further acts of "intimidation" by WFM members, Sheriff Cruse took out a December 20 advertisement in the *Daily Mining Gazette*, stating:

> To the Public in General and Every Working Man in Particular:
>
> Houghton County for the last four months has been the scene of lawlessness and disorder. Working men have been assaulted and intimidated, and the sacred right of citizenship violated.

> Charles H. Moyer has been notified that the right to work must be respected. Violence and intimidation must stop. Every man who wants to work will be protected, and the Sheriff and his deputies, with the co-operation of the citizens, will make this guarantee effective.[42]

Cruse makes no mention of protection for the strikers' rights to freedom of assembly and speech, or the fact that both sides had used violence within the last four months. Surely, the two men shot and killed in Seeberville would have posthumously appreciated an article in the *Gazette* from the sheriff when company men fired repeatedly into the Putrich house. The above passage leaves little doubt about which "side" Sheriff Cruse was on, and in this case, Justice, who should remain blind, had become very keen-sighted for the mining bosses' interests. Perhaps the most important phrase in Sheriff Cruse's warning is "with the co-operation of the citizens, will make this guarantee effective." Seemingly, Sheriff Cruse was falsely alleging that the citizens of the Copper Country were wholly on the side of the mining companies' interests, or perhaps implying that he would unleash the power of the fervently pro–mining company Citizens' Alliance to stem the tide of the Copper Country's most intense and longest-lasting labor disruption.

The Italian Hall Tragedy

The 1913–1914 Copper Strike caused open class conflict, sometimes bloody confrontations between strikers, the Citizens' Alliance, and hired mining-company "thugs," but there was no more distressing event during the strike than the Italian Hall disaster of December 24, 1913. In the crowded Red Jacket (today Calumet) pro-labor Italian Hall, approximately seventy three to seventy nine people suffocated when a crowd of hundreds pushed from the second floor of the hall toward a stairway that led to a first floor exit when someone purportedly exclaimed, "FIRE!" There was no fire.[43] *Työmies* was quick to print the workers' version of the event in Finnish and English in a special impromptu edition published on Christmas Day. The beginning of the English-language version of the article read:

The most appalling disaster in the history of Michigan occurred last evening at the Italian Hall in Calumet where hundreds of men, women and children had gathered to witness Christmas exercises for the strikers children. The program which was quite lengthy had just begun when a strange man ascended the stairway, yelled "fire" and quickly made his escape to the street. Several persons who stood near the entrance where this man appeared, state that he had his cap pulled down over his eyes, and that pinned to the lapel of his coat was a Citizens' Alliance button. At the cry of fire, the great crowd arose as one and made a mad rush for the exit in the front of the building. In the rush down the stairway, many fell and being unable to regain their feet were trampled to death, their bodies acting as stumbling blocks for others who followed, until the hallway was entirely blocked by the dead and dying. The fire alarm was soon sounded and those responding were forced to gain entrance to the hall by ladders at the front windows. Firemen entered the building in this manner and stopped the panic stricken crowd from further crowding into the hallway upon the dead bodies of their friends in a frantic effort to escape. The bodies in the hallway were so tightly packed that they could not be released from below, and firemen were compelled to remove the dead from the top of the stairway carrying the dead and dying back up into the hall before the stairs could be cleared. At the time the cry of fire was sounded in the hall Mrs. Annie Clemenc was making a talk to the little ones present who naturally were crowded as near the stage as possible, their little faces beaming with happiness, their hearts bounding with Christmas cheer. In less than three minutes afterward fifty of their frail little bodies were jammed and crushed in the hallway being used as a roadway over which their companions were vainly endeavoring to escape. The scene was a horrible one, and will never be effaced from the minds of those who witnessed the terrible tragedy.

The bodies of the dead were taken to a temporary morgue established in the town hall as soon as they were removed from the building. As soon as identifications were made, the bodies were removed to their homes. In some homes the mother and all the children lie cold in death, the husband and father crazed with grief. In others the mother being the only one spared has been plunged into despair and sorrow that yet dazes her, the full truth not yet dawning upon her terrified brain.[44]

Herman Kallungi was in Red Jacket (Calumet) when the fire whistles blew:

> I got up by that big Austrian Church by the depot there and I heard the fire whistles start blowing and I could tell where the fire was by the time they blew. The location . . . I stopped there because I could tell by the whistles it was in town. When I got down a little ways I could not see the smoke. There was no smoke. There was a big crowd of people in front of the Italian Hall on Seventh Street.
>
> They had a strike breaking gang there and one thing. When I got there . . . Waddell were strikebreakers. When I got there one of them on horseback was riding in front of the door. There was a narrow stairway coming down there. People were piling down. There was a door going into the tavern and they pulled a lot of them in there. But those that come down they could have saved a lot more but that goddamned Waddell man was riding back and forth in front of the door. Wouldn't let anybody help out.[45]

The Italian Hall disaster brought incredible misery to thousands of people. The final count of the dead is difficult to determine because of the enormous amount of chaos surrounding the event and generally poor documentation processes of the time. A somewhat agreed-upon number of deaths is seventy-three or seventy-four, but reviewing Työmies Publishing Company sources gives an oft-overlooked insight into the gruesome toll of the dead. On December 25 and December 26, *Työmies* included named lists of the Italian Hall dead, including addresses and relations of the dead. On December 31, the *Miners' Bulletin* published a list of the Italian Hall dead, complete with addresses and ages for many of the dead. From these somewhat incomplete and provisional lists, combined with a record of the dead from the Houghton County coroner's inquest, we come to the possibility of a slightly higher total of seventy-five to seventy-nine persons deceased. Of these persons, fifty or more were children under the age of thirteen; at least two of the fifty children were babes in arms. Twenty-nine mothers and children died together on the stairway. Five groups of siblings died in the hall: the three Heikkinen brothers, the three Klarich girls, the three Mihelchich siblings, the three or possibly four Montanen siblings, and the two Myllykangas boys sadly all rushed toward the stairs together and to their deaths.[46]

Because of the number of "Finns" involved with striking factions, persons of Finnish ethnicity were especially affected by the sorrowful events at Italian Hall. Around fifty of the Italian Hall dead were of Finnish ancestry. The Niemalä, Manley (Manni in Finnish), and Kotajärvi families had heartbreaking stories to tell after the disaster. Mr. and Mrs. Niemalä, who lived by No. 4 Shaft in Wolverine Location, died while holding their small child above their heads as they plummeted into the mass of bodies flowing down the hall's steep stairway. The child survived; Mr. and Mrs. Niemalä did not. The Manley family of North Tamarack Location lost four-year-old Wesley, mother Elina, and Elina Manley's ten- or eleven-year-old sister, Saida Raja. Especially tragic was that thirty-five-year-old Elina was pregnant at the time of her death. She left behind a husband, Herman, who had stayed home with the couple's two-and-a-half-year-old son, Neil, and seven-month-old baby, Wilfred. The Kotajärvi family of 353 Franklin Street, Florida Location, lost at least four and possibly five persons. Annie Kotajärvi died along with her four-year-old daughter, Annie, and possibly another three-year-old daughter, Amy. Along with mother Annie, daughter Annie, and perhaps Amy, two more girls from the family died. These two young women were from Annie's first marriage to a man with the surname Rytilahti. Emilia and Heli Rytilahti died with their mother Annie Kotajärvi, but for all these years were separated in the coroner's inquest because of differing surnames.[47]

Työmies accused their principal noncompany adversary in the strike, the Citizens' Alliance, of orchestrating the disaster. No named instigator(s) of the disaster ever emerged, no one from the Citizens' Alliance was ever called to testify or dispel allegations, and no person or persons ever faced criminal legal action, though sworn testimony, certified statements in *Työmies*, and local rumor directly implicated the Citizens' Alliance. People did go to jail for the events at Italian Hall, though—but these people were from the Työmies Publishing Company.

So, what exactly did *Työmies* print that got them in so much trouble? In accounts of the event, *Työmies* explicitly blamed an individual associated with or the Citizens' Alliance as a group for orchestrating the event. The special issue Christmas Day extra directly laid culpability on someone with a Citizens' Alliance pin: "Several persons who stood near the entrance where this man appeared, state that he had his cap pulled down over his eyes, and that pinned to the lapel of his coat was a Citizens' Alliance button." Then on December 26, *Työmies* printed: "The money offered from the Citizens Alliance will not be accepted," ostensibly because "a Citizens Alliance thug [*huligaani*] yelled the fire alarm and gun hounds closed the exit path, which was overrun by people in terror."[48]

Then on December 27, *Työmies* published oath-sworn certification of the Italian Hall events in a ten-point list. This list was damning toward the Citizens' Alliance and Sheriff's deputies. In the list, *Työmies* claimed that a man dressed in good clothes donning a sealskin hat screamed fire at the door twice, which created a panic and sent people rushing toward the stairway. As a result of this children and women formed about a four-foot-high heap in the stairwell, and from a couple of questionable testimonies, it was stated that something was dropped or left in the women and children's path before they began to flow down the stairs. The list then indicated that men from the Citizens' Alliance and Houghton County deputies pushed away onlookers trying to help and in a couple of instances deputies did not begin to help where aid was needed foremost by untangling the heap, but actually restrained others that were helping to untangle the heap, so that more and more victims crashed into the heap. The article also stated that deputies jammed the doors shut, so that the rescue work could only be made from the top of the stairs, causing the heap of people to remain there for a long time and therefore people suffocated. The article went on to state that deputies and Citizens' Alliance members stood around jeering and shaking their heads at strikers plugged up at the bottom of the pile while upstairs in the hall a deputy twisted a 5–6-year-old child's neck and drug a man by the neck so to stricken the man's last breath of life leaving thumbprints around his throat.[49]

This list was likely the last straw for those who wanted the events of Italian Hall and the implication of wrongdoing by the Citizens' Alliance, sheriff's deputies, and mining-company thuggery to go away. So, for their corroborated reports of the Citizens' Alliance and Houghton county deputies' actions, *Työmies*'s editor Severi Alanne and four others from *Työmies* were arrested and charged with publishing maliciously false statements on December 27, 1913.[50] On December 29, the newspaper detailed arrest events in a timeline:

> On Saturday at 10 am, Työmies' Calumet correspondents were reporting that something was going to happen to Työmies' workers.

> At 10.10, we began to confer on what to do.
>
> At 4.00 pm, deputies rushed Työmies' offices arresting Alanne, Nummivuori, Kokko and Vuorela and later in the evening came for machine apprentice Väisänen, as well as numerous others.[51]
>
> Immediately after the phone call from Työmies, a news agency in Duluth reported the event and telegraphed the event to several other places.
>
> At 9.35 pm, Marttila contacted Chicago to bring our party headquarters [Socialist Party of America] in on the murders in Calumet, that we had received sworn certificates of the events and to inform on Työmies' fate and status in general.
>
> On Sunday, all was peaceful. In the afternoon, we received telegraph requests asking for further information on how Työmies was targeted for persecution.
>
> At 6.30 pm, a telegram from [Victor] Berger came in which he stated that the Milwaukee Leader's shop is at Työmies' disposal or we can have two Finnish pages in the Milwaukee Leader.
>
> At a 7 pm consultation meeting, we decided to accept the offer of Berger and began to organize for the necessary implementation.
>
> At 10 pm, we determined that it would be disreputable to be on the move.
>
> Sunday, the day after, we quietly manufactured a makeshift Työmies; which meant this event will be known worldwide. What if this number would not have been published.[52]

These arrests perhaps would have been valid *if* the Työmies Publishing Company printed the accounts without citing sources, but the articles about Italian Hall were journalistic reporting using oath-sworn accounts. Additionally, it is certain that *Työmies*'s had at least one first-hand account from someone in the hall, which was gathered by Heimer Mikko and WFM organizer Mor Oppman from a grieving mother named Anna Lustig. From her testimony during a December 31, 1913, Houghton County coroner's inquest, Anna Lustig, who was of Finnish ethnicity and had lost a five-year-old son in the panic, clearly indicated that she had the first-hand knowledge about events in Italian Hall to provide Mikko and Oppman, and thus *Työmies* and the *Miners' Bulletin*. Lustig testified at the inquest that Mikko and Oppman visited her house after the disastrous night. She told examiner Anthony Lucas during her testimony that Mikko and Oppman asked her to recount the night's events; Lustig then repeated to Lucas what she had previously told Oppman and Mikko: "A man called, 'FIRE!' and then another man, I did not hear, it was so loud; and a man with a Citizens' Alliance button on . . ." Lucas went on to question, "Where did he have the button?" Lustig replied, "Right here on his left side. A little above his pocket." "Did you hear him cry fire?" asked Lucas. Lustig testified, "Yes sir." Lucas then asked, "How far from him were you?" Lustig said, "About 9 or 10 feet."[53]

While important members of *Työmies* staff were under arrest for phony reasons, other members of the newspaper's staff led the crusade to release their imprisoned fellow workers by circulating a cutout petition addressed to Governor Woodbridge Ferris. The petition read:

> I am one of the 12,000 subscribers of the "Työmies," an 8 page 7 column Finnish daily newspaper, published at Hancock, Michigan. Instead of my daily paper I received today this leaflet containing the most astonishing information that the publishers, editors and even the employees of the office and print shop of Työmies were arrested on the 27th day of December and that the paper cannot be published. They are charged with publishing inflammatory articles contained in the issues of December 25th and 26th in connection with the great copper strike which began July 23, more than five months ago. I have read this paper every day, and every time the imported gunmen at Copper Country had done some outrages this paper advised the strikers to be calm and peaceful. It is apparent, that this wholesale arrest of the printers, bookkeepers and even office boys is an unwarranted action to suppress this paper because it dares to speak for the striking miners. This action is a direct violation of the Constitution of the United States and therefore I ask you as Governor of the State to protect the constitutional rights of the publishers of Työmies and my right to read this paper which I have subscribed for.[54]

While the petition aimed for the release of those arrested and getting the newspaper press rolling again, it was also a way to draw attention to those who were vulnerable to the integrity of the Copper Country's slanted legal process. Because while *Työmies*'s presses were out of commission for one day (December

28, 1913), this day was a Sunday, a regular day off at the publishing company. The TPC printed newspapers on the 27th and the 29th, not missing a regular day of publication. While the paper did not miss a beat in printing the workers' side of the strike story, the arrests likely had more of a psychological effect, creating a sense of martial law being declared on the newspaper, its staff, and supporters. Arrested *Työmies* staff members had to come up with the exorbitant amount of $1,000 dollars for bail and were then released days later. The case against *Työmies*'s was also let go because a violation of constitutional rights was inherent in the trumped-up charges.[55]

In the aftermath of the Italian Hall tragedy, Charles Moyer, WFM president, arguably made one of the biggest blunders in the history of his WFM leadership. Moyer refused to accept any public donations of sympathy, monetary or otherwise, unless they were from card-carrying union members.[56] This act likely alienated thousands of people who had no affiliation with the mining companies—people who were potential sympathizers of the union, especially in light of the tragic events at Italian Hall. While this was an attempt to provide strong leadership in a troubled time, it infuriated the local public and swung public opinion for the last time away from the WFM. Moyer's act also nearly got him killed. On December 26, 1913, a number of men, many of whom had some association with the Citizens' Alliance, rushed Moyer's hotel room in Hancock. The vigilantes beat and nonfatally shot Moyer and then placed him on a train to Chicago. A Houghton County grand jury inexplicably chose to exonerate the group of men responsible for the beating and shooting.[57] Justice seemed to be a backward concept in the strike-ravaged Copper Country.

The most heart-wrenching consequence of the misery at Italian Hall was the great number of dead children. As would be expected, the Christmas Eve party at the hall had hundreds of kids, who were hoping to reap the bounty of candy and presents available on the hall's stage. In what must have been an incredibly tough time to be a child among the sporadic violence, hours-long parades, and deep divisions within the Copper Country, this was a night for festivity, frivolity, and escape from the strike area's polarized realities. The WFM Women's Auxiliary sponsored the Christmas Eve party, and it was supposed to be a chance for the children of strikers to be "kids" again, if only for a short time. After the present distribution, funded in part by the WFM national and in part by donations procured by the Women's Auxiliary, there was to be a Mother Goose–style play that evening. That all went to hell in a few short moments.[58]

It would seem that a great sort of injustice was done to "just being a kid" that night, but Houghton County's prosecuting attorney, Anthony Lucas, found a despicable way to further ruin the night for the working-class children. During the coroner's inquest, examiner Lucas did not do much for the cause of determining the identity of an assailant, or even establishing if a crime had indeed been committed at Italian Hall. Lucas's bumbling of the inquest perhaps could be forgiven in light of events at the Italian Hall being so frantic and distressed if not for a most contemptible act that occurred while he was questioning Mrs. Louis Lesch (surname also seen as Lesh), an organizer of the Christmas Eve festivities. After recalling Lesch to the stand, Lucas began a line of questioning that attempted to focus the blame for the mass panic on the children. Lucas questioned Lesch with queries that tried to insinuate that the children were becoming restless due to the length of the gift-giving procedures. When Lesch refused to acquiesce and say that the children were in fact getting impatient, Lucas then rhetorically questioned, "The purpose of this jury is to find out what caused this and what brought it on and *probably the children themselves are to blame?* We got to get all the facts we can."[59]

On the heels of the arrests of *Työmies*'s workers, Moyer's abduction, and the bungled inquest, the funerals for the Italian Hall victims happened in a solemn, somber setting. The Old Apostolic Lutheran Church on Pine Street in Calumet hosted the funerals for many of the Finnish ethnic contingent. The Apostolic Lutherans, often referred to as Laestadians, were pious and antimaterialistic adherents of an Old Country Lutheran revivalism introduced to the indigenous people (Sámi) of arctic Finland and Scandinavia by naturalist Lars Levi Laestadius in the mid-1800s. It is possible that many of the Laestadians saw the excesses and materialism of the mining companies as sinful and joined the ranks of striking workers. Thus, a number of Laestadian families were likely at the Italian Hall on Christmas Eve, and a number of the dead children from Italian Hall were probably from families with Sámi roots in the northern reaches of Finland.[60]

It is also possible that some of the strikers with Sámi ancestry saw the horrible events of the night in supernatural terms. As Asbjörn Nesheim wrote in his survey of Sámi culture, "In other [Sámi] legends disasters are caused by children making merry during the Christmas season or by work being done on Christmas Eve, with the result that either the moon or the stallo [a cannibalistic monster] or Christmas spirits come and devour the culprits."[61] It is unlikely that anyone associated with the striking workers saw the tragic events of the night as the children's fault, but the overwhelming grief of the night did perhaps beckon some to look for otherworldly explanations regarding the tragic events.

Regardless of causation, ethereal or otherwise, Calumet was once again a scene of absolute misery as a long funeral procession of around 5,000 mourners moved through an estimated twenty thousand people who watched as the caskets of the Italian Hall deceased moved through the city streets and out to Lakeview Cemetery. The somber march led to two mass graves in Protestant and Catholic sections of the cemetery. Altogether, thirteen undertakers assisted in preparing the bodies for burial. The ceremonies at Lake View Cemetery lasted until nightfall. Frank Aaltonen gave the eulogy for the Finnish contingent.[62]

A newsreel photographer captured the woeful events and luckily had the foresight to create "dummy films" of his work, because someone or some group stole the films from the photographer's hotel room in Red Jacket. A rumor among strike sympathizers held that the Citizens' Alliance stole the films, leaving many to wonder if "the Citizens' Alliance would stop at nothing."[63] The WFM and strikers struggled to regroup and looked to the home of Hancock's Finnish immigrant socialist-unionists to do so: "Protest Meeting: A meeting of the strikers is called for tomorrow afternoon at 2 P.M. at Kansankoti Hall. This meeting is to be held for the purpose of protesting against the tyranny of the mining companies and injustice of Houghton County Officials. Prominent speakers will be present."[64] Could the pieces be put back together again after a dreadful event like Italian Hall?

Regionally, the lawlessness of pro–mining company factions did not go unnoticed in areas of vested proletarian interests. On January 21, 1914, the *Miners' Bulletin* ran an article titled "General Strike Threatened," which outlined a resolution threatening a solidarity strike on the Upper Peninsula's Marquette Iron Range. Members of the Negaunee and Ishpeming Miners' Union locals passed resolutions designed to compel an investigation by the U.S. Congress regarding the "conditions in the strike district of the copper regions." Wording of the resolution left no doubt regarding the disgust felt by the Negaunee and

Ishpeming unions. Ethnic bonds probably accentuated wage-worker solidarity in these unions. The signers of the resolution were all "Finns"—Ishpeming Miners' Union president Ivar Ikkela, Ishpeming vice president Oscar Kuoppala, Negaunee Miners' Union president Arvid Anderson, and Negaunee vice president K. A. Saaristo. The Ishpeming and Negaunee unions also likely had a large number of Finnish immigrant rank-and-filers with strong ties to the Finnish Socialist Federation. The resolution read in part:

> Whereas the brutal assault of an apparently well organized and well protected gang in the copper district of Michigan, upon Charles H. Moyer, president of the Western Federation and his colleague, Charles Tanner, and their deportation from the state, together with the death of the 74 men, women and children on Christmas eve, under suspectable [*sic*] circumstances; and the lawless persecution of the Finnish daily Tyomies, and the arrest of its editors and the robbing of a private boarding house occupied by the miners on strike, by men who were supposed to be the officers of the law, and the deliberate killing of strikers in the district, clearly show that there is no longer any safety for life or property in the copper mine region of Michigan.
>
> Whereas, men have been assaulted upon and beaten in, and thrown out of the United States post office . . . Whereas threatening "black hand" letters have been sent through the United States mail . . . Whereas, the complicity of the sheriff of Houghton County in some of these outrages and the existence of a lawless organization, the so-called "Citizens Alliance," sworn to acts of violence against the miners of that district, and the refusal and neglect of the state government and all its agencies . . . show that the local powers are subservient to the mine owners and have become part of the conspiracy.[65]

Työmies also attempted to mobilize national support for a congressional investigation. J. W. Sarlund, translator and secretary of the "Finnish Socialist Organization" penned this message in Chicago to United States socialists:

> National Secretary Socialist Party calls upon all locals to hold mass meetings Immediately and send resolutions to the President and their Congressman demanding congressional investigation of Michigan strike. Secretaries of

> all foreign speaking federations do likewise. Recent developments, Calumet catastrophe as one, prove we must take nation wide action in name of million socialists and of their respective organizations. National Secretary and foreign secretaries have each wired President Wilson.[66]

The threat of the Negaunee and Ishpeming Miners' Unions general strike was a show of solidarity that came too late, but a congressional investigation was made, though it did little to bolster the diminishing strike efforts. At this point, a general strike threat was more likely a bit of general theater on the part of sympathetic fellow workers attempting to draw attention to and salvage a disintegrating, ever-isolated labor action. The month of January proved to be the beginning of the end for Copper Country strikers. The wheels were slowly falling off the WFM machinery: the WFM was hemorrhaging money, men were walking back on the job, and the Copper Country winter exacted an icy toll on both bodies and morale. The WFM's epic struggle, catalyzed by Finnish immigrant workers and their fellow workers from other ethnicities, was ending in a slow burn.

The Strike's End

The exact catalyst for the strike's end is unclear—whether it was Moyer's comments, the tragedy at the Italian Hall, disillusionment with the course of the strike, or just plain exhaustion on the part of the strikers—but it seemed that the proletarian surge had been turned back. In January 1914, nearly eight thousand men went back to work. There were congressional investigations into the various events, and union organizers spread through the Copper Country attempting to trumpet support for an ostensibly broken instrument, the WFM. The mining companies had not changed their stance throughout the strike, as Puotinen wrote: "On March 2, a Calumet and Hecla superintendent reiterated a company position stated forty years earlier by Alexander Agassiz during the strike of 1874. Die-hard union men 'can find employment elsewhere. If they do not want to subscribe to the conditions that we impose, they are perfectly free to go to other places.'"[67]

There were small hints of an emerging end to the strike, bolstered by admonishments to listen for official union news only from official union sources: "Attention Striking Miners: The strike will not be 'called off' by the Daily Mining Gazette, Copper Journal, Calumet News nor by bulletins posted in the 'Rexall Drug Store.' Any information relative to the strike will be forthcoming from authoritative sources. DO NOT BE DECEIVED."[68] Even union-perceived concessions from the mining companies in April seemed to indicate that strike actions were close to ending: "Another Victory—Abolishment of the heavy one-man drill better known as the widowmaker. Every demand except the recognition of the union has now been granted." According to the *Miners' Bulletin*, mines were switching to the lighter Baby Leyner drill, which weighed approximately 90 lbs.—down from previous models of the heavier one-man drill (150–190 lbs.) in use before the strike. The *Bulletin* added, "Not only is the Baby Leyner lighter, but it is dustless and easily operated."[69] The WFM's April rhetoric and rather technical machinery descriptions were much different from the heavily inspired proletarian-themed rhetoric that had come at the beginning of the strike; energy was lost, no matter how the WFM tried to spin it.

Every indication seemed to point to the strike ending in April, and on April 14, it did. The *Miners' Bulletin* reported:

> At a meeting of the District Union held Wednesday April 8th in which every local of the Federation in this district was represented, it was decided that if the strike was to be continued the relief benefits would have to be reduced, and that accommodations would have to be furnished for several hundred families now living in company houses. After thoroughly debating the subject it was decided to put the matter before the men on strike. Meetings were arranged for the Ahmeek and Calumet locals on Friday and the Hancock and South Range on Saturday when the strikers were informed of the proposed reduction in benefits and of other obstacles confronting them.
>
> Two propositions were put to the men viz: To either make further sacrifices regarding benefits, or return to work which was put to a referendum vote on Sunday with the result that the men decided on the latter. At the meetings held prior to taking a referendum of the proposition, the question was thoroughly discussed, and the men realizing that all the concessions asked at the time

> of calling the strike had been granted by the Mining Companies with the exception of recognition of the union, they felt as though this demand might be waived, and that they could return to work with the feeling that the strike had been practically won.[70]

WFM district secretary Charles Hietala divulged that a vote on continuing the strike found that of the 4,740 men voting, the overwhelming majority—3,104—voted to go back to work. Mining companies required that strikers turn in their red WFM union cards to regain employment in the area copper mines. For many, giving up the fight and returning to the mines was just too much to bear. There are no statistical analyses of the out-migration from the Copper Country during this time, but it is common knowledge that many strikers left for other mining districts, such as the Minnesota iron-ore ranges; left for Detroit factories; joined logging operations deep in the Upper Peninsula forests; or moved to rural agricultural areas on the Copper Country's industrial periphery.[71]

With the culmination of the strike actions, the *Miners' Bulletin* sounded a conciliatory yet defiant tone:

> To the striking miners we say: Return to your work with a firm determining to do your full duty to your employer, an Honest days work for the compensation agreed upon. Give him full value of service, but do not permit yourselves to sink down into dumb indifference as to your future welfare, and the welfare of your children.
>
> Educate yourselves that you may be better prepared to aid in the great battle that is soon to be fought for your own freedom, a battle that will require your services in the front ranks, a battle from which you cannot escape . . .
>
> Don't imagine that your enemies are going to free you. Their interests lie in keeping the chains of wage slavery about your limbs. You and your class are the only ones that you should consider, the other fellow will take mighty good care of his. The lessons that have been taught you in this terrific struggle of the past nine months has been a great educator and should never be forgotten. It will no doubt better fit you in the future. What many consider a defeat for the striking copper miners is merely a truce in the battle between capital and labor which must wage until the banner of labor shall triumph over the bulwarks

> of capitalism which will join its predecessors of chattel slavery, serfdom and feudalism, to be buried forever in the past.[72]

It was in this last hour of concession that the Finnish Anti-socialist League officially organized in the Copper Country. The first formal meeting of Hancock's Anti-socialist League met on April 9, 1914, in Rouleau Hall. Calumet Finns organized a branch of the Anti-socialist League on May 10 of the same year, holding a large gathering in the Calumet National Guard Armory.[73] Twenty-two people attended the Hancock League's first meeting. The second meeting saw Swaby Lawton, Hancock City attorney and brother of Quincy Mine superintendent Charles Lawton, join the group as a new member of "good social standing." The second meeting attracted thirty-eight new members, the third meeting forty-one new members, the fourth sixty-three; and then by the fifth meeting, women joined the ranks. This co-ed meeting drew forty-two new members, but after that, numbers of new members began to drop off dramatically. Altogether, the league's ranks comprised roughly 285 members, who met at the Rouleau Hall, Kauth Block Hall, and after the fourth meeting, exclusively at Pohjantähti Temperance Hall.[74]

Predictably, the group focused almost solely on socialist-unionist activities in Hancock. Whether the League was jumping on Copper Country Finnish socialist-unionists after the strike or reacting to a perceived threat, it seemingly was working to thwart any future disturbances that might again bring about another strike-like event. Ever vigilant, the group utilized the power of the mining companies through the local company-influenced media:

> We discussed the ball [dance] at Kansankoti. Secretary E. Saastamoinen suggested that we should make a petition for the city council of Hancock to keep an eye on the event. At this time, it was considered to be enough to write an article about it to the *Mining Gazette*. A. Braum took responsibility for the task. Secretary E. Saastamoinen was asked to write about the same thing to *Amerikan Suometar*.[75]

The Hancock League was, however, a short-lived organization: the last meeting entry for the Hancock Anti-socialist League occurred only a half year later, on September 12, 1915.[76]

The mining companies, Citizens' Alliance, and Copper Country Finnish anti-socialists had turned back the WFM, and more specifically, the Finnish immigrant socialist-unionists. Make no mistake, though—the mining companies suffered financially as well as publicly because of the strike. What toll did the strike take on the mining companies? In the months following the strike, the companies made some changes that were beneficial to wageworkers. An eight-hour day became standard in many copper mines, though it was widely speculated that the eight-hour day was coming to the copper mines before the 1913–14 strike. Some companies instituted a better system for worker grievance reporting, and in some cases, wages received a slight bump up. For the mining companies, dividends shrank precipitously. In 1912, the mining companies paid out $9 million—but in 1913, $7 million, and only $1.6 in 1914.[77] The strike certainly had a great effect on the mining companies, but most historians count the strike a loss for organized labor because mining companies never recognized the WFM. Predictably, the *Miners' Bulletin* was not so defeatist in their summation of the strike:

> Had it not been for the work of the Western Federation of Miners since coming into the district you would still be working from eleven to thirteen hours in super heated dungeons a mile below the surface of the earth. You would still be getting starvation wages, and work under the most deplorable conditions existing for the past half century, with no joy and no hope beyond your daily toil. You can now return to work with the feeling that the fight you have made for better pay, shorter hours and more humane working conditions has been granted, although far from being just, but was all you asked. While you were wresting these few concessions from the Mine Owners, organized labor through the Western Federation of Miners fed and clothed you and your family. Almost a half million dollars was poured into the copper country for your benefit, besides a trainload of clothing.[78]

The efforts of organized labor in the Copper Country were valiant if a person subscribes to the union ideal, but there was no sugarcoating the outcome: the strike was unceremoniously broken and the WFM unrecognized. The WFM was even more "broke," as it sank a small fortune into the strike. "The Western Federation had lost hard fought battles before, but this one proved particularly devastating. The strike left the union buried in debt. It spent $800,000 in an attempt to organize the Michigan copper workers, including $125,000 borrowed from other labor organizations; $275,000 that had come as voluntary contributions; and nearly $400,000 of mandatory assessments paid in by WFM members," wrote Larry Lankton.[79] Still, many Finnish immigrant labor organizers planned and plotted ways to continue the challenge against the copper oligarchy, and some felt that the WFM did not fully commit to the strike.

Socialist-unionist sentiment was still very strong in areas of the Copper Country. The Quincy Mining Company remained vigilant because although they had defeated the WFM, the ideal persisted. Blacklisted workers, sympathizers, and those who were just fed up with the industrial milieu left Copper Country mining areas in droves, sometimes settling in rural areas on the mining companies' industrial periphery.

At times, this settlement was too close for comfort, as we find with Paavola (formerly Concord City), a rural hamlet sandwiched in between the Quincy Mining Company's industrial core. In a letter from Quincy Mining Company general manager Charles Lawton to Quincy Mining Company president W. R. Todd, Lawton warned Todd that union men and socialists were leaving company property and heading to Paavola. Possibly fearing eviction from company houses, Finnish immigrant socialist-unionists retreated to this ethnic enclave to reorganize, reenergize, or simply escape. Paavola was unique in that it was almost adjacent to company property without being on company property, and as it was off company property, many of the strikers, members of the Western Federation of Miners, took refuge in Paavola. This troubled Lawton, as is clear from an April 4, 1914, letter to Todd: "In checking up on the voters of Franklin Township, we find that a great many of the Federation men who have left company houses, have gone over to Concord City to live, and still remain in Franklin Township. Therefore, the outlook for eliminating the Socialists and Federation men in the election of Monday next is not over bright. The idle labor vote seems to be very strong."[80]

Though the strike was off, a torch continued to burn for many who deplored wages, conditions, and labor-management relations in the Copper Country. The WFM national and its 16th District Union agreed that calling off the strike had left some incomplete business in the Copper Country. Dan Sullivan, president of the 16th District Union, WFM, and C. E. Hietala, secretary of the same, authored a summation, thank you, and defiant promise to various supporters of the strike, which included the United Mineworkers of America, the American Federation of Labor, and the Socialist Party of America:

> The eight-hour workday and increased wage would never have been granted by the employing companies. The help which you gave has enabled us to stay with the struggle until our demands for improved working conditions were granted at least in part.
>
> We wish to again express our appreciation and thanks to all who aided us and to assure you that while our victory at this time will be regarded as only partial our struggle for improved working conditions will continue until the banner of organized labor shall wave triumphant over the copper mines of Michigan.[81]

In July 1914, Hietala implored the WFM national: "There are still men in the Copper Country who believe they were sold to the companies and believe that the Federation [WFM] had enough money to support them until the battle was won."[82] Like many socialist-unionist Finnish immigrants, Hietala remained true to the cause and was unwilling to give up on efforts in the Copper Country, as a final letter to the WFM national asserts:

> Now as to the organizing work in this district, I will say that in my opinion after 5–6 months the organizing work can be done with good success if the conditions little improve in the Iron district. At the present time every day number of men are coming from Iron Country to this district looking for work and that makes conditions to the local miners miserable or in other words hard to keep their jobs because hundreds of men are always looking for work round the mining company offices. The Anti-socialist movement will loose their foothold soonest the conditions little improve and they have already lost good number of their dues paying members according to their own newspaper reports.[83]

Included in the letter was Hietala's inventory of the remaining materials at the Kansankoti Hall: "1 office desk, 1 high stool, 1 check protector, 1 paper fastener, 1 safe, 1 cabinet, 1 Ferrer picture, 2 picture frames, 1 Y&E office filing system, 2 waste baskets, 3 window curtains, 1 Acme wire letter tray, rubber stamps, stationary, books, papers, WFM reports, 1 hammer, 1 gavel, 1 ballot box, 1 banner stick, 1 American flag and 13 editions of *The Fighting Editor*."[84]

Conclusion

In April 1914, after nearly 265 days of striking, the Copper Strike was over. In the days, weeks, and months following the strike, the proverbial wheels began to come off for the Finnish immigrant socialist-unionists. Much like the cold winter currents of Lake Superior that begin to rise with the heating of the big lake in spring, the undertow of animosity and division present within the movement as early as 1905 began to flow upward and then boiled over. The tense solidarity that had been built up for the last decade came crumbling down under the weight of a failed collective labor action. The work of the early grass-roots organizers, the careful constructing of the Työmies Publishing Company, and the power of dual-union solidarity took over a decade to build, but less than a year to demolish. This meteoric decade-long rise was significant because it illustrated what an immigrant people could do against seemingly insurmountable odds; it was a challenge accepted by Finnish immigrant socialist-unionists. This rise would also soon illustrate what could happen with a fall. The Finnish immigrant socialist-unionists were not broken, were not bankrupt, but they were bereft. The search for new directions hindered the movement. A semblance of the unified movement returned for the 1916

Industrial Workers of the World Minnesota Iron Ore Miners' strike, but the Finnish immigrant socialist-unionists never fully assembled the pieces back together and certainly never achieved a more unified response than the one presented when confronting the Michigan copper bosses.

The Strike's Aftermath

During the course of the Copper Country Strike, the WFM had run out of money to support a strike, and increasingly, internal factions within the WFM began to argue over its future. With the exception of holdout strikers, the copper mines were back in nearly full production by early May.[1] The Työmies Publishing Company and the Kansankoti Hall threw everything into the strike, but as was the case with the WFM, the publishing company and the hall began problematic and terminal internal disputes over the direction of their own political and labor efforts.[2]

A month earlier, and after a failed appeal, John Nummivuori and Jukka Salminen went to jail for the 1912 *Lapatossu* obscenity ruling. At roughly 10:00 P.M. on March 19, a crowd of around two hundred comrades met them at the Hancock train station. Even at this grim hour, Salminen was concerned about tension in the Finnish Socialist Federation, as he wrote from jail: "At 10.50 P.M. the train slowly got underway and friends from both 'yellow' and 'radical' socialist factions shouted words of encouragement."[3] Nummivuori and Salminen headed to Marquette's jail after preparing for their incarceration in true Finnish fashion: "So, on Friday to cleanse ourselves thoroughly, we stepped into Kalle Hakala's sauna . . . while delightful superheated steam rose to the ceiling, we contentedly puffed and panted knowing that it'd be sixty days before we again enjoyed a sauna."[4] After overcoming the initial claustrophobia of their cell, the two men seemed to settle quite well into the life of inmates. They paid the jailers to receive extra food rations, received gifts of flowers and nicotine, received cards and letters from well-wishers, and were let out of Marquette's subterranean cells for three minutes to pose with guests in a group photo. This was the only time the two inmates were able to inhale "God's free air."[5] But the

Finnish Socialist Federation Nummivuori and Salminen came back to was not the same organization they had left.

Nineteen-fourteen's annual Työmies Publishing Company and stockholders' meeting in May was an exercise in arguing inconsequential ideologies. The rancor between groups was likely accentuated by the apparent loss of the 1913–14 Copper Strike. The divisions within the TPC centered around radical supporters of the IWW, who were attempting to wrest power and the TPC away from less radical "yellow" elements. The radical Finns in the Finnish Socialist Federation supported IWW syndicalist methods of labor agitation and wanted to steer the federation toward an association with the IWW. A seemingly irreconcilable division within the TPC was evident as early as the February 21–28, 1914, yearly gathering. Minutes from the Duluth FSF meeting show that the "factionalism over the IWW question penetrated into branches of the federation and even into the editorial staff of *Työmies*."[6]

The split in the Työmies Publishing Company mirrored a split in the Finnish Socialist Federation, and the Finnish Socialist Federation's factionalism mirrored a split in the overall Socialist Party of America.[7] As aforementioned, the Finnish Socialist Federation grew rapidly from 1906 to 1912, but as the federation grew, the chasm between competing ideologies created rival internal factions. Perhaps the most tangible element of this internal dissension in the Finnish Socialist Federation was the Negaunee Labor Temple injunction. For a time in 1913, the Negaunee Finnish Socialist Federation local became the center of attention in Finnish immigrant working-class circles. The Labor Temple, once a place of proletarian promise and pride intended as "a building which the bourgeoisie and their stooges view in a cold sweat,"[8] became a battleground between comrades. The battle for ownership of the hall was the first open volley between the IWW radicals and the parliamentary socialists, as Auvo Kostiainen wrote:

> The first open split came in the Finnish socialist branch of Negaunee, Michigan. The losers, those driven out of the meeting hall, soon started openly supporting the IWW and its ideas. From there the disputes gradually spread all over the United States to almost every Finnish workers' association.[9]

The "Negaunee Injunction," as it came to be known, transfixed Finnish Socialist Federation locals, and the growing division estranged radical and parliamentary elements of the locals' membership. Parliamentary Finns became known within the federation groups as the "Opportunists" and passed resolutions condemning anarchist methods. The IWW Finns, known as the "Impossibilists," argued for one industrial, syndicalist union and the right to impose direct economic action through strikes and sabotage. The Impossibilists saw politics as a tool for the bourgeoisie, while the Opportunists saw politics as a tool for change.[10]

Debate over the Finnish Socialist Federation's future colored the proceedings of the Finnish Socialist Federation from 1909 to 1914. When the Impossibilists established a majority, they called for a vote in 1914. By a vote of 48 to 42, the federation district delegates accepted radical industrial-style unionism—in short, the IWW. After the 1914 vote, the radical element of the Finnish Socialist Federation began to purge the Opportunists from the ranks of the Federation.[11] Thus began the splitting of assets as federation locals had to decide which side of the fence they were on and, according to their allegiance, which hall or publishing company would become the voice of their movement. *Työmies* and the publishing company were an especially sought-after item:

> The spring of 1914 saw an attempt by the radicals to seize control of *Työmies* at the annual meeting of the publishing company by purchasing shares. The board of directors of *Raivaaja*,[12] however, was quicker and bought a controlling share of the newspaper's capital and thereafter started financially supporting *Työmies*.[13]

In a seemingly unrelated set of events, the Socialist Party of America (SPA) was also in the midst of a division in their membership. The SPA had always celebrated the fact that their organization was a highly diverse group of socialist adherents. The SPA was a heterogeneous group, consisting of Christian Socialists, Marxian Socialists, representatives of the American intelligentsia, and various other groups of immigrant workers. This diversity of background had its benefits and problems. One benefit of the SPA's diversity was the ability to increase its numbers rapidly by accepting varied forms of socialist ideology.

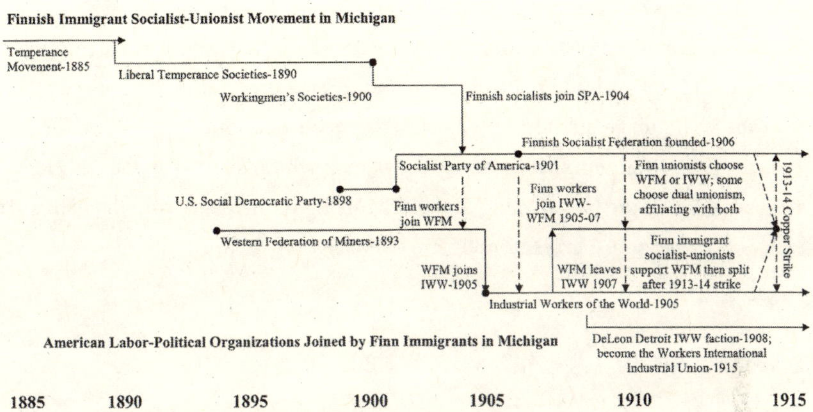

Finnish Socialist-Unionist Organizations, 1885–1915. Flow chart representing the merging of Finnish immigrant socialist-unionist organizations with American labor-political movements in Michigan, 1885–1915. (Gary Kaunonen.)

This benefit also detracted from unity within the SPA. The SPA, in order to remain politically viable in elections, could not entertain dissension within its ranks. A dissenting faction within the ranks was the IWW. By 1914, the SPA had purged most of the radical, syndicalist IWW members from its organization.[14]

In an astounding turn of events in 1914, two radical proletarian organizations, members of the radicalized Finnish Socialist Federation and the cast-out Wobblies, were now free from the bonds of their parliamentarian socialist comrades. It should come as no surprise that these two similar segments of radical ideology quickly gravitated toward each other. With a unique synergy, the unionist elements of the radicalized Finnish Socialist Federation combined with the industrial-labor character of the IWW to foment a unique brand of labor organization in the Finnish socialist-unionist population.

Leo Laukki, director and professor of the Work People's College in Duluth, Minnesota, was the most conspicuous figure associated with the IWW wing. The political faction portrayed Laukki as having hijacked the labor movement and literally riding it to Minnesota. From Edith A. Koivisto's interview with Douglass Ollila, it is clear that in some people's minds, Laukki surreptitiously rose to the head of the IWW ranks:

Ollila: He was most often regarded as the real leader of the Industrialisti faction of the Finns, the IWW faction. Do you regard him as the leader of that group?

Koivisto: He was a leader, but I tell you, at the last he was of the opinion that there should be political activity as well as economic, but the rank and file, the majority of Finnish people didn't want anything to do with politics. He switched at the last meeting of the organizing of the paper, and that's the way he became a leader among the IWWs.[15]

The TPC Moves to Superior, Wisconsin

The realities of the split in the Finnish Socialist Federation pressed the TPC into relocating to Superior, Wisconsin. The legalities of the move appear in a revision of the publishing company's Articles of Association. However, the 1915 revisions to the Articles of Association were a mere formality, as *Työmies* had been in publication from its new Superior headquarters since early October 1914.[16] Hancock's Jousi took a major hit when the publishing company left town. As Holmio related, "During the years 1904–1914, when *Työmies* was being published in Hancock, *Jousi,* the local socialist organization, was the leading Finnish organization in the state."[17] Local rumor and innuendo had the publishing company moving to Superior for various reasons, including being run out of town by angry antisocialist businesses, local advertising revenues falling to unprofitable levels, and/or financial distress over the vast amounts of money put into the 1913–14 Copper Strike.

Previous scholarship has not agreed either on the exact catalyst for the Työmies Publishing Company's move to Superior, Wisconsin. P. George Hummasti theorized that "businessmen in and around Hancock initiated an advertising boycott," which, coupled with the competition for readers by *Sosialisti,* forced the Työmies Publishing Company to seek a "more favorable atmosphere" for its publication.[18] Thurner opined that "Its relocation marked an important change in the Copper Country's role as a publishing center for Finnish radicals. Many blamed *Työmies* for generating hatred. Financially distressed, the newspaper was denied credit."[19] Puotinen is probably more accurate when he writes, "Because of financial reasons and power struggle going on within the Finnish Socialist Federation, the *Työmies* was moved to the Duluth-Superior area."[20]

An examination of the publishing company's minutes for the fiscal year 1913–1914 showed that the company had $118,697.07 in assets. The next fiscal year after the strike, and after the publishing company moved to Superior, the company had $121,306.49 in assets. Additionally, in fiscal year 1913, *Työmies* made $2,607.55 in advertising profits. In the next year, when fiscal reports would show the effects of the strike, *Työmies* took in $5,378.02 in advertising and subscriptions.[21] Unfortunately, 1914's financial records do not give specific numbers for advertising revenue, but there appears to be no discernable or disastrous drop in advertising revenue or in company assets between 1913 and 1915. It is likely that the absence of Copper Country advertisers did not have as large an impact as ascribed by some historians because *Tyomies* was a regional publication, and advertisements from across the Midwest ran in its pages. Copper Country advertisers were only a portion of the ad revenue and likely easily offset with new revenue from other areas of the Midwest.

This indicates that the internal divisions, and perhaps a migration to find more fertile organizational territory in Minnesota's booming iron ranges, led to the Työmies Publishing Company's departure from Hancock. This search for a following likely precipitated the move to Superior, rather than locally induced financial troubles in Hancock. *Työmies* had a following throughout the Midwest, the United States, and into Canada, which could easily sustain a readership. In fact, according to running subscription tallies on the upper right-hand side of *Työmies*'s front page from January 12, 1914, to May 16, 1914, subscriptions trended upward throughout the strike, reaching the highest levels ever recorded even as the strike actions ended.[22]

Regardless of causation for the TPC's departure, Thurner is correct in his assessment that an important change took place within the Copper Country with the publishing company's exit. While the publishing company retained a business office and bookstore in Hancock, it was likely that the energy it had generated was simply gone from the area.[23] The socialist-unionist movement remained in the area, taking a variety of forms, such as workers' cooperatives and a Young Communist League chapter in the 1920s and '30s, but Hancock never regained the prominent place it once had in either the Finnish immigrant socialist-unionist movement or the American labor movement.

A certain type of malaise seemed to affect Finnish immigrant proletarians in the coming years. A cooperative store run by Finnish immigrants took over the Työmies Publishing Company's quarters. The co-op was quite successful, and by 1917, it had 568 members and four branch stores in Calumet, South Range, Bruce's Crossing, and Arnheim. The Kansankoti continued to host meetings and was a place of business where Wilhard Aho worked as a tailor. There was still activity in the buildings, but for some, there seemed an energy lost in Copper Country working-class circles.[24] The corner of Franklin and Tezcuco in Hancock, dare we say once the seat of revolution in the Copper Country, apparently settled into a rather mundane existence:

> Father still works in the cooperative store. The times are bad because they have closed the mine in Hancock. Men have been put out of work and wages have gone down. Single men and farmers have been fired. Mother has been so lazy that she has not visited Kansankoti all winter. Now her back is so bad she can hardly walk.
>
> We have had a room empty [no boarder] all winter because we don't have a restroom indoors and here people are so spoiled that they want to shit indoors even though there was nothing to shit. The Viljamaas moved near Kansankoti because there is a restroom indoors and the Hall is so close they can spend all their time there.[25]

Final Thoughts on the Finnish Immigrant Socialist-Unionists

Many Finnish immigrants came to America with a history of subjugation by Swedish and Russian rule fresh in their collective minds. The Finnish immigrants' challenge to the Copper Country's industrial milieu varied among different ideological segments of the Finnish immigrant population, but the socialist-unionist immigrant Finns actively fomented social and economic change for over a decade. The Finnish immigrant socialist-unionist cultural organization in Hancock, Michigan, was a primary actor in the agitation for, and organization of, a challenge to industrial life as dictated to workers by Copper Country mine owners.

The truly impressive growth of the Finnish immigrants' socialist-unionist cultural organization in Hancock can be related by the growth of its physical attributes in the Finnish Transitional Neighborhood. Between 1900 and 1910, the early meeting places of Hancock's Finnish Socialist Federation local were rented meeting spaces. Within seven years of entrance into the Copper Country, the Finnish immigrant socialist-unionists had the funding and need, because of increased membership, to build their own large hall, which notified Copper Country capitalists that socialist-unionist Finnish immigrants were a force to be reckoned with in Michigan's Copper Country. The consolidation of the Työmies Publishing Company's operations with the Jousi's grand hall was a further declaration to the Copper Country public that the Finnish immigrants' socialist-unionist movement was an enduring, tangible force supporting the area's working class.

Hancock's Finnish immigrant socialist-unionists opened their halls and publications and gave of their own labor to advance the goals and initiatives of the greater American labor movement. In their response to the Copper Country bosses, Finnish immigrant socialist-unionists sought to participate in and join the American labor movement, but did so while maintaining their cultural and ethnic identity. The Työmies Publishing Company served an integral role as the disseminator of the socialist-unionist message, and the breadth of the company's published offerings to support the proletarian effort was impressive. The Hancock socialist local and Työmies Publishing Company jumped headfirst into this confrontation with capitalism, devoting their considerable accrual of monetary and physical resources to the effort to change the social and labor conditions in the Copper Country, Midwest, and greater United States.

The culmination of these efforts came in 1913, when Finnish immigrant socialist-unionists led the fight in a class conflict that engulfed the entire Copper Country. At the height of their maturity as a cultural organization, Hancock's Finnish immigrant socialist-unionists wagered their growth and stake in the American labor movement to bust the hold of monopoly capital in the Copper Country. This wager turned out to be a losing proposition that cost Hancock and the Copper Country effective union representation for the next thirty years. It was not until 1943 that the International Union of Mine, Mill and Smelter Workers (which was a reorganization of the WFM) organized Copper Country workers under the favorable auspices of the Franklin Roosevelt administration. It should be noted that it was a Finnish American named Gene Saari who led the local fight to bring industrial democracy to the area.[26]

We have taken a unique look at the Finnish American labor-political movement in this book. Analyzing the course of the Finnish immigrants' socialist-unionist movement, using both the historical and material record of Hancock's Finnish immigrant socialist-unionist organizations, provides a textured and intimate account of an exciting, yet extremely turbulent time in Copper Country history. Through the analysis of the Jousi, Kansankoti Hall, and Työmies Publishing Company's buildings, machinery, organizations, and publications, we can better comprehend the rather meteoric growth of the socialist-unionist movement in the Copper Country.

The Työmies Publishing Company and the Finnish Socialist Federation hit a high point of sorts during *Työmies*'s time in Hancock. At no other time was *Työmies* or the federation larger or more unified than when the newspaper was being published in the Copper Country. The composition of Finnish immigrant and Finnish American political and labor organizations changed for good after the 1913–14 Copper Country Strike, and as it went, the ideological pieces were never put back together again. Finnish immigrant and Finnish American political and labor organizations certainly went on to play major roles in other labor-capital conflicts, such as the 1916 IWW strike on Minnesota's Iron Range, but "Finns" never regained the political-labor synergism that led to a collective, ideologically inclusive proletarian effort that challenged the perceived inequalities of the early twentieth-century industrial setting.

The story of the Finnish immigrants' socialist-unionist movement in Hancock adds to the overall American labor literature a detailed perspective on how an ethnic neighborhood coalesced around industrial issues to organize a significant challenge to corporate mining power. Today, Finnish ethnic identity in the Copper Country is celebrated with festivals and food samplings. Yet little memory is left of the working-class identity created between 1904 and 1914 in the Hancock Finnish community around the struggle for industrial democracy.

Perhaps one of the more salient points of this story, however, is that while Finnish immigrant socialist-unionists worked to maintain ethnic solidarity and identity through their publications and social-hall activities, they also reached out to "other" Copper Country workers. By printing non-Finnish-language publications, by translating English-language publications into Finnish, and by opening the doors of their hall and publishing company to Copper Country proletarians in a time of great tumult, the Finnish immigrant socialist-unionists succeeded in gaining the interest of, and joining with, other working ethnicities in the Copper Country.

In sum, possibly the most noteworthy accomplishment of the Finnish immigrant socialist-unionists in the Copper Country was that as a largely unskilled group of immigrant laborers, newspaper employees, and "hobo" socialists, they had a very considerable impact on the history of a place that was dominated by powerful mining companies and the men who ran those companies. Finnish immigrant socialist-unionists in Hancock grew a small upstart cultural organization, with a small upstart publishing company, into a force that could contend with the power of monopoly capital in the Copper Country. This was truly remarkable, a challenge accepted by Finnish immigrant socialist-unionists to have a say in their own working conditions in a place dominated by a mining oligarchy; but embedded in this study of ethnic political-labor history is also a story of division and decline that ultimately and terminally fractured a truly proletarian movement dedicated to working-class solidarity. This demise is significant when recounting the capabilities and vulnerabilities of the American labor movement in the early twentieth century.

Epilogue

So, what became of some other major "players" in the Finnish immigrant socialist-unionist saga? It can be deduced that the vestiges of the Finnish immigrant socialists and the members of the Finnish-American labor movement in Hancock continued to congregate at the Kansankoti Hall, though likely on a smaller organizational scale and certainly never as unified as when *Työmies* had its headquarters in Hancock. The Kansankoti Hall became the home of the communistic Finnish Americans, who supported revolutionary, "dictatorship of the proletarian" political actions. While many of the major "players" in the early socialist-unionist movement left the area, some die-hard socialist-unionist elements from the TPC's days in Hancock remained. Men such as Herman Louko and John Nummivuori, both members of the publishing company while in Hancock, stayed to manage, respectively, the Kansankoti Hall and the Farmer's Co-op Trading Company, which sold groceries, farm implements, and a full line of general merchandise.[1]

The Farmer's Co-op and Trading Company took over the mercantile space that the Työmies Publishing Company once occupied at 201–203 Franklin Street.[2] Research has not indicated how long the Kansankoti Hall was in operation, but people were still living in apartments there as of 1917. The hall underwent demolition sometime between 1917 and 1938, and the store with frontage at 201–203 Franklin was demolished sometime after 1938.[3] At the site once known as the Finnish socialist-unionist cultural center of the Midwest, there is now Neil's Taxicab stand.

Leo Laukki maintained his close association with the Work People's College. After he became head of the Finnish American wing of the IWW, he was imprisoned as part of the IWW's Chicago 166 in 1918. Jail changed his ideological views, and Laukki came out of jail a Communist and escaped to Russia in 1921. He rose to prominence in Soviet Russia, but died during a Stalinist purge.[4]

V. S. Alanne, capable but bourgeois-branded editor of *Työmies*, went on to a rather stellar career educating, managing, organizing, and writing in the Finnish American cooperative movement. Alanne was also a respected editor and translator of books. He continued to work on his Finnish-English dictionary, adding to its voluminous size. Alanne seems to have continued his efforts in the workers' movement, but never again claimed affiliation with any particular group.[5]

Martin Hendrickson, socialist orator and original Apostle of Finnish Socialism, continued in the Finnish American labor-political movement. Hendrickson bought into the ill-fated Russian policy to populate the Soviet Republic of Karelia in the mid to late 1930s with Finnish North Americans and Finnish nationals. Hendrickson left for Karelia, just across the border from northeastern Finland, and was never heard from again. He likely died in the Stalinist purges of 1938, known as the horrifying "Karelian Finns' year of terror."[6]

John Välimäki continued to work in the Finnish immigrant socialist-unionist movement. After the split, Välimäki moved east and joined the staff of the Raivaaja Publishing Company in Fitchburg, Massachusetts. In the split, many of the eastern U.S. Finnish Socialist Federation locals sided with the Socialist Party of America. Apparently, Välimäki stayed with the socialists and was a lifelong member. His years as an organizer appeared to have ended when the Western Federation of Miners folded.[7]

Evert Björklund, type composer for the Työmies Publishing Company, followed the company to Superior in 1914. His wife Laina (Ollila) Björklund attempted to keep the family together while Evert was away. The family, now composed of three children, alternated homes between Superior and Hancock. Libby Koski-Björklund, oral history subject for this book, was born in 1919—which was also the last year Laina made the attempt to move back and forth between households. For a time, Evert maintained contact with his family, sending postcards and the occasional money order.

During the early 1920s, Laina and the children moved from Hancock to a farm near Oskar Bay in the small Finnish American agricultural community of Heinola. According to Libby, after the early to mid-1920s Evert seldom made trips back to the Copper Country. When he did, he would stay in a cabin away from his wife and children on the family's property near Oskar Bay along the Portage Lake Canal. Laina and the children had to perform the daily tasks and upkeep of the farm without Evert's help. When he retired from the publishing company, Evert moved back to the Copper Country, but never resumed normal relations with his family, living with a bachelor fisherman in the cabin on the Canal. Laina, possibly out of disgust with the failed relationship, left the socialist-labor movement and cancelled all subscriptions to Työmies Publishing Company publications. Libby does not remember ever seeing the name *Työmies* in their household.[8]

It is easy to become fascinated with the large-scale episodes and events of major movements within American history, but events like the Copper Country Strike also had very real impacts on individual people and their families. Libby Koski-Björklund never knew her father, because of his association with the Työmies Publishing Company and their commitment to the working-class struggle. All Libby has to remember of her father are the recollections of relatives (who considered Evert to have very beautiful handwriting), a journal, photographs, and a handful of small landscape paintings Evert created as a younger man.[9]

Lastly, what became of the Finnish immigrants' socialist-unionist press in the Midwest? After the loss of *Työmies*, in 1914 the Finnish Socialist Federation's IWW faction began to publish its own newspaper, titled *Sosialisti* (The Socialist), in Duluth, Minnesota. In the early years of the newspaper's publication, likely because of the freshness of the split, it was quite similar in ideology to *Työmies*. At a 1915 meeting, the paper became an official organ of the IWW, and left the Finnish Socialist Federation soon after.[10] The paper underwent two name changes in the next two years. The change in name reflected a hard turn to the radical "left," and in 1916 the name of the paper became *Teolisuustyöläinen* (Industrial Worker). The newspaper and its supporters were now united in support of revolutionary industrial unionism and eschewed political action. The next year, 1917, saw the paper change its name once again, becoming the *Industrialisti* (The Industrialist). At this time, the paper was available for subscription to members of the IWW only. By 1919, *Industrialisti* had over 10,000 subscribers. Its popularity declined after World War I, and readership fell off incrementally thereafter. However, *Industrialisti* maintained enough of a base to continue publication into the 1970s.[11]

As for one of our major "characters" in this story, after leaving Hancock the Työmies Publishing Company continued its assault on capitalism for over eighty years. For the Työmies Publishing Company, the pace of change in Superior was incremental, but eventually *Työmies* became "a loyal servant of the Communist Party in America," though it never became an officially sanctioned newspaper of the Party.[12] On August 20, 1950, *Työmies* joined ranks with an eastern United States communist Finnish-language newspaper known as the *Eteenpäin* (Forward). The merger was likely the result of declining readership through loss of its older, loyal subscription base. The *T-E*, as its readers knew it, continued publication at various frequencies until its last issue, a monthly, came out in July 1998. For much of its life, *T-E* remained a predominantly Finnish-language publication. The *Finnish American Reporter* was an English-language offshoot publication of *T-E*, begun in 1986. The Työmies Society of Superior, Wisconsin, deeded the *Finnish American Reporter* to Finlandia University, the former Suomi College, in 2000. The *Reporter* is currently published on the campus of Finlandia University in Hancock, Michigan.[13]

While in Superior, the Työmies Publishing Company later became the Työmies Society, headquartered in a building at 601 Tower Avenue in Superior that stands to this day. In its later life, and after the last issue of *Työmies-Eteenpäin* came off the press, the Työmies Society building became the Työmies Bar, still serving a decidedly working-class clientele. I shudder to think what the early members of the Jousi might have thought about their newspaper's former home, born out of temperance ideals, being home to a bar, working-class clientele or not. The former Työmies building sits in a ramshackle, postindustrial setting, adjacent to at least two strip clubs. There is a palpable irony in the fact that a building that was once unquestionably in a Red *enlightenment* district is now in a decidedly red-light *entertainment* district.

APPENDIX 1

Työmies Publishing Company Staff and Contributors, 1909

NAME	BORN/IMMIGRATED	EDUCATION
Aaltonen, Frank	Hämeenlinna 1885/1905	Kansankoulu*
Joined SDP in Finland, 1901; worked in mines in U.S.; lecturer; WFM organizer		
Alatalo, Kalle	Puolanka 1882/1907	People's College
Attended Liminka People's College in Finland, 1901–02; wrote for *Helsingin Sanomat*; SDP agitator and organizer, 1907; joined SPA, 1907; worked in American mines; wrote for *Työmies* and annual publications		
Askeli, Henry	Hailuoto 1886/1901	Art school
Attended Lockwood-Stoltz Art School in U.S.; joined SPA in 1907; wrote and drew comics for *Työmies* and other special editions		
Gröndahl, K. E.	Eurajoki 1882/1902	Valparaiso
Attended English-language courses at Valparaiso, 1907; joined SPA, 1904; worked in woods and iron mining; editor *Työkansa*; *Työmies* office manager; socialist lecturer; translator and writer *Työmies*		

Haataja, Kalle L. Paltamo 1872/1904 Oulu lyseo

Worked in woods, mines, at a pharmacy, and for a newspaper; studied mathematics and geology in college; instructor and board member of Kansan Opisto (name before WPC); joined SPA, 1907; formerly an instructor at a mining college in Rolla, Mo.

Hahl, Moses Liperi 1879/1886 Kansankoulu

Joined SPA; worked with printing machines before coming to the TPC; noted writer of socialist press in America

Hantula, Herman Lapua 1866/1889 None stated

Worked as a miner and farmer in America; joined Sointula commune; after Sointula fire he left with his wife and four children to farm in the Dakotas; wrote about party news

Hautamäki, Alfred Kymi 1885/1901 None stated

Alternative last name Jacobson; joined workers' movement in Finland, 1900; lectured and wrote on workers' issues; attended Cleveland and Hancock organizational meetings; was a member of *Työmies* in Worcester; spent 5 years lecturing on East Coast and Midwest, including in Chicago, Ill., Quincy, Mass., Negaunee and Ironwood, Mich.

Hendrickson, Mart. Kivijärvi 1872/1889 None stated

One of the early Finnish socialist immigrants; editor of *Työmies*; lectured across the Midwest and East Coast

Hiltunen, Toivo Oulu 1880/1901 Commercial school

In America, first worked in Hancock; joined the Hancock Jousi; moved to Minnesota, 1902–03; migrated to Astoria, Oregon, 1903, and joined Socialist local; moved back to Hancock, 1906, and worked at TPC as a type composer, editor, and translator

Holland, Selma Lohtaja 1882/1883 None stated

Maiden name Jokela; joined SPA, 1908; writer for *Työmies* and other socialist party publications; became editor for *Toveritar* as Selma Jokela McCone

Hukkala, Emil Savonlinna 1867/Unk Kansankoulu
Noted publisher, worked as a publisher in Finland for 11 years; member of the Canadian Socialist Party

Jokinen, Henry Tampere 1885/1902 Kansankoulu
Wrote for *Kansan Lehti* in Finland; wrote poetry and party news for *Työmies*

Kainu, Matti Veteli 1883/1900 Work People's Coll.
Joined SPA, 1905; attended WPC, 1908–09; worked in mines; wrote stories and about party news and events

Kankaanpää, Sak. Kannus 1879/1889 Kansan Opisto
Became interested in socialism in 1904; joined SPA, 1906; wrote for *Toveri* and *Työmies*; attended Kansan Opisto before it became WPC and was a leading figure in criticism of religious instruction at Kansan Opisto

Kannasto, Sanna Ylihärmä 1878/1899 None stated
Joined SPA, 1905; organizer in East and Midwest, 1907; lectured throughout Canada and the U.S.; very active in FSF affairs; wrote for *Työmies*, *Raivaaja*, and *Työkansa*

Karvonen, Juho Kuopio 1867/1904 None stated
Store worker in Finland; worked 2 years at *Raivaaja*; joined workers' movement in Finland, 1889, and SPA in 1906; writer for publications since 1890

Kolu, John Muola 1877/1888 English lang. school
Wrote for Ashtabula, Ohio, newspaper, 1891–92; worked in Ohio coal mines; got his "schooling" during big strikes of coal regions in 1891–92; joined SPA, 1902; worked in northern Minnesota mines; lecturer, striker, and WFM organizer; wrote for *Raivaaja* and *Työmies*; instructor at WPC; and joined IWW

Korpi, John Ruovesi 1884/1905 Kansankoulu +
Joined workers' movement in Finland, 1902; worked mines in America, which brought him to socialism; writer and poet; organizer in the Midwest

Laukki, Leo Helsinki 1880/1907 Lyseo

Editor at *Raivaaja* and *Työmies*; instructor at Work People's College; socialist theorist; edited *Kansan Lehti* for 6 years in Finland; worked in Russia and Germany

Leikas, Wilho Pieksämäki 1879/1904 Kansankoulu

Joined Imatra League in Calumet, Mich., then the SPA; writer and lecturer; attended Hibbing Conference to found FSF; set up a number of FSF locals in the Midwest and was an effective organizer

Leino, Leo Karttula 1882/1903 Agitation courses

Attended agitation courses in Turku via stipend, 1903; joined labor movement in Finland, 1899; worked in Russia and Sweden; spent time lecturing in Oulu; representative in Forssa SDP meetings; lectured western U.S. and Canada, 1906; returned to Finland in 1906, but returned to U.S. in 1907; wrote about party news and activities

Nieminen, Alex Laukaa 1865/1903 Kansankoulu

Joined workers' movement in Finland, 1894; Helsinki workers' group, 1895; editor of strike publications in Tampere; joined SDP; involved in early efforts to establish the TPC and served as board member, *Työmies* editor, contributor, and business manager

Pasanen, Ida Asikkala 1872/1903 None stated

Joined the SDP in Finland, 1898; active in and helped to found the women's section of the SDP; lectured in Finland and America; joined the FSF in America; organized FSF locals in Minnesota; maiden name Nurminen

Pesola, Richard Kaustinen 1886/1905 None stated

Joined Socialist Party of America (SPA), 1906; lecturer; wrote for and helped the Työmies Publishing Company's editorial staff; author of several Finnish titles

Rauhala, Jaakko Vimpeli (unknown) Kansankoulu

Worked in copper and iron mines; joined SPA, 1903; lecturer and writer for *Työmies* and other publications; organizer in western United States

Saari, Onni Kauhava 1887/1905 Work People's Coll.

Joined SPA, 1908; wrote about party news and activities; attended WPC, 1908–09; worked in mines for a while

Saarimaa, Hem. Alajärvi 1885/1903 Work People's Coll.

Worked in woods and rock quarries; joined SPA, 1906; attended WPC, 1907–08; wrote about party news and activities

Salmi, Adolf Veteli 1882/1904 None stated

AKA Matti Aatto Salmela; joined SPA, 1906; worked in coal mines; wrote about party news and events, penned poetry, and drew illustrations

Salmi, John E. Kotka 1884/1906 Work People's Coll.

Joined SDP, 1904; wrote in Finnish press and lectured in Finland; worked iron and coal mines in U.S.; attended WPC, 1908; wrote about party news and activities

Salminen, John Hämeenlinna 1875/1903 Work People's Coll.

Worked several industrial jobs; joined SPA, 1905; writer for *Työmies* and *Raivaaja*; attended Work People's College, 1907–08; editor at TPC, 1908

Sarell, Antti O. 1881/1901 Confirmation school

Joined Imatra League, 1904 and the SPA, 1905; TPC editor, 1908; member of Finnish Socialist Federation and Midwestern organization committee

Savela, Evert Huittinen 1875/1902 None stated

Joined workers' movement in Finland, 1898; member of Sointula commune, 1902; joined SPA, 1904; wrote poetry, lectured, wrote party news, and was an organizer in the Midwest

Syrjälä, Frans J. Kauvatsa 1880/1903 None stated

Joined workers' movement in Finland, 1897; began writing for socialist press, *Kansan Lehti*, and *Työmies* in Finland; editor at *Raivajaa* for 3 years; lecturer

Toivola, Kalle Terijoki 1884/1907 None stated

AKA Tolle Kaivola; joined SPA, 1907; wrote about party news in Finland before coming to the U.S.

Välimäki, John Lapua 1884/1901 Kansankoulu

Western Federation of Miners agitator and organizer; member of SPA; editor at Työmies Publishing Company

Wierikko, Edw. Ruovesi 1877/1902 Kansankoulu

Worked in woods, mines, and steel industry; joined SPA, 1906; involved in organization of Marquette, Mich., FSF local; in Marquette, led general boycott against mine owners during spring of 1909 and organized the iron dock workers' strike in autumn of 1909; wrote American national party and SPA news

Source: Köyhälistön Nuija 4 (1910): 160–178.

ABBREVIATIONS
FSF–Finnish Socialist Federation, America
IWW–Industrial Workers of the World
SDP–Social Democratic Party, Finland
SPA–Socialist Party of America
WFM–Western Federation of Miners
WPC–Work People's College

*Kansankoulu was the early Finnish version of public school. It consisted of either a four- or an eight-year primary education. In the cases above, no distinction is made as to duration of education in the Kansankoulu system.

APPENDIX 2

Työmies Publishing Company Interior Use of Space

THIS IS AN AUTHOR RECREATION OF LIKELY ELEMENTS OF THE SPATIAL LAYOUT of the TPC publishing buildings. This layout and subsequent floor plans are the "best educated guess" of the author according to historic photos assembled from *Työmies 10 Vuotias* and the Immigration History Research Center's COLLAGE online database.

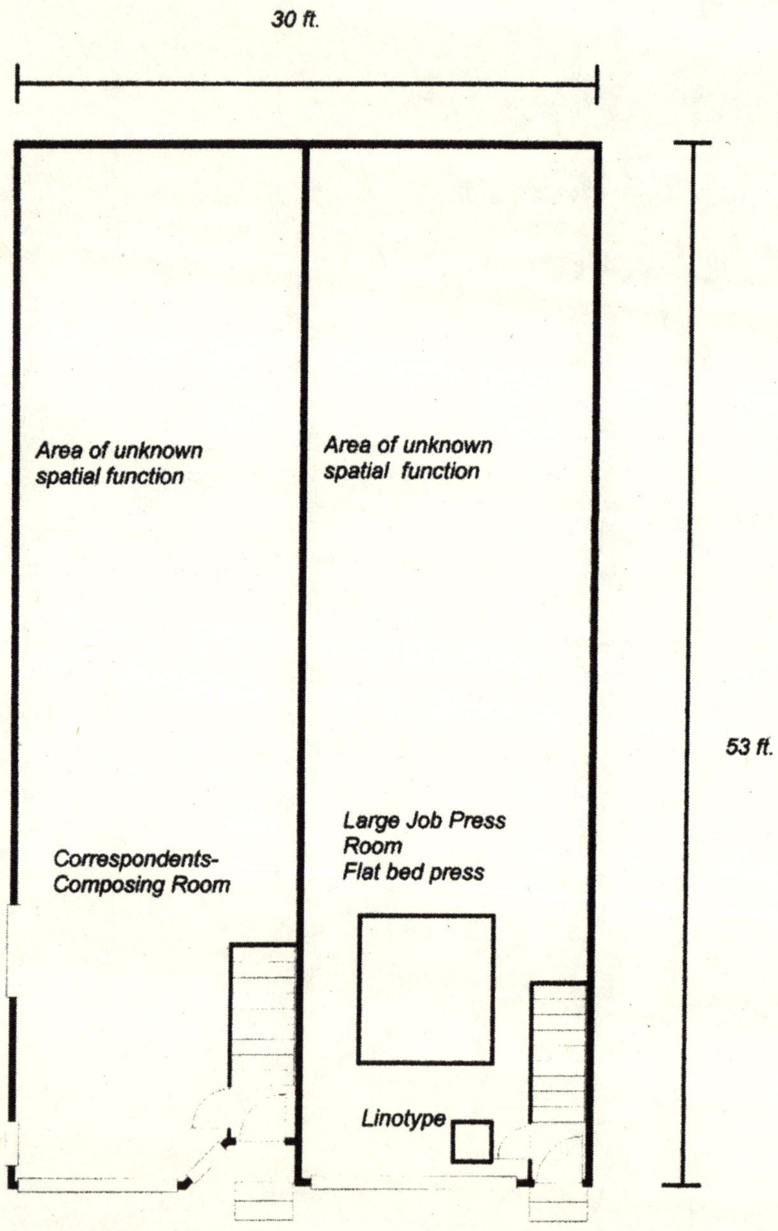

Työmies Office Building, First Floor. (Gary Kaunonen.)

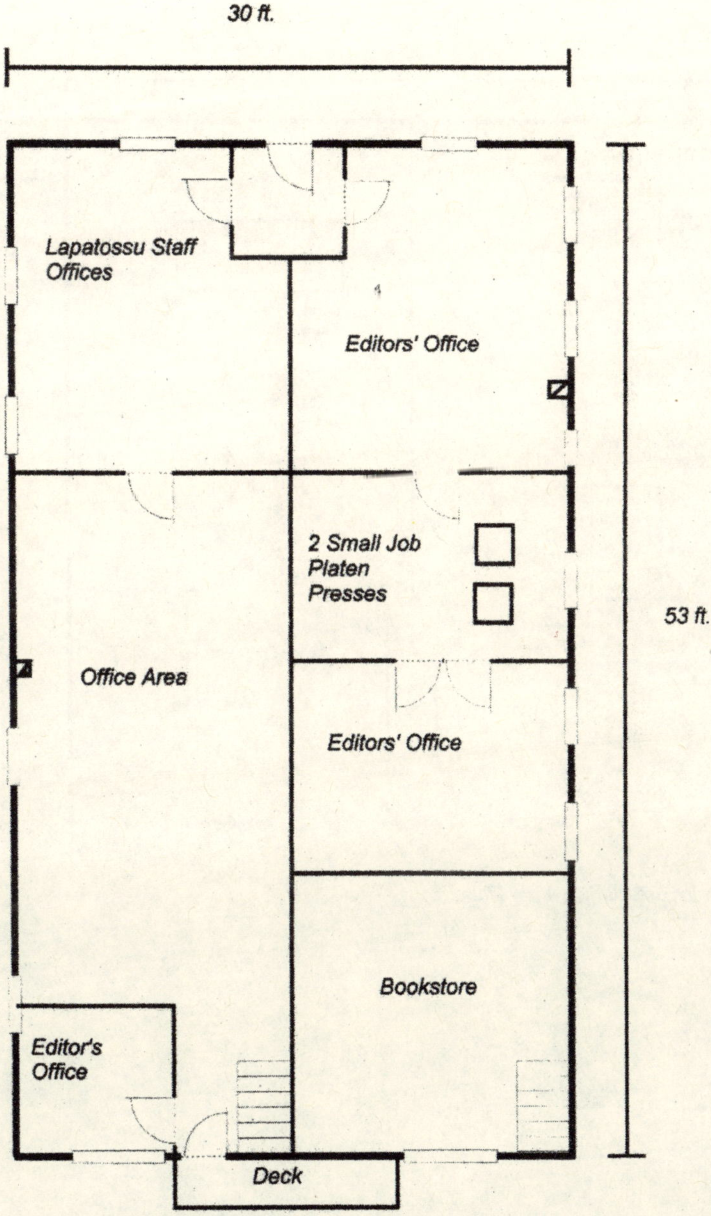

Työmies Office Building, Second Floor. (Gary Kaunonen.)

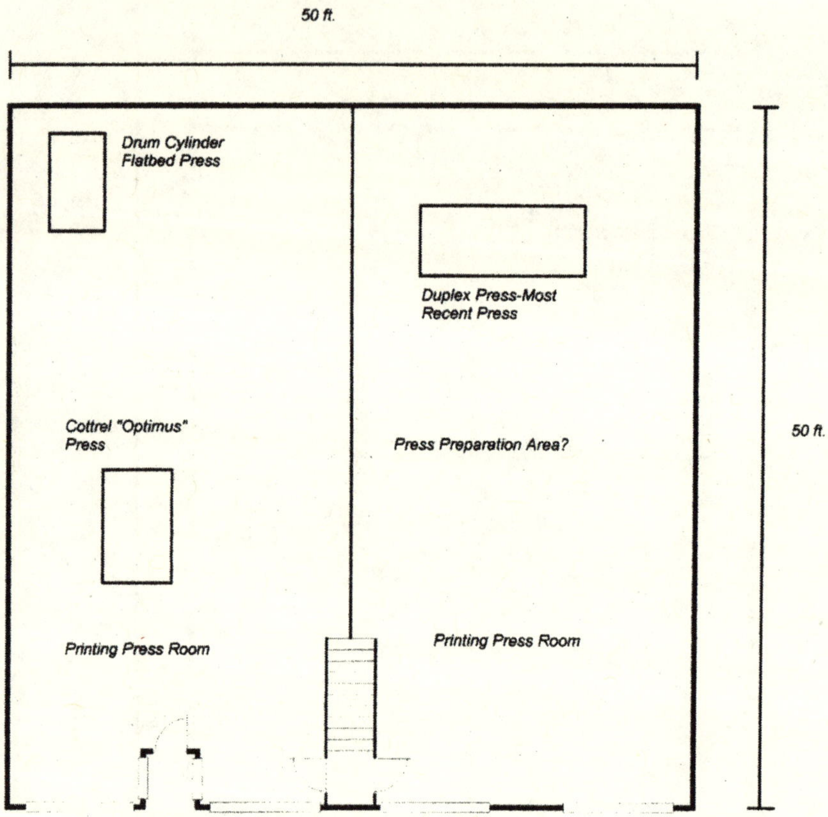

Työmies Press Building, First Floor. (Gary Kaunonen.)

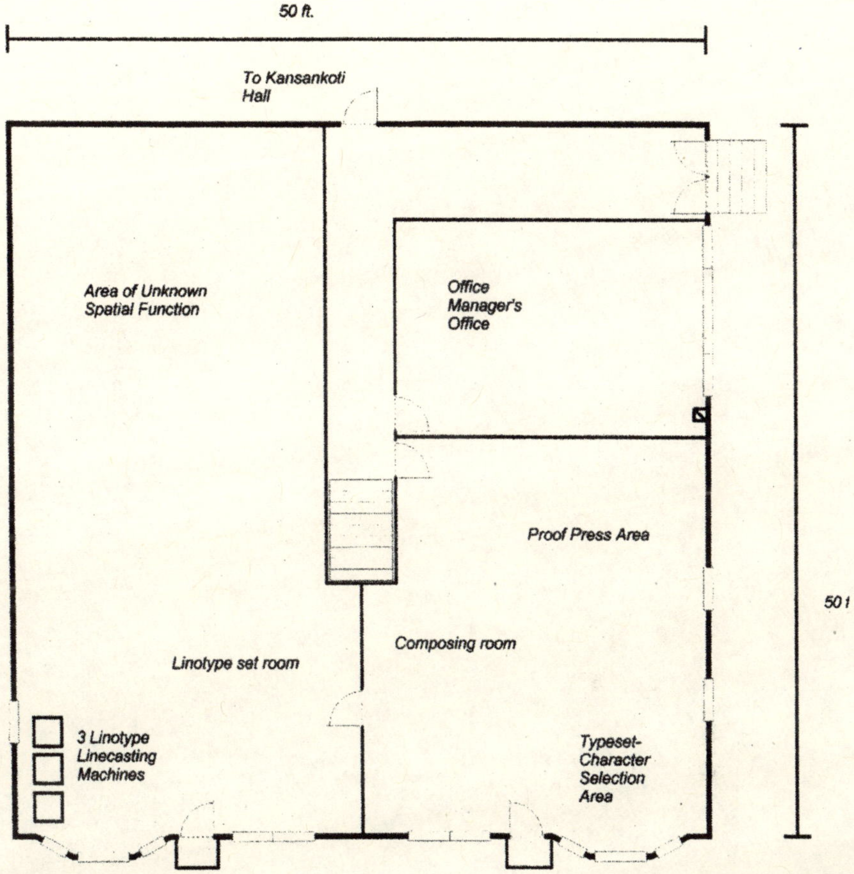

Työmies Press Building, Second Floor. (Gary Kaunonen.)

APPENDIX 3

Copper Territory Strikers' March, 1913

March of the Copper Territory Strikers

(Tune: *Varsovalainen*)

Copper miners have gallantly risen
To fight against oppression and exploitation
From a long dream like a wintry bear
To demand human rights
We have slept enough already and been slaves
Just kissing MacNaughton's whip
Let's rise brothers and throw the chains
Into the dirty oppressors faces

To the fight for human rights
For our bread
Off, off miners off you go!

Copper Island the cradle of darkness
The "promised land" of scabs
All 'round America the cry has been shouted
We guarantee it will not continue
God does not help, that time has gone
We gallantly raise our heads high
Though there are many languages,
there is only one mind
When rising quickly to fight

To the fight for human rights
For our bread
Off, off miners off you go!

Long has the American working class
Waited for the fight,
MacNaughton has mockingly given potato peels
To feed to his slaves
Are still suffering as toiling brothers
The dirty mocking of the Masters?
We swear, the fight will not end
Until mine magnates are on their knees

To the fight for human rights
For our bread
Off, off miners off you go!

Source: "March of the Copper Territory Strikers," *Työmies*, 1913 (translated by Anna Leppänen).

APPENDIX 4

Työmies Publishing Company's Composite List of Italian Hall Deceased, 1913

THOSE IN ITALICS ARE NOT LISTED IN THE CORONER'S INQUEST, AND INFORMATION in brackets are alternatively listed names.[1] NG = Not given.

	NAME [ALTERNATE NAME(S)]	AGE	ADDRESS
1.	Ala, Herman	50–66	16 Bust Street, Tamarack
2.	Aho, Lempi [Lempi Ala]	8	366 Caledonia St., Calumet[2]
3.	Aaltonen, Wilma	7	548 Wyandot, Florida Location
4.	Aaltonen, Sanna [Mrs. Oscar]	30	548 Wyandot, Florida Location
5.	Aaltonen, Sylvia	5	548 Wyandot, Florida Location
6.	Branze, Mrs. Kate [Bronzo]	28	108 Calumet St., Laurium
7.	Bueff, Ilka [Blof]	4	4994 Waterworks St., Calumet
8.	Butala, Joseph	8	118 3rd St., Centennial Heights
9.	Burcar, Victoria [Burcer]	12	126 North Kearsarge
10.	Gregorich, Kate	10	17 Back St., Centennial Mine
11.	Heikkinen, John [Eino]	9	Water St., Wolverine
12.	Heikkinen, Edward	5	Water St., Wolverine
13.	Heikkinen, Isaac	7	Water St., Wolverine

14.	Isola, Mrs. Henry [Tilma]	35	2516 D St., Raymbaultown[3]
15.	Isola, Philemina [Ina]	baby	2516 D St., Raymbaultown
16.	Jesick, Mrs. Barbara [Jesit]	35	2406 B St. Raymbaultown
17.	Jesick, Rosie	baby	2406 B St. Raymbaultown
18.	Jackoletti, Jenni [Jacoletto]	6	369 7th St., Wolverine
19.	Jokipii, Uno [Sam]	16	Raymbaultown
20.	*Kempi, John*	*4*	*120 1st St., Centennial Heights*[4]
21.	Kiemunki [Johan E. Kremanki]	boy	Centennial Heights
22.	Klarich, Christina	5	Waterworks St., Calumet
23.	Klarich, Mary	—	Waterworks St., Calumet
24.	Klarich, Kate	—	Waterworks St., Calumet
25.	Kotajärvi, Anna [Mrs. Matt]	—	353 Franklin St., Florida Location[5]
26.	Kotajärvi, Anna [girl]	4	353 Franklin St., Florida Location
27.	*Kotajärvi, Amy*	*3*	*353 Franklin St., Florida Location*
28.	Rytilahti, Emelia	NG[6]	
29.	Rytilahti, Heli	NG	
30.	Kalunki, Mrs. Peter [Brida Liisa]	35	364 3rd St., Centennial Heights
31.	Kalunki, Efia	6	364 3rd St., Centennial Heights
32.	Kalunki, Anna E.	4	364 3rd St., Centennial Heights
33.	Kärkelä, John	—	Copper City
34.	Krunich, Mary [Mary Krentz] [Kranjac, Marija, 10][7]	12	22 Tamarack Jr. Location
35.	*Krunich, Mrs.*	—	*22 Tamarack Jr. Location*
36.	Lauri, John [Sula Rubet]	4	350 Centennial Heights
37.	Lesar, Ralph [Rafael]	5	229 7th St., Red Jacket
38.	Lesar, Mary [Mamie]	11	229 7th St., Red Jacket
39.	*Lesar, Rachel [Mrs. Rachel]*	—	*229 7th St., Red Jacket*
40.	Lustig, Jacob [Alper C. W.]	5	Raymbaultown
41.	Lindström, Arthur	12	Pine St., Calumet
42.	Luomi, Lydia [Luoma]	5	124 3rd St., Centennial Heights
43.	Lantto, Mrs. [Mary G. Lanto]	35	Lake Linden Road, Dover Farm
44.	Lantto, girl [Hilja K.]	girl	Dover
45.	Manley, Wesley	4	North Tamarack Location
46.	Manley, Elina [Mrs. Herman]	35	North Tamarack Location[8]

47.	Manly, girl [Saida Raja]	11	North Tamarack Location[9]
48.	Mihelchich, Agnes	—	Waterworks St., Calumet
49.	Mihelchich, Paul	5	Waterworks St., Calumet
50.	Mihelchich, Elizabeth	NG	
51.	Montanen, Ella E. [Elfreda]	NG	
52.	Montanen, Mathias E. [Eddie]	NG	
53.	Montanen, Geza H. [George]	NG	
54.	*Montanen, Albert*	*3*	*22 Cherry St., No. 5 Tamarack*[10]
55.	Murto, Matt [Walter]	6	Walnut St., No. 5 Tamarack
56.	Myllykangas, boy [Johan W.]	5	County Road, Osceola
57.	Myllykangas, boy [Edward Emil]	3	County Road, Osceola
58.	*Nauer, Samma*	*5*	*Not given*[11]
59.	Niemala, Abram	—	No. 4 Shaft, Wolverine
60.	Niemala, Mrs. [Mary E.]	35	No. 4 Shaft, Wolverine
61.	Papsh, Annie [Mrs. Antone]	52	307 (305) High St., Osceola
62.	Papsh, Mary	20	307 (305) High St., Osceola
63.	Peteri, Mrs. Kate	60–66	4016 Portland St., Calumet
64.	Piira, William [Piri]	5	Residence unknown
65.	Renaldi, Tracy [Terresa]	13	46 North Tamarack
66.	Ristell, Ellen [Elena W. Ristelli]	5	Iroquois St., Laurium
67.	Saari, John [Yalmer]	5	Iroquois and 7th St., Laurium
68.	Saatia, Alina [Elida, Alita]	6	Centennial Heights
69.	Smuk, Mamie [Mary]	7	2406 B St., Raymbaultown
70.	Staudahar, Frances [Antonia]	10	288 Mine St., Osceola
71.	Cvelkovich, Nick [Svetkovich]	—	8 Butler House, Red Jacket
72.	Taipalus, Sandra M.	5	Centennial Heights
73.	Taipalus, Elena [Elina Taipalos]	6	Centennial Heights
74.	Takala, Henry [Edward Takola]	—	310 Iroquois, Laurium
75.	Talpaka, Ida [Juto Tallbach]	4	26 Chestnut St., Tamarack
76.	Tulppo, Mrs. Henry [Kaisa G.]	42	123 N. Iroquois, Florida Location
77.	Tulppo, Mamie L.	4	123 N. Iroquois, Florida Location
78.	Wuolukka, Helga [Hilja]	42	366 Caledonia St., Calumet
79.	Westola, John P. [J. P.]	48	Secretary Farmers' Mutual Ins.

Notes

Introduction

1. Houghton County, State of Michigan, "Coroner's Inquest Transcript," December 31, 1913, Labor and Political Collection, Italian Hall Materials, manuscript box K-17, Finnish American Historical Archive: Hancock, Michigan, 150–151.
2. Ibid., 133–134.
3. Ibid., 63.
4. Ibid., 35–36.
5. Ibid., 165–166 and 168.
6. Ibid., 131.
7. Ibid., 94.
8. Ibid., 37–38.
9. Ibid., 157–158.
10. Ibid., 1–4.
11. This letter also made its way to the United States secretary of labor. Larry Lankton, *Cradle to Grave: Life, Work and Death at the Lake Superior Copper Mines* (New York: Oxford University Press, 1991), 211–212.

12. For a socio-technological history of paternalism in the Copper Country, see Lankton's *Cradle to Grave.*
13. In this book, we will use the term *capital* and *monopoly capital* interchangeably to explain that a few large mining companies, such as Calumet and Hecla, Quincy, and Copper Range had great influence on both the industrial and social milieu. Thus, capital and monopoly capital are used as descriptive words, originating from Harry Braverman's discussion of monopoly capitalism in which he writes, "Monopoly capital had its beginnings . . . in the last two or three decades of the nineteenth century. It was then that the concentration and centralization of capital, in the early form of trusts, cartels and other forms of combination began to assert itself." Harry Braverman, *Labor and Monopoly Capital: The Degradation of Work in the Twentieth Century*, 25th anniversary edition (New York: Monthly Review Press, 1998), 175.
14. Thomas J. Schlereth, "Social History Scholarship and Material Culture Research," in *Material Culture: A Research Guide* (Lawrence: University Press of Kansas, 1985), 156.
15. Ibid., 157.
16. Ibid., 156–157.

Chapter 1. Finnish Immigration and Settlement in a Hancock, Michigan, Neighborhood

1. Michael G. Karni, *For the Common Good* (PhD diss., University of Minnesota, 1975), 35–38; and Arthur Puotinen, *Finnish Radicals and Religion in Midwestern Mining Towns* (New York: Arno Press, 1979), 24–26.
2. Osmo Jussila, Seppo Hentilä, and Jukka Nevakivi, *From Grand Duchy to Modern State: A Political History of Finland since 1809*, translated from Finnish by David and Eva-Kaisa Arter (Carbondale: Southern Illinois University Press, 1999), 79–83, 90.
3. Elis Sulkanen, *Amerikan Suomalaisen Työväenliikkeen Historia* (Fitchburg, Mass.: Amerikan Suomalainen Kansanvallan Liitto ja Raivaaja Publishing Company, 1951), 485–503.
4. Ibid.

5. Fred Torma, interview by Douglas Ollila, August 3, 1973, oral history interview transcript, Finnish American Historical Archive, Finlandia University, Hancock, Michigan, 19–20.
6. Peter Kivisto, "The Decline of the Finnish-American Left," *International Migration Review* 17, no. 1 (1983): 68.
7. Clemens Niemi, *Americanization of the Finnish People in Houghton County, Michigan* (Duluth, Minn.: Finnish Daily Publishing Company, 1921), 9.
8. Ibid., 8–12.
9. Auvo Kostianen, *The Forging of Finnish-American Communism, 1917–1924: A Study in Ethnic Radicalism* (Turku, Finland: Turun Yliopisto, 1978), 19.
10. The English ethnicity accounted for 4,459, the Italians 2,634, and French Canadians 2,616 of Houghton County's total population. The Department of Commerce and Labor, *The 13th Census of the United States of America: Bulletin Population Michigan* (Washington, D.C.: Government Printing Office, 1910).
11. Charles K. Hyde, *Historic American Engineering Report: Quincy Mining Company* (Washington, D.C.: Department of the Interior, 1978), 196–200.
12. Larry D. Lankton and Charles K. Hyde, *Old Reliable: An Illustrated History of the Quincy Mining Company* (Hancock, Mich.: Quincy Mine Hoist Association, 1982), 152.
13. Hyde, *Historic American Engineering Report*, 196–200.
14. Lankton, *From Cradle to Grave*, 154–155.
15. The Village of Hancock, platted in 1859, was also originally QMC land, but was parceled into lots early and became a municipality separate from the QMC, but not devoid of latent QMC influence. Lankton and Hyde, *Old Reliable*, 35.
16. Keith P. Baird and Erin C. Timms, "Quincy Hillside Addition," unpublished National Historic District Nomination, 2005, Copper Country Historical Archive, Michigan Technological University, Houghton, Michigan, 3.
17. G. Walton Smith, "Houghton County Census," unpublished report, "Vertical Files: Finnish Immigration," Copper Country Historical Collections, Michigan Technological University, Houghton, Michigan.
18. Niemi, *Americanization of the Finnish People*, 40.
19. The designation "Finnish" includes Swedish-Finnish as well.
20. R. L. Polk & Co., Houghton County Directories, Hancock and Red Jacket City Directories, 1912, 257–412.

21. It is unclear what became of Maria's husband and Laina's father. There are no records of him ever joining his wife and daughter in America. Perhaps he died, or maybe he left his family. For whatever reason, Maria felt compelled to make the voyage to America with her daughter alone. Libby Koski-Björklund, interview by Gary Kaunonen, oral history interview, Finnish American Historical Archive, Finlandia University, Hancock, Michigan, March 2006.
22. Institute of Migration, Turku Finland, *Passenger Records*, www.migrationinstitute.fi/pl_engdetail.asp?snimi=QYH0R002Q (accessed August 18, 2006).
23. Both residential-district businesses and commercial-district businesses were included in this category.
24. Houghton County Tax Rolls, Hancock First Ward, 1911, Copper Country Historical Archive, Michigan Technological University, Houghton, Michigan.
25. R. L. Polk & Co., Houghton County Directories, Hancock Directory, 1912, 436. There were 471 data sets considered in this neighborhood study. Determination of ethnicity was by surname. Surnames were categorized as either Finnish, Swedish-Finnish, or non-Finnish. Those names that were indistinguishable were not included in the analysis. Ownership records for property in the neighborhood are found in Houghton County Tax Rolls, 1909 and 1914.
26. Houghton County Tax Rolls, Hancock First Ward, 1909 and 1914, Copper Country Historical Archive, Michigan Technological University, Houghton, Michigan.
27. Ibid.
28. Ibid.
29. Ibid.
30. Quincy Mining Company, "Scheme for Shanty Town," 1899, Quincy Mining Company Collection, Quincy Drawing 2019, Copper Country Historical Archive, Michigan Technological University, Houghton, Michigan; Houghton County Articles of Association, book 5, Copper Country Historical Archive, Michigan Technological University, Houghton, Michigan, 90–91.
31. *Työmies* and the TPC had been in Hancock at various locations since 1903. Michael M. Passi, "Finnish Immigrants and the Radical Response to Copper Country," in *For the Common Good: Finnish Immigrants and the Radical Response to Industrial America*, ed. Michael G. Karni and Douglas J. Ollila Jr. (Superior, Wisc.: Työmies Society, 1977).
32. Quincy Mining Company, "Quincy Hillside Addition Property Deeds," n.d.,

Quincy Mining Company Collection, Copper Country Historical Archive, Michigan Technological University, Houghton, Michigan. In 1909, Block B, Lot 5 was the site of a boarding house owned by Jacob Olgren. Olgren resided in the boarding house and worked at a blacksmith shop in the eastern adjacent lot owned by Henry Hendrickson. Olgren maintained ownership of the lot until 1914, when Hendrickson is listed as property owner; Houghton County Tax Rolls.

33. Antilla's Saloon was at 412 Tezcuco Street, two doors down from the KH-TPC's Block B, Lot 1; Houghton County Tax Records 1909 and Sanborn Insurance Company, "Hancock Sanborn Map," 1917, Copper Country Historical Archive, Michigan Technological University, Houghton, Michigan. In 1906, trammers led a strike at QMC; No. 5 to Quincy Mining Company, August 20, 1906.
34. N. A. Sampson to Quincy Mining Company, September 4, 1906, Quincy Mining Company Collection, box 341, folder 006, Copper Country Historical Archive, Michigan Technological University, Houghton, Michigan. Funkey's Hall was at 238 Quincy Street.
35. No. 5 to Quincy Mining Company, September 7, 1906.
36. Sampson to Quincy Mining Company, Chicago, September 17, 1906.
37. Sanborn Insurance Company, "Hancock Sanborn Map," 1893 and 1900, Copper Country Historical Archive, Michigan Technological University, Houghton, Michigan.
38. R. L. Polk & Co., "Hancock City Directories," Polk's Houghton County Directory (Detroit: R. L. Polk and Co.), 1906–1907.
39. Sanborn Insurance Company, "Hancock Sanborn Map," 1917, Copper Country Historical Archive, Michigan Technological University, Houghton, Michigan.
40. Houghton County Tax Rolls, Hancock First Ward, 1909.
41. Sanborn Insurance Company, Hancock Map, 1917. The KH-TPC complex spanned three addresses from 201–207 Franklin Street.
42. R. L. Polk & Co., Houghton County Directory, 1912, 257–412.
43. Ibid.
44. Ibid.
45. Ibid.
46. R. L. Polk & Co., Houghton County Directories 1912; Sanborn Insurance Company, Hancock Map, 1917; and Houghton County Tax Records, 1914.
47. No. 5 to Quincy Mining Company, September 7, 1906.

48. R. L. Polk & Co., Houghton County Directory, 1912; and Sanborn Insurance Company, Hancock Map, 1907 and 1917.

Chapter 2. Finnish Immigrant Cultural Organizations and the "Finn Hall"

1. Karni, *For the Common Good*, PhD diss., 12–13.
2. Helen K. Leiviska, interview by Arthur Puotinen, June 26, 1973, oral history interview transcript, Finnish American Historical Archive, Finlandia University, Hancock, Michigan, 6.
3. Karni, *For the Common Good*, PhD diss., 72–75.
4. Ibid.
5. Map 2 shows the spatial distribution of Finnish organizations from 1890–1915. The large gray circle represents the 15-mile radius around Hancock. Sanborn Insurance Co., Local City Maps for Hancock, Houghton (South Range), and Red Jacket, 1907–1917; Armas K. E. Holmio, *History of the Finns in Michigan*, translated by Ellen M. Ryynanen (Detroit: Wayne State University Press, 2001); Suomalaisten Socialistijärjestön Edustajakokouksen, *Pöytäkirja 1912* (Fitchburg, Mass.: Suomalainen Sosialisti Kustannus Yhtiö, 1912); and Reino Hannula, *An Album of Finnish Halls* (San Luis Obispo, Calif.: Finn Heritage, 1991).
6. The Knights of Kaleva were a Finnish immigrant version of the Free and Accepted Masons. The organizational group began in Montana in 1898 and grew to include thirty lodges with three thousand members by 1909. As the group was a secretive fraternal order that sought very few new members, and as social issues became a focus of Finnish cultural organizations, the Knights of Kaleva began to shrink in membership. "Kaleva Temple National Register of Historic Places Inventory—Nomination Form" (1977), Vertical Files Keweenaw National Historical Park, Calumet, Michigan, 1.
7. Holmio, *History of the Finns in Michigan*, 306–310.
8. Kaleva Temple National Register Form, 1.
9. Sanborn Insurance Company, Houghton (South Range) Map, 1907 and 1917.
10. Sarah Mimnaugh, "National Register of Historic Places Nomination Form, The South Range Finnish Socialist Hall," unpublished (2008), Finnish American

Historical Archive, Finlandia University, Hancock, Michigan, section 8, page 4, and section 7, page 1.

11. Holmio, *History of the Finns in Michigan*, 244.
12. Houghton County Tax Records, Hancock, Ward 1, 1909; and R. L. Polk & Co., Houghton County Directories, Hancock listings, 1903–1917. The Pojhantähti's former hillside home likely continued to function as a hall, listed in the 1910 and 1917 Polk's Directories as "the Old Finn Temperance Hall"; R. L. Polk & Co., Houghton County Directories, Hancock listings, 1910 and 1917. The Valon Sade Temperance Society organized in 1891, but had no listings of hall ownership; Holmio, *History of the Finns in Michigan*, 244.
13. Mrs. Hugo Klemetti, interview by Eero Ranta, July 22, 1973, oral history interview transcript, Finnish American Historical Archive, Finlandia University, Hancock, Michigan, 4.
14. A. William Hoglund, *Finnish Immigrants in America: 1880–1920* (Madison, Wisc.: University of Wisconsin Press, 1960), 44.
15. Carl Ross, "Essays on the Finnish American Community: 1865–1914, Part 2, The Finnish American Community Matures, 1885–1900," unpublished, n.d., Carl Ross Papers, Immigration History Research Center, University of Minnesota, Minneapolis, Minnesota, 5–6.
16. Holmio, *History of the Finns in Michigan*, 255–261.
17. Salomon Ilmonen, "Raittiusseura Pohjantähden 25–Vuotis Historia," translated by E. Olaf Rankinen (1994), in *Raittius Kalenteri 1911* (Hancock, Mich.: Suomalais-Luteerilaisen Kustannusliikkeen Kirjapaino, 1910), 12–13.
18. Holmio, *History of the Finns in Michigan*, 7–8.
19. Karni, *For the Common Good*, PhD diss., 112.
20. Kruth-Leiviska, oral history interview transcript, 9.
21. Helen Kruth, "How the Finnish Federations Functioned," in *Työmies 85: 1903–1988* (Superior, Wisc.: Työmies Society, 1988), 9; Auvo Kostiainen, *The Forging of Finnish-American Communism, 1917–1924: A Study in Ethnic Radicalism* (Turku, Finland: Turun Yliopisto, 1978), 29; and Holmio, *History of the Finns in Michigan*, 276–277.
22. *Wage Slave*, May 22, 1908.
23. Holmio, *History of the Finns in Michigan*, 296.
24. Michael G. Karni, "The Founding of the Finnish Socialist Federation and the

Minnesota Strike of 1907," in *For the Common Good: Finnish Immigrants and the Radical Response to Industrial America*, ed. Michael G. Karni and Douglas J. Ollila Jr. (Superior, Wisc.: Työmies Society, 1977), 70–71; and Holmio, *History of the Finns in Michigan*, 278. Holmio, *History of the Finns in Michigan*, 277–281.

25. *Wage Slave*, May 22, 1908.
26. Ibid.
27. Hoglund, *Finnish Immigrants in America: 1880–1920*, 44.
28. Nor did this mean that the temperance movement died out; on the contrary, it was a strong organizational contemporary of the socialist movement growing into the Prohibition Era.
29. Thiel Detective Service to Quincy Mining Company, August 15, 1906, Quincy Mining Company Collection, box 341, folder 006, Copper Country Historical Archive, Michigan Technological University, Houghton, Michigan.
30. Operative K to Thiel Detective Service Company, September 7, 1906, Quincy Mining Company Collection, box 341, folder 006, Copper Country Historical Archive, Michigan Technological University, Houghton, Michigan. The hall in question was likely the Pohjantähti's Hall, which in 1906 was perched on the side of Quincy Hill in the Quincy Hillside Second Addition; Sanborn Insurance Company, Hancock Map, 1900 and 1907.
31. Operative P to Quincy Mining Company Manager, September 21, 1906, Quincy Mining Company Collection, box 341, folder 006, Copper Country Historical Archive, Michigan Technological University, Houghton, Michigan.
32. Fred Torma, oral history transcript, tape 1, Finlandia University's Finnish American Historical Archive, Finlandia University, Hancock, Michigan, 26–27.
33. Arnold Alanen, "Finns and the Corporate Mining Environment of the Lake Superior Region," in *Finnish Diaspora II: United States* (Toronto: Multicultural History Society of Ontario, 1981), 44.
34. *Wage Slave*, May 22, 1908.
35. Arthur Puotinen, "Transitions for Finnish-American Workers in Temple and Marketplace," unpublished paper (December 7, 1970), Immigration History Research Center, University of Minnesota, Minneapolis, Minnesota, 12.
36. Hoglund, *Finnish Immigrants in America: 1880–1920*, 98.
37. Karni, *For the Common Good*, PhD diss., 82.
38. Hannula, *An Album of Finn Halls*, 23.

39. Timo Riipa, "The Finnish American Radical Theatre of the 1930s," in *Finnish Americana*, vol. 9, *A Journal of Finnish American History and Culture*, ed. Michael Karni (New Brighton, Minn.: Finnish Americana, 1992), 28–29.
40. Torma, oral history transcript, tape 1, 35–40.
41. Ibid.
42. *Työmies*, January 4, 1914.
43. Torma, oral history transcript, tape 1, 1–4.
44. *Työmies*, November 1910.
45. Ibid.
46. *Työmies*, December 1910.
47. Kaarlo Pölkki to Hilja Fräki, personal correspondence, July 24, 1915, Hilja Fräki-Regan Family Collection, manuscript box T-38-a, Finnish American Historical Archive, Finlandia University, Hancock, Michigan.
48. *Työmies*, June 1913.
49. Hoglund, *Finnish Immigrants in America: 1880–1920*, 91–98; and Frank Walli, "The Midwest: Cradle of the LSU," in *Työmies 85: 1903–1988* (Superior, Wisc.: Työmies Society, 1988), 19–22.
50. Suomalaisten Sosialistijärjestön Edustajakokouksen, *Pöytäkirja 1912* (Fitchburg, Mass.: Suomalainen Sosialisti Kustannus Yhtiö, 1912), 29–53; and K. Marianne Wargelin Brown, "Three Founding Mothers of Finnish America: Ida Pasanen: Socialist Agitator and Women's Advocate," in *Women Who Dared: The History of Finnish American Women*, ed. Wargelin Brown and Carl Ross (New York Mills, Minn.: Parta Printers, 1986), 126.
51. Suomalaisten Sosialistijärjestön Edustajakokouksen, *Pöytäkirja 1912*, 29–53.
52. Wargelin Brown, "Three Founding Mothers of Finnish America," 136–140.
53. Ibid.
54. Ibid., 126–133.
55. Ibid., 139.
56. *Wage Slave*, April 17, 1908.
57. *Pöytäkirja 1912*, 37–44. Gender numbers for the example cities: New York City, 226 women and 157 men; Brooklyn, 78 women and 94 men; Cleveland, 89 women and 99 men; Detroit, 57 women and 60 men; Chicago, No. 1, 126 women and 155 men; Chicago No. 2, 17 women and 13 men. Minneapolis, Minnesota, is the exception to the exception, as the membership in Minneapolis's Finnish Socialist

Federation local counted 52 women and 124 men.

58. *Työmies 10 Vuotias*, 159–160.
59. Sulkanen, *Amerikan Suomalaisen Työväenliikkeen Historia*, 438 and 318–319.
60. "Työmies Kustannusyhtiön vuosi-ja tilikertomus, tiliuotena 1912–1913," in *Työmiehen Vuosikok: Pöytäkirjat, 1912–1924* (Hancock, Mich. and Superior, Wisc.: Työmies Publishing Company, 1913), 43.
61. Sulkanen, "Midwestern Locals and Marquette Local," translated by Tanja Aho, *Amerikan Suomalaisen Työväenliikkeen Historia*, 347–484 and 439–443.
62. Frank Aaltonen, "The Gallant Women of the Copper Strike," translated by Jarno Heinilä, in *Työmiehen Joulu, 1913* (Hancock, Mich.: Työmies Publishing Company, 1913), 24–25.
63. Hilja's relatives in Hancock were the Fräkis. Gust Fräki was a member of the Hancock Jousi and constituent of the Työmies Publishing Company.
64. Kalle Pölkki to Hilja Fräki, personal correspondence, October 6, n.d., Hilja Fräki-Regan Family Collection, manuscript box T-38a, Finnish American Historical Archive, Finlandia University, Hancock, Michigan.
65. Hilma Fräki to Hilja Fräki, personal correspondence, September 15, 1918, Hilja Fräki-Regan Family Collection, manuscript box T-38a, Finnish American Historical Archive, Finlandia University, Hancock, Michigan.
66. Matt Thompson to Hilja Fräki, personal correspondence, September 29, 1918, Hilja Fräki-Regan Family Collection, manuscript box T-38a, Finnish American Historical Archive, Finlandia University, Hancock, Michigan.
67. Kaarlo to Hilja Fräki, personal correspondence, November 1, 1918, Hilja Fräki-Regan Family Collection, manuscript box T-38a, Finnish American Historical Archive, Finlandia University, Hancock, Michigan.
68. Carl Antti to Hilja Fräki, personal correspondence, November 1, 1918, Hilja Fräki-Regan Family Collection, manuscript box T-38a, Finnish American Historical Archive, Finlandia University, Hancock, Michigan.
69. Karni, *For the Common Good*, 82.
70. James A. Roe, "Virginia, Minnesota's Socialist Opera: Showplace of Iron Range Radicalism," in *Finnish Americana*, vol. 9, *A Journal of Finnish American History and Culture*, ed. Michael Karni (New Brighton, Minn.: Finnish Americana, 1992), 38.
71. Ibid.

72. Ibid, 39.
73. Ibid., 38.
74. Ibid., 38–40.
75. Hoglund, *Finnish Immigrants in America: 1880–1920*, 98.
76. Roe, "Virginia, Minnesota's Socialist Opera," 40–41.
77. Daisy's biological father (Walkama) was a conscientious objector during World War I. He died in prison in Washington State. Daisy's mother moved to Virginia, Minnesota, in 1922, when Daisy was three years old. Her mother worked in the Jukkola boarding house in Virginia before meeting John Partanen, who was heavily involved in the unionist movement. Partanen was an Industrial Workers of the World member and served on the Työmies Publishing Company board of directors, possibly operating the Työmies branch office in Virginia, Minnesota. Daisy Nelson-Walkama, interview by Gary Kaunonen, July 20, 2006, oral history interview, Hancock, Michigan, Finnish American Historical Archive, Finlandia University, Hancock, Michigan.
78. Ibid.
79. Ibid.
80. Roe, "Virginia, Minnesota's Socialist Opera," 38.
81. Ibid., 41.

Chapter 3. Finnish Immigrant Socialist-Unionists in Hancock

1. Sulkanen, *Amerikan Suomalaisen Työväenliikkeen Historia*, 489–490.
2. Arthur Puotinen, "Early Labor Organizations in the Copper Country," in *For the Common Good: Finnish Immigrants and the Radical Response to America*, ed. Michael G. Karni and Douglas J. Ollila Jr. (Superior, Wisc.: Työmies Society, 1977), 133.
3. The Jousi Seura officially associated on June 1, 1900, allowing "any respectable Finnish laboring male or female over fifteen years of age" to "join all Finnish laborers with combined forces to elevate the material and intellectual condition of labor by all honorable means which are not against any existing laws of the State or County or against the good conscience of men." Jousi Society Articles of Association, Houghton County, book 6, Copper Country Historical Archive,

Michigan Technological University, Houghton, Michigan.

4. Ibid. The Germania Hall was in the Finnish Transitional Neighborhood at 309–313 Quincy Street.
5. Holmio, *History of the Finns in Michigan*, 275.
6. Ilmonen, "Raittiusseura Pohjantähden 25–Vuotis Historia," 15.
7. Holmio, *History of the Finns in Michigan*, 276–277 and T. H., "Katsus Liikkeeseemme," in *Köyhälistön Nuija I, 1907* (Hancock, Mich.: Työmiehen Kustannusyhtiön Kustannuksella, 1906), 40–41.
8. Holmio, *History of the Finns in Michigan*, 292.
9. Ilmonen, "Raittiusseura Pohjantähden 25–Vuotis Historia," 15.
10. This was mandated by the SPA in 1906. Karni, *For the Common Good*, 72.
11. As mentioned in chapter 1, the Kansankoti Real Estate venture associated on September 16, 1907. The venture associated for the purpose of "acquiring, holding, leasing, selling and buying real estate and for the erection of building there on." The Kansankoti Real Estate Corporation started with capital stock amounting to $15,000 and had fifteen stockholders with fifty shares a person; Kansankoti Real Estate Corporation, Articles of Association, book 5, Copper Country Historical Archive, Michigan Technological University, Houghton, Michigan.
12. Hoglund, *Finnish Immigrants in America, 1880–1920*, 91.
13. Hämeenlinna was a southern urban center, just north of Helsinki. World War I Draft Registration Card, Form Card C, Federal Government, United States of America, www.ancestry.com (accessed August 17, 2006); and Institute of Migration, Turku, Finland, website, www.migrationinstittute.fi/emreg/ml_enfdetail.asp?snimi=_QYH0Q7NZ9 (accessed August 17, 2006).
14. Ilmonen, "Raittiusseura Pohjantähden 25–Vuotis Historia," 14.
15. Libby Koski-Björklund oral history interview.
16. Thirteenth Census of the United States of America, 1910, www.ancestry.com (accessed August 17, 2006).
17. Holmio, *History of the Finns in Michigan*, 280.
18. *(Hancock, Mich.) Evening Journal*, Monday, July 29, 1907.
19. Ibid.
20. Ibid.
21. Ibid.
22. *(Hancock, Mich.) Evening Journal*, Monday, August 3, 1907.

23. Ibid.
24. Ibid.
25. Ibid.
26. Holmio, *History of the Finns in Michigan*, 277–278.
27. Ilmonen, "Raittiusseura Pohjantähden 25–Vuotis Historia," 15–16.
28. Holmio, *History of the Finns in Michigan*, 278.
29. Puotinen, "Early Labor Organizations," 145.
30. Ibid., 144–145.
31. Holmio, *History of the Finns in Michigan*, 278.
32. Ibid. In 1910, the TPC moved to Block B, Lot 1 at 201–203 Franklin Street. Nieminen was also an editor of *Työmies* at this time, as well as a key figure in the Kansankoti Real Estate Corporation.
33. Klemetti, oral history interview transcript, 3. It is unclear from current research whether the Kansankoti Real Estate Corporation financed the acquisition of Block B, Lot 1 at 201–203 Franklin Street, but there are indications that the purchase of land for a new socialist-unionist Finn hall did not happen without some inside facilitation.
34. The $30,000 figure is from the back of a postcard from the Quincy Mining Company Collection, box 1, folder 8, Copper Country Historical Archive, Michigan Technological University, Houghton, Michigan.
35. Klemetti, oral history interview transcript, 3.
36. Nick Hendrickson and John Palosaari, interview by Arthur Puotinen, July 14, 1973, oral history interview transcript, Finnish American Historical Archive, Finlandia University, Hancock, Michigan, 19.
37. R. L. Polk & Co., Houghton County Directories, Hancock Directory 1912.
38. T. H., "Työmiehen uusi koti," translated by Aino Utriainen (2005), *Työmiehen Joulu VII* (Hancock, Mich.: Työmies Publishing Company, 1910), 10.
39. Jousi Society Articles of Association, book 6; and R. L. Polk & Co., Houghton County Directories, Hancock Directory 1917, 479.
40. Jousi Society Articles of Association, book 6.
41. Arvid Tianen, "Socialist Party of America Christmas Card in Finnish," 1911, Hilja Fräki-Regan Collection, manuscript box T-38a, Finnish American Historical Archive, Finlandia University, Hancock, Michigan.
42. *Köyhälistön Nuija* 6 (1912).

43. Suomalaisten Sosialistijarjeston Edustajakokouksen, *Pöytäkirja 1912*, 40.
44. Socialist Party of Michigan, State Bulletin, July 1914 (Harbor Springs, Mich.: Socialist Party of Michigan, 1914), 1–2.
45. Sulkanen, *Amerikan Suomalaisen Työväenliikkeen Historia*, 439–440.
46. Two thousand to two thousand-five hundred is an approximation because seven locals did not provide statistics in the *Pöytäkirja 1912*. The locals that did not provide membership statistics were Calumet, Chassell, Kaleva, Negaunee, Princeton, South Range, and Verona. Of these locals, Calumet, Negaunee, Princeton, South Range, and Verona were all mining industry communities and thus would likely have significant numbers of membership, but were perhaps reluctant to register membership numbers due to the close proximity to mining company oligarchy; Suomalaisten Sosialistijarjeston Edustajakokouksen, *Pöytäkirja 1912*, 39–40.
47. Ibid, 41. In contrast, the Minnesota FSF locals had seventeen agitation committees.
48. T. H., "Katsus Liikkeeseemme," 40–41.
49. Ibid.

Chapter 4. The Early Existence of the Työmies Publishing Company, 1904–1909

1. Puotinen, "Early Labor Organizations," 134–36.
2. Ibid.
3. Työmies Publishing Company Articles of Association, book 4, Copper Country Historical Archive, Michigan Technological University, Houghton, Michigan.
4. Ibid.
5. Larry Lankton, *Cradle to Grave*, 214.
6. Ibid.
7. Ibid., 215–216.
8. Superintendent James McNaughton to Alexander Agassiz, personal correspondence, May 23, 1904, Copper Country Historical Archive, Michigan Technological University, Houghton, Michigan.
9. Holmio, *History of the Finns in Michigan*, 276–278. The SPA divided the circulation of Finnish immigrant socialist newspapers into three United States regions. *Työmies* served the Midwest. *Raivaaja* (Pioneer) served the eastern United States,

and *Toveri* (Comrade) served the western United States. *Työkansa* (Work People) was a Canadian Finnish-language publication.

10. Ibid., 277.
11. Holmio, *History of the Finns in Michigan*, 277; R. L. Polk & Co., Houghton County Directories, Hancock Directory, 1905–06, 463; and historic photo in *Työmies 10 Vuotias*.
12. John I. Kolehmainen, *The Finns in America: A Bibliographical Guide to Their History* (Hancock, Mich.: Finnish Lutheran Book Concern, 1947), 92.
13. Sanborn Insurance Company, Hancock Map, 1907, sheet 4.
14. R. L. Polk & Co., Houghton County Directories, Hancock Directory, 1899–1900, 355.
15. R. L. Polk & Co., Houghton Country Directories, Hancock Directory, 1901–1902, 460.
16. R. L. Polk & Co., Houghton County Directories, Hancock Directory, 1903–04, 384.
17. While Kosonen was not likely an anarchist, he was decidedly a devout Marxist. John I. Kolehmainen, "The Inimitable Marxists: The Finnish Immigrant Socialists," *Michigan History* 36 (1952): 396.
18. Ibid., 279.
19. R. L. Polk & Co., Houghton County Directories, Hancock Directory, 1905–06, 38. Pine Street was a Finnish immigrant enclave in Calumet, Michigan. Ahlman's editorship of *Päivälehti* ended with his move to Chicago in 1907 or 1908. O. J. Larson was president of the Päivälehti Publishing Company at this time; ibid., 1907–08.
20. Holmio, *History of the Finns in Michigan*, 279.
21. Taisto T. Holm, "Local Correspondents: Paikkakuntakirjeet," in *Työmies 85: 1903–1988* (Superior, Wisc.: Työmies Society, 1988), 12–14.
22. R. L. Polk & Co., Houghton County Directories, Hancock Directory, 1905–06.
23. Kolehmainen, *The Finns in America*, 91–94.
24. A single story of the 421 Michigan Street building is 1,500 sq. ft. From historic photos, it appears as if the TPC used two floors for their printing operations. The Polk's Directory for 1907–08 places the TPC building at 415 Michigan Street, but research with the 1907 Sanborn Insurance Company Maps shows no evidence of a printing press or publication building at such an address. The 1907 Sanborn maps

do indicate that there were "print shops" at both 421 and 425 Michigan Street. From historic photos in *Työmies 10 Vuotias*, it appears that the TPC building was at 421 Michigan Street due its proximity to a large-looking shed-type structure to the right of the TPC building. Sanborn Maps corroborate the historic photos as to relative proximity to each other and building types.

25. Sulkanen, *Amerikan Suomalaisen Työväenliikkeen Historia*, 490, and Holmio, *History of the Finns in Michigan*, 279.
26. Sulkanen, *Amerikan Suomalaisen Työväenliikkeen Historia*, 499, and Holmio, *History of the Finns in Michigan*, 279.
27. Edith A. Koivisto, interview by Douglas Ollila, August 3, 1973, oral history interview transcript, Finnish American Historical Archive, Finlandia University, Hancock, Michigan, 4.
28. Ibid., 4–5.
29. Holmio, *History of the Finns in Michigan*, 279–280.
30. Thiel Detective Service Company to Quincy Mining Company, business correspondence, August 31, 1906, Quincy Mining Company Collection, box 341, folder 006, Copper Country Historical Archive, Michigan Technological University, Houghton, Michigan.
31. Ibid., Chicago, September 21, 1906.
32. Ibid.
33. R. L. Polk & Co., Houghton County Directories, Hancock Directory, 1907–08, 473.
34. Työmies Publishing Company Articles of Association Amendment, book 5.
35. R. L. Polk & Co., Houghton County Directories, Hancock Directory, 1907–08, 473.
36. *S. Juntilla v. Työmies Publishing Company*, 1907, Houghton County Court transcript microfilm, Copper Country Historical Archive, Michigan Technological University, Houghton, Michigan.
37. F. S—n, "Amerikan kansalliskymni (Mukaelma)," translated by Gary Kaunonen (2008), *Köyhälistön Nuija* 4 (Hancock, Mich.: Työmies Publishing Company, 1910): 118. In the original poem, the English rhymed with the Finnish, creating a type of spoken meter, but the rhythm of the rhyme is lost in the English translation.
38. James Moran, *Printing Presses: History and Development from the 15th Century to Modern Times* (Los Angeles: University of California Press, 1978), 123–124, 157.

39. According to Holmio, the TPC had one linotype machine as early as 1904, "which meant that its linotype machine was in operation twenty-four hours a day"; Holmio, *History of the Finns in Michigan,* 279. In this same sentence, Holmio wrote that *Työmies* was a triweekly, which is most likely false as Polk's Directory ads relate that *Työmies* was a weekly until sometime in 1907–08.
40. For a description of how the linotype machine worked, see Richard E. Huss, *The Developments of the Printers' Mechanical Typesetting Methods, 1822–1925* (Charlottesville: University Press of Virginia, 1973), 9.
41. *Wage Slave,* March 20, 1908.
42. Ibid.
43. There have been a number of the *Vanguard* serial titles, but the likely *Vanguard* offered along with the *Wage Slave* was a newspaper published in Green Bay, Wisconsin, November 1902–October 1908 by Vanguard Press, and in Milwaukee, Wisconsin, by the Social-Democratic Publishing Company, August 1904–October 1908 (imprint varied). University of Wisconsin-Madison Library online listing at: http://www.worldcat.org/oclc/45966017?pgload, accessed August 13, 2008.
44. *Wage Slave,* May 1, 1908.
45. *Wage Slave,* May 1, 1908; "The Miehle: Two Revolution Presses," The Press Gallery On-line, http://letterpressprinting.com.au/page8.htm (accessed September 2008); and Moran, *Printing Presses,* 157–159.
46. *Wage Slave,* May 1, 1908. The above article also hints as to why the editorial leadership was in constant flux: seemingly, the TPC expected a lot from its editors, and when an editor underachieved, a critique in a TPC publication was sure to follow. It is unclear from current research how long the *Wage Slave* ran as a publication, but it is certain from accounts of the 1913–1914 Copper Strike that the *Wage Slave* was still in publication during the strike; Puotinen, "Early Labor Organizations," 154.
47. Stirton, described in the *Wage Slave* as "a former educator and minister . . . now an Industrial Union Socialist," was a well-traveled socialist lecturer; *Wage Slave,* May 1, 1908.
48. *Wage Slave,* May 1, 1908, and March 20, 1908. "*Cead Mille Failte*" is an old Irish-Gaelic colloquialism meaning "A hundred million welcomes."
49. Alanen, "Finns and the Corporate Mining Environment," 4–5.
50. Ibid.

51. *Wage Slave,* March 20, 1908.
52. *Wage Slave,* April 17, 1908; May 1, 1908; May 29, 1908; and May 29, 1908.
53. Debs polled less than 3 percent, while Taft won the election polling almost 52 percent to Bryant's 43 percent. James MacGregor Burns, J. W. Peltason, Thomas E. Cronin, and David B. Magleby, *Government by the People,* national version, 18th edition (Upper Saddle River, N.J.: Prentice Hall, 2000), appendix A-10.
54. *Wage Slave,* April 17, 1908.
55. Ibid., May 29, 1908, and June 19, 1908.
56. Ibid., June 19, 1908.
57. Ibid., May 1, 1908.
58. Ibid., April 17, 1908.
59. Ibid.
60. Ibid., March 20, 1908.
61. Ibid., May 22, 1908.
62. Ibid., March 20, 1908.
63. Ibid., June 19, 1908.
64. Kolehmainen, *The Finns in America,* 91–94.
65. Ibid., 97.
66. *Amerikan Matti* 1, no. 1 (April 1910): 10.
67. "Calumetin Mainari," translated by Anna Leppänen (2008), *Amerikan Matti,* April 1910.
68. While *Amerikan Matti* ceased publication in 1910, another satirical magazine, titled *Lapatossu,* began publication in 1911. *Amerikan Matti* returned in 1917. This second *Matti,* published in Hancock after the TPC moved to Superior, had much the same satirical character, but new publishers. The new publishers were J. G. Tuira and T. Hiltunen.
69. Holmio, *History of the Finns in Michigan,* 280; and *Köyhälistön Nuija* 4 (1910): 160.
70. *Köyhälistön Nuija* 4 (1910): 160–178. A listing of the TPC staff/contributors and short biographical information from the article is in appendix 1.

Chapter 5. The Työmies Publishing Company Reaches Maturity, 1910–1913

1. R. L. Polk & Co., Houghton County Directories, Hancock Directory, 1910, 413.
2. Sanborn Insurance Company, Hancock Map, 1907 and 1917.
3. Holmio, *History of the Finns in Michigan*, 280.
4. This article likely came before the TPC's rental of the neighboring Coughlin Building at 207 Franklin Street; T. H., "Työmiehen uusi koti," 10–11.
5. Being well "armed" may have two meanings, a literal meaning and a figurative one. There were Marxists on staff—were they agitating for an armed rebellion, or were they using armed as a figurative term? Possibly the article was written as to be open to both operational definitions.
6. The TPC had other bookstores in Duluth, Minnesota; Ishpeming, Michigan; and Virginia, Minnesota.
7. This is an unidentified press, but the press's function was probably as a large jobbing press.
8. An author recreation of likely elements of the spatial layout of the TPC publishing buildings is in appendix 2. It is important to note that this layout and subsequent floor plans are the "best educated guess" of the author according to historic photos assembled from *Työmies 10 Vuotias* and the Immigration History Research Center's COLLAGE online database.
9. *The Wage Slave*, May 1, 1908.
10. *Työmies*, January 4, 1914.
11. For a description of the Duplex, see Moran, *Printing Presses*, 205–206.
12. Sulkanen, *Amerikan Suomalaisen Työväenliikkeen Historia*, 493.
13. Douglas J. Ollila Jr., "The Work People's College: Immigrant Education for Adjustment and Solidarity," in *For the Common Good*, ed. Michael G. Karni and Douglas J. Ollila Jr. (Superior, Wisc.: Työmies Society, 1977), 87–112.
14. Kostiainen, *The Forging of Finnish-American Communism*, 38–39.
15. Sulkanen, *Amerikan Suomalaisen Työväenliikkeen Historia*, 502.
16. Ibid.
17. R. L. Polk & Co., Houghton County Directories, Hancock Directory, 1910 and 1912.
18. Union contract between the Työmies Publishing Company and the International

Printing Pressmen and Assistants' Union, September 18, 1911, Työmies Society Collection, Finnish American Historical Archive, Finlandia University, Hancock, Michigan.

19. Ibid.
20. Ibid.
21. Ibid.
22. *Työmies*, May 14, 1914.
23. Kristiina Markkanen, "K. A. Suvanto: Political Satirist," in *Finnish Americana: A Journal of Finnish American History and Culture*, vol. 9, ed. Michael G. Karni (New Brighton, Minn.: Finnish Americana, 1992), 7–8.
24. Ibid., 10.
25. Ibid.
26. "Työmies Kustannusyhtiön vuosi-ja tilikertomus, tiliuotena 1911–1912," in *Työmiehen Vuosikok: Pöytäkirjat 1912–1924* (Hancock, Mich., and Superior, Wisc.: Työmies Publishing Company, 1912), 57–58.
27. Sulkanen, *Amerikan Suomalaisen Työväenliikkeen Historia*, 494.
28. Kolehmainen, *The Finns in Michigan*, 91–95.
29. John I. Kolehmainen, "The Inimitable Marxists," 399.
30. Holmio, *History of the Finns in Michigan*, 278.
31. "Työmies Kustannusyhtiön vuosi-ja tilikertomus, tiliuotena 1912–1913," in *Työmiehen Vuosikok: Pöytäkirjat 1912–1924* (Hancock, Mich., and Superior, Wisc.: Työmies Publishing Company, 1913), 43.
32. Ibid.
33. This drastic jump is likely from an infusion of Western Federation of Miners money for the 1913–14 Michigan Copper Miners Strike, which will be discussed in chapter 6. It is of interesting note, though, that in adjusted value, the TPC's $126,000 would equal over $3,000,000 today.
34. "Työmies Kustannusyhtiön vuosi-ja tilikertomus, tiliuotena 1912–1913," 44–48. Again, the TPC managed to break even, making a profit of $64,860.79 and registering losses of $64,860.79.
35. United States of America, Western District of Michigan, Northern Division, *People of the United States v. The Työmies Publishing Company, John Nummivuori and John Salminen*, filed January 15, 1913, copy of Indictment, Työmies Society Collection, Finnish American Historical Archive, Finlandia University, Hancock, Michigan.

36. Ibid.
37. Ibid.
38. United States Circuit Court of Appeals for the Sixth Circuit, Cincinnati, Ohio, January 6, 1914, the *Työmies Publishing Company, John Nummivuori and John Salminen, Defendants in Error v. The United States Government, Defendant in Error*, Työmies Society Collection, Finnish American Historical Archive, Finlandia University, Hancock, Michigan.

Chapter 6. The 1913–14 Copper Country Strike

1. Sarell, born in 1881 in Hapanranda, Sweden, a far-northern hamlet just across the Finnish border on the Tornio River's Swedish banks, immigrated to the United States in 1901. Upon arrival in America, he worked in Copper Country mines and joined the Finnish Socialist Federation in 1905. In 1908, he became an editor at the Työmies Publishing Company and for a time served as its editor-in-chief; Sulkanen, *Amerikan Suomalaisen Työväenliikkeen Historia*, 500.
2. Arthur Thurner, *Rebels on the Range: The Michigan Copper Miner's Strike of 1913–14* (Hancock, Mich.: Book Concern Printers, 198), 33.
3. Ibid.
4. Arthur Puotinen, "Early Labor Organizations in the Copper Country," in *For the Common Good: Finnish Immigrants and the Radical Response to Industrial America*, ed. Michael G. Karni and Douglas J. Ollila Jr. (Superior, Wisc.: Työmies Society, 1977), 124.
5. Ibid. 124–125.
6. Ibid., 125.
7. Larry Lankton, *From Cradle to Grave: Life, Work and Death at the Lake Superior Copper Mines* (New York: Oxford University Press, 1991), 203.
8. Ibid.
9. Lankton, *From Cradle to Grave*, 203–204; and Puotinen, "Early Labor Organizations in the Copper Country," 125.
10. Lankton, *From Cradle to Grave*, 202.
11. Puotinen, "Early Labor Organizations in the Copper Country," 130.
12. Lankton, *From Cradle to Grave*, 202.

13. Puotinen, "Early Labor Organizations in the Copper Country," 130.
14. Lankton, *From Cradle to Grave*, 204–206.
15. Ibid., 208
16. Paul F. Brissenden, *The IWW: A Study of American Syndicalism* (New York: Russell & Russell, 1957), 57–149.
17. Lankton, *From Cradle to Grave*, 204–206.
18. No. 5 to Quincy Mining Company, business correspondence, August 10th, 1906, Quincy Mining Company Collection, box 341, Copper Country Historical Archive, Michigan Technological University, Houghton, Michigan.
19. Operative P to Quincy Mining Company, business correspondence, n.d., Quincy Mining Company Collection, box 341, Copper Country Historical Archives, Michigan Technological University, Houghton, Michigan.
20. Ibid.
21. Puotinen, "Early Labor Organizations in the Copper Country," 137–138.
22. Puotinen, "Early Labor Organizations in the Copper Country," 137–138 and Lankton, *Cradle to Grave*, 208–209. While Thurner devotes a sentence to this critical labor action in *Rebels on the Range*, both Lankton and Puotinen gave the events of the Rockland strike their due credence in the annals of Copper Country labor history.
23. Puotinen, "Early Labor Organizations in the Copper Country," 138–139.
24. Ibid., 138–139.
25. Ibid.
26. Ibid.
27. Ilmonen, "Raittiusseura Pohjantähden 25-Vuotis Historia," 15.
28. Puotinen, "Early Labor Organizations in the Copper Country," 139–140.
29. Ibid., 139–140.
30. Unknown operative Thiel Detective Agency to Quincy Mining Company, "Re: Employees," October 15, 1906, Quincy Mining Company Collection, box 341, Copper Country Historical Archives, Michigan Technological University, Houghton, Michigan, 2.
31. Operative P, Thiel Detective Agency to Quincy Mining Company, "Re: Employees," September 21, 1906, Quincy Mining Company Collection, box 341, Copper Country Historical Archives, Michigan Technological University, Houghton, Michigan, 1.
32. Unknown operative Thiel Detective Agency to Quincy Mining Company, "Re: Employees," October 6, 1906, Quincy Mining Company Collection, box 341,

Copper Country Historical Archives, Michigan Technological University, Houghton, Michigan.

33. Albert Gedicks, *Working Class Radicalism among Finnish Immigrants in Minnesota and Michigan Mining Communities*, photocopy (Ann Arbor, Mich.: University Microfilms International, 1980), 123–124; and Lankton, *From Cradle to Grave*, 209.
34. Lankton, *From Cradle to Grave*, 220.
35. Lankton, *From Cradle to Grave*, 219–222; and *Työmiehen Joulu 1913*.
36. Thurner, *Rebels on the Range*, 45; and U.S. Department of Labor, *Michigan Copper District Strike: Bulletin of the United States Labor Statistics* (Washington, D.C.: Government Printing Office, 1914), 11–21.
37. Contract between the Työmies Publishing Company and the Hancock Local No. 229 of the International Printing Pressmen and Assistants' Union, 2–4.
38. Ibid.
39. Ibid.
40. U.S. Department of Labor, *Michigan Copper District Strike*, 106.
41. Ibid., 106–115.
42. Ibid.; and Lankton, *Cradle to Grave*, 38–39.
43. William B. Gates Jr., *Michigan Copper and Boston Dollars: An Economic History of the Michigan Copper Mining Industry* (Cambridge, Mass.: Harvard University Press, 1951), 219.
44. William Parsons Todd, interview by Ralph Jalkanen, October 1974, oral history recording and interview transcript, Finnish American Historical Archive, Finlandia University, Hancock, Michigan, 1831–1833. Todd did relate later in the interview that some small grievances did occur.
45. Ibid.
46. Ibid.
47. Ibid., 1839–1841. Todd felt that the introduction of the one-man drill into the Copper Country was the sole instigator of the 1913–14 strike.
48. Gedicks, *Working Class Radicalism among Finnish Immigrants*, 124–125.
49. *Työmies*, July 15, 1913.
50. Ibid., July 16, 1913.
51. Libby Koski-Björklund, oral history interview.
52. Lankton, *Cradle to Grave*, 221.

53. Ibid., 221–222.
54. Ibid.
55. Douglas J. Ollila, Jr., "From Socialism to Industrial Unionism (IWW): Social Factors in the Emergence of Left-Labor Radicalism among Finnish Workers on the Mesabi, 1911-19" in *The Finnish Experience in the Western Great Lakes Region: New Perspectives*, (Turku, Finland: Institute for Migration), 1975, 156-158.
56. J. Peter Campbell, "The Cult of Spontaneity: Finnish-Canadian Bushworkers and the Industrial Workers of the World in Northern Ontario, 1919–1934," *Labour/Le Travail* 41 (Spring 1998): 121.
57. Sanborn Insurance Company, Calumet, Michigan, Map, sheet 2, 1908.
58. Thurner, *Rebels on the Range*, 133. Thurner identifies WFM headquarters in South Range as the Finnish Socialist Federation's Socialist Hall, 130–132.
59. *Miners' Bulletin*, various editions.
60. *Työmies*, December 11, 1913.
61. Ibid.
62. Articles of Association, book 5, 463–464.
63. Puotinen, "Early Labor Organizations in the Copper Country," 154.
64. *Työmies*, July 25, 1913.
65. Lankton, *Cradle to Grave*, 224–225.
66. A. O. Sarell, "The Copper Country Strike: Its Features so Far," translated by Jarno Heinilä (2006), *Työmiehen Joulu 1913* (Hancock, Mich.: Työmies Publishing Company, 1913), 13.
67. Lankton wrote the WFM claimed 9,000 men out (Lankton, *Cradle to Grave*, 222–223).
68. The complete song lyrics are in appendix 3. Jukka S., "March of the Copper Territory Strikers," translated by Anna Leppänen, *Työmies*, 1913.
69. U.S. Department of Labor, *Michigan Copper District Strike*, 66–67.
70. Sarell, "The Copper Country Strike," 13.
71. U.S. Department of Labor, *Michigan Copper District Strike*, 43–44.
72. William Parsons Todd, oral history transcript, 1846–1847.
73. Sarell, "The Copper Country Strike," 19; and *Työmies*, December 19, 1913.
74. Lankton, *Cradle to Grave*, 222–225.
75. Ibid.
76. U.S. Department of Labor, *Michigan Copper District Strike*, 67.

77. Sarell, "The Copper Country Strike," 14–15.
78. *Miners' Bulletin*, August 28, 1913.
79. Puotinen, "Early Labor Organizations," 152.
80. Sarell, "The Copper Country Strike," 15.
81. Thiel Detective Service Co. to C. L. Lawton, General Manager Quincy Mining Co., business correspondence, August 5, 1913, Quincy Mining Company Collection, box 341, Copper Country Historical Archive, Michigan Technological University, Houghton, Michigan.
82. Ibid.
83. *Miners' Bulletin*, August 14 and September 13, 1913.
84. Ibid., October 11 and September 13, 1913.

Chapter 7. Gun Hounds, Scabs, and Tragedy

1. *Työmies*, October 27, 1913.
2. Ibid., August 18, 1913.
3. Sarell, "The Copper Country Strike," 15.
4. *Miners' Bulletin*, October 2, 1913.
5. Sarell, "The Copper Country Strike," 15.
6. Ibid. The six defendants eventually returned to stand trial and were given varying sentences; for a complete account, see Alison K. Hoagland, "The Boardinghouse Murders: Housing and American Ideals in Michigan's Copper Country in 1913," *Perspectives on Vernacular Architecture: The Journal of the Vernacular Architecture Forum* 11 (2004).
7. Hoagland, "The Boardinghouse Murders," 6.
8. U.S. Department of Labor, *Michigan Copper District Strike*, 69.
9. Sarell, "The Copper Country Strike," 16. Lankton cites the number as closer to approximately 5,000 mourners; Lankton, *Cradle to Grave*, 228–231.
10. Puotinen, "Early Labor Organizations," 153.
11. *Miners' Bulletin*, August 23, 1913.
12. U.S. Department of Labor, *Michigan Copper District Strike*, 70.
13. Ibid., 69–70.
14. *Työmies*, August 22, 1913.

15. U.S. Department of Labor, *Michigan Copper District Strike*, 63–64.
16. William Parsons Todd, oral history interview, 1848–1850.
17. U.S. Department of Labor, *Michigan Copper District Strike*, 63–64.
18. Ibid.
19. Sarell, "The Copper Country Strike," 19.
20. *Työmies*, September 17, 1913.
21. Sarell, "The Copper Country Strike," 20.
22. Ibid.
23. Lankton, *Cradle to Grave*, 229.
24. Nick Hendrickson and John Palosaari, oral history interview transcript, 23.
25. *Miners' Bulletin*, November 15, 1913.
26. Ibid., September 27, 1913. The Finnish Workmen's Cooperative was a dealer in general merchandise located on County Road, Kearsarge Location. The co-op's president was Matt Tossava; Isaac Uitti was vice president, Gustav Johnson was treasurer, and William Uitti was secretary. The cooperative store seems to be a part of a Finnish Socialist Federation local in that area of Keweenaw County. There were two Finnish halls in that area. One was also on County Road, North Kearsarge Location, and was likely a Finnish Socialist Federation local hall. The other "Finnish Hall" was at 100 Wolverine Location, which was likely a Temperance or Knights of Kaleva hall; R. L. Polk & Co., Houghton County Directories, Calumet Directory, 1905–06 and 1907–08.
27. Sarell, "The Copper Country Strike," 19–20.
28. Ibid., 19–20.
29. *Miners' Bulletin*, November 15, 1913.
30. Quincy Mining Company, "Wanted Poster," Andrew Curto Photograph Collection, Keweenaw National Historical Park Archive, Calumet, Michigan, 1913.
31. Lankton, *Cradle to Grave*, 234–235.
32. *Miners' Bulletin*, November 15, 1913.
33. Puotinen, "Early Labor Organizations," 121.
34. Sarell, "The Copper Country Strike," 2.
35. Leo Blom, "Eulogy for Heimer Mikko, February 1982," Vertical Files, Finnish American Historical Archive, Finlandia University, Hancock, Michigan.
36. *Miners' Bulletin*, April 14, 1914.
37. Thurner, *Rebels on the Range*, 130–133. The arrested men were charged with carrying

concealed weapons. Thurner wrote that the siege occurred at the "hall shared by socialists and the union local." Thurner cites a December 11, 1913, *Daily Mining Gazette* article for this assertion, but a day later the *Gazette* refers to the building as a "house." Additionally, in their December 11, 1913, edition, *Työmies* referred to the building under siege as an office (*konttorin*) and not a hall. It is likely that the raid occurred at the balloon-framed, house-like structure and not at the Finnish Socialist Federation's Socialist Hall.

38. Thurner, *Rebels on the Range*, 130–133.
39. Ibid.
40. Thurner, *Rebels on the Range*, 130–133; and *Työmies*, December 11, 1913. It should be noted that Thurner's sources for description of all these events come from English, pro-company newspapers, such as the *Mining Gazette* and the *Calumet News*.
41. *Työmies*, December 11, 1913.
42. *Daily Mining Gazette*, Houghton, Michigan, December 20, 1913.
43. Lankton, *Cradle to Grave*, 236–239.
44. *Työmies*, December 25, 1913.
45. Herman Kallungi, interview by Harold L. Mathieu, July 18, 1973, oral history interview transcript, Finnish American Historical Archive, Finlandia University, Hancock, Michigan, 34–36.
46. A composite list of the Italian Hall dead and a comparison of the coroner's inquest list with lists from *Työmies* and the *Miners' Bulletin* is in appendix 4. On December 31, 1913, *Työmies* printed another list of the Italian Hall deceased, using the coroner's report as a source. The newspaper makes no mention of the credibility of this source as compared with their earlier accounts of the Italian Hall deceased.
47. Allied Printing, Houghton, Michigan, "No. 13, Niemalä Stereoscope," Immigration History Research Center Photograph Collection, University of Minnesota, Minneapolis, Minnesota, 1913; Ed Stewart, *Neil's Story*, unpublished family memoir of Neil Manley (Manni in Finnish), n.d., Finnish American Historical Archive, Finlandia University, Hancock, Michigan, 10–11; and *1910 United States Census*, HeritageQuest Online, www.heritagequestonline.com/hqoweb/library/do/index (accessed May 2008).
48. *Työmies*, December 25 and 26, 1913.
49. *Työmies*, December 27, 1913.

50. Thurner, *Rebels on the Range*, 166.
51. While others were targeted for arrest, it appears as if only five of *Työmies*'s staff were taken into custody. Thurner wrote, "Warrants were also served charging other Tyomies employees with 'conspiracy to publish mis-statements calculated to incite riot.'" These warrants were apparently withdrawn. Thurner, *Rebels on the Range*, 166.
52. *Työmies*, December 29, 1913.
53. Houghton County, State of Michigan, "Coroner's Inquest Transcript," December 31, 1913, Italian Hall Materials, manuscript box K-17, Finnish American Historical Archive, Finlandia University, Hancock, Michigan, 111–112.
54. *Työmies*, December 29, 1913.
55. Arne Halonen, "The Role of Finnish-Americans in the Political Labor Movement," (master's thesis, University of Minnesota, 1945), 86; and Thurner, *Rebels on the Range*, 165–166.
56. Lankton, *Cradle to Grave*, 237–238; and Puotinen, "Early Labor Organizations," 160.
57. Puotinen, "Early Labor Organizations," 159–161.
58. Houghton County, State of Michigan, "Coroner's Inquest Transcript."
59. Ibid., 179. Emphasis added by author.
60. *Työmies*, December 25 and 26, 1913, and "Coroner's Inquest" for lists of names; Engel and Mantel, *Calumet*, 211 (photograph of inside of Old Apostolic Lutheran Church); Pirjo Mikkonen and Sirkka Paikkala, *Sukunimet* (Helsinki, Finland: Otava, 1992); and Lankton, *From Cradle to Grave*, 238.
61. Asbjörn Nesheim, *Introducing the Lapps* (Oslo, Norway: Johan Grundt Tanum Forlag, 1963), 40.
62. Thurner, *Rebels on the Range*, 165–167.
63. Ibid.
64. *Miners Bulletin*, December 31, 1913.
65. *Miners' Bulletin*, January 21, 1914.
66. *Työmies*, December 27, 1913.
67. Puotinen, "Early Labor Organizations," 162; and Thurner, *Rebels on the Range*, 229–232.
68. *Miners' Bulletin*, March 12, 1914.
69. *Miners' Bulletin*, April 1, 1914.

70. *Miners' Bulletin*, April 14, 1914.
71. Puotinen, "Early Labor Organizations," 162–163.
72. *Miners' Bulletin*, April 14, 1914.
73. Armas K. E. Holmio, "Notes on the Finnish Anti-socialist League," Anti-sosialistien Liitto, manuscript box O-43, Finnish American Historical Archive, Finlandia University, Hancock, Michigan.
74. Anti-sosialistien Liitto, *Pöytäkirja*, Huhtikuu 9, 1914–Syyskuu 12, 1915, translated by Anna Leppänen and Gary Kaunonen (2008), manuscript box O-43, Finnish American Historical Archive, Finlandia University, Hancock, Michigan.
75. Ibid.
76. Ibid.
77. Lankton, *Cradle to Grave*, 240–241; and Thurner, *Rebels on the Range*, 229–232.
78. *Miners' Bulletin*, April 14, 1914.
79. Lankton, *Cradle to Grave*, 239.
80. Charles Lawton to W. R. Todd, business correspondence, April 4, 1914, Quincy Mining Company Collection, box 342, Copper Country Archives, Michigan Technological University, Houghton, Michigan.
81. *Miners' Bulletin*, April 14, 1914.
82. Thurner, *Rebels on the Range*, 230.
83. Charles E. Hietala to Mr. Ernest Mills, business correspondence, June 7, 1915, Papers of the Western Federation of Miners/International Union of Mine, Mill and Smelter Workers, box 1, folder 29, University Archives, University of Colorado-Boulder, Boulder, Colorado.
84. Ibid.

Conclusion

1. Lankton, *Cradle to Grave*, 239.
2. Halonen, *The Role of Finnish-Americans in the Political Labor Movement*, 88.
3. Jukka Salminen, "Behind Bars: Written in the Marquette County Jail," in *Työmies*, April 2, 1914, translated by Taisto T. Holm, *Työmies-Eteenpäin* (July 1998): 3.
4. Ibid.
5. Ibid.

6. Halonen, *The Role of Finnish-Americans in the Political Labor Movement*, 71 and 87–89.
7. Passi, "Finnish Immigrants and the Radical Response," 11–12.
8. Holmio, *History of the Finns in Michigan*, 294.
9. Kostiainen, *The Forging of Finnish-American Communism*, 40.
10. Ollila, "The Work People's College," 162–164.
11. Ibid.
12. *Raivaaja* was an eastern United States socialist publication associated with the yellow parliamentary Finns.
13. Kostiainen, *The Forging of Finnish-American Communism*, 41.
14. Ibid., 22.
15. Koivisto, oral history audio tape.
16. Articles of Association, book 6. Thurner wrote that the publishing company printed its final issue of *Työmies* in Hancock in October 1914; Thurner, *Rebels on the Range*, 240.
17. Holmio, *History of the Finns in Michigan*, 292.
18. P. George Hummasti, "The Workingman's Daily Bread: Finnish-American Working Class Newspapers, 1900–1921," in *For the Common Good*, ed. Michael G. Karni and Douglas J. Ollila Jr. (Superior, Wisc.: Työmies Society, 1977), 185.
19. Thurner, *Rebels on the Range*, 240.
20. Puotinen, "Early Labor Organizations," 163.
21. Työmies Publishing Company, *Pöytäkirja 1914* (Hancock, Mich.: Työmies Publishing Company), 34–35; and Työmies Publishing Company, *Pöytäkirja 1915* (Hancock, Mich.: Työmies Publishing Company), 16–17.
22. *Työmies*, January 14–May 16, 1914. January 14 subscription numbers were 13,200 and May 16 numbers were 15,241 subscribers. Perhaps these numbers are exaggerated, but the Työmies Publishing Company's financial books seem to indicate that there was in fact no drop in revenue or subscription numbers.
23. Työmies Publishing Company, *Pöytäkirja 1914* and *Pöytäkirja 1915*.
24. *Amerikan Matti*, September 1917, Hancock, Michigan, front inside cover and back inside cover.
25. Wilma Fräki to Hilja Fräki, personal correspondence, March 16, 1919, Hilja Fräki-Regan Collection, manuscript box T-38a, Finnish American Historical Archive, Finlandia University, Hancock, Michigan.

26. Arthur Thurner, *Strangers and Sojourners: A History of Michigan's Keweenaw* Peninsula (Detroit: Wayne State University Press, 1994), 261–262.

Epilogue

1. R. L. Polk & Co., Houghton County Directories, Hancock Directory, 1917, 519 and 552.
2. Ibid.
3. Sanborn Insurance Company, Hancock, Michigan Map, 1917 and 1938.
4. Kostiainen, *The Forging of Finnish-American Communism*, 222–223.
5. Holmio, *History of the Finns in Michigan*, 334, 337, and 354.
6. Ibid., 300–301.
7. Sulkanen, *Amerikan Suomalaisen Työväenliikkeen Historia*, 502–503.
8. Libby Koski-Björklund, oral history interview.
9. Ibid.
10. Kostiainen, *The Forging of Finnish-American Communism*, 41–42.
11. Hummasti, "The Workingman's Daily Bread," 182–186 and 192.
12. Halonen, *The Role of Finnish-Americans in the Political Labor Movement*, 88. Though *Työmies* was never officially an organ of the Communist Party in the United States of America, it maintained close ties with that party. While it can be said that *Työmies* was a small "c" communist paper, it cannot be stated that it was officially a big "C" Party-sanctioned newspaper.
13. "A History of the *Finnish American Reporter*," *Finnish American Reporter*, 20th anniversary issue, October 2006.

Appendix 4. Työmies Publishing Company's Composite List of Italian Hall Deceased, 1913

1. List compiled from the Houghton County Coroner's Inquest; *Työmies*, December 25, 1913; *Työmies*, December 26, 1913; and the *Miners' Bulletin*, December 31, 1913.
2. In the 1910 Census, Gust Ala lives at 366 Caledonia St., Calumet Township. Of his six children, he and wife Hilda have a 7-year-old daughter named Lempi. Ala

and Aho may have been easily mistaken, especially in written form. United States Census, *1910 United States Census*, Heritage Quest Online, www.heritagequestonline.com/hqoweb/library/do/index (accessed May 2008).

3. In some lists, Henry Isola, Tilma's husband, is listed as dying in the hall, but he probably did not die there. The 1920 Census lists Henry Isola, a widower living in Calumet Township. This was likely the husband of Tilma and father of Philemina Isola; United States Census, *1920 United States Census*, Heritage Quest Online, www.heritagequestonline.com/hqoweb/library/do/index (accessed May 2008).
4. Ibid. John Kempi (4) is a probable addition to the Coroner's Inquest list. Not only does John Kempi appear with the same address on all three of *Työmies*'s publications, but also there were two Kempi families living in Calumet at the time, according to the 1910 U.S. Census. One family had a 3-month-old son in 1910 named Orville, which could be a middle name.
5. Ibid. In 1910, Annie Kotajärvi lived with her husband Matt at 318 Franklin St., Florida Location, Calumet Township. Though he is listed in one source as doing so, Matt Kotajärvi did not die in the hall. The 1920 census lists a Matt Kotajarvi living at 353 Franklin St., Florida Location, Calumet Township, with a new wife, Olga, and six children—two of whom are William and Arthur from his first marriage with Annie, who did die in the hall. Matt was Annie's second husband. Annie had four daughters from a previous marriage to a man with the surname Rytilahti. Two of these girls died in the hall, listed with the surname Rytilahti. The 1910 Census lists Matt and Annie having three children together, a son William and twins Arthur and Annie. Annie, the daughter, died in the hall. Therefore, Annie Kotajärvi and three of her daughters died in the disaster at Italian Hall. There is also a chance that a fourth daughter, Amy (3), died in the hall. Both *Työmies* and the *Miners Bulletin* list additional Kotijärvi children dying in the hall, and Amy would have been born after the 1910 Census.
6. Ibid. Emilia and Heli Rytilahti were the daughters of Annie Kotajärvi from her first marriage. In 1910, they lived at 318 Franklin St., Florida Location, Calumet Township, with Matt and Annie, three half-siblings, and two other Rytilahti siblings (both sisters).
7. This spelling comes from a headstone in Lakeview Cemetery, Calumet, Michigan.
8. Elina Manley was pregnant at the time of her death; Ed Stewart, *Neil's Story*, 10–11.

9. Ibid. Saida Raja was the sister of Elina Manley, but is listed in *Työmies* and the *Miners Bulletin* as a Manley.
10. *1910 United States Census.* The 1910 Census confirms that George (10), Edward (7), and Alfreda (4) lived with father Henry, mother Alice, and two older siblings at 18 Hemlock St. in Osceola Township. Albert—3 at the time of the hall disaster—would not have been listed in the census, so it is possible that he could have been in attendance. Both *Työmies* and the *Miners Bulletin* list an Albert Montanen.
11. Samma Nauer (5) may be an unlikely addition, but she is included in the *Miners Bulletin* list of the Italian Hall deceased. There are, however, no Nauer families listed in the 1910 U.S. Census in the Upper Peninsula, and no Samma Nauer in any census entries searched.

Bibliography

Books and Archival Materials

Aaltonen, Frank. "The Gallant Women of the Copper Strike." Translated by Jarno Heinilä. In *Työmiehen Joulu 1913*. Hancock, Mich.: Työmies Publishing Company, 1913.

Agassiz, Alexander, to James MacNaughton, personal correspondence, May 27, 1904. Copper Country Historical Archive, Michigan Technological University, Houghton, Michigan.

Alanen, Arnold. "Finns and the Corporate Mining Environment of the Lake Superior Region." In *Finnish Diaspora II: United States*. Toronto: Multicultural History Society of Ontario, 1981.

Ancestry.com. *Thirteenth Census of the United States of America, 1910*. www.ancestry.com. Accessed August 17, 2006.

———. "Evert Björklund, World War I Draft Registration Card, Form Card C, Federal Government, United States of America." Www.ancestry.com. Accessed August 17, 2006.

Anti-sosialistien Liitto. *Pöytäkirja*, Huhtikuu 9, 1914–Syyskuu 12, 1915. Manuscript box O-43, Finnish American Historical Archive, Finlandia University, Hancock, Michigan.

Baird, Keith P., and Erin C. Timms. "Quincy Hillside Addition." Unpublished National Historic District Nomination, 2005. Copper Country Historical Archive, Michigan Technological University, Houghton, Michigan.

Blom, Leo. "Eulogy for Heimer Mikko," February 1982. Digital Vertical Files Collection, Finnish American Historical Archive, Finlandia University, Hancock, Michigan.

Braverman, Harry. *Labor and Monopoly Capital: The Degradation of Work in the Twentieth Century.* 25th anniversary edition. New York: Monthly Review Press, 1998.

Brissenden, Paul F. *The IWW: A Study of American Syndicalism.* New York: Russell & Russell, 1957.

Campbell, J. Peter. "The Cult of Spontaneity: Finnish-Canadian Bushworkers and the Industrial Workers of the World in Northern Ontario, 1919–1934." *Labour/Le Travail* 41 (Spring 1998).

Engel, Dave, and Gerry Mantel. *Calumet: Copper Country Metropolis.* Rudolf, Wisc.: River City Memoirs, 2002.

Engle, Eloise. *The Finns in America.* Minneapolis: Lerner Publications, 1977.

Finnish American Reporter Staff. "A History of the *Finnish American Reporter.*" In *The Finnish American Reporter*, 20th anniversary issue, October 2006.

Gates Jr., William B. *Michigan Copper and Boston Dollars: An Economic History of the Michigan Mining Industry.* Cambridge, Mass.: Harvard University Press, 1951.

Gedicks, Albert. *Working Class Radicalism among Finnish Immigrants in Minnesota and Michigan Mining Communities.* Photocopy. Ann Arbor, Mich.: University Microfilms International, 1980.

Halonen, Arne. *The Role of Finnish-Americans in the Political Labor Movement.* Master's thesis, University of Minnesota, 1945.

Hannula, Reino. *An Album of Finnish Halls.* San Luis Obispo, Calif.: Finn Heritage, 1991.

Hendrickson, Nick, and John Palosaari. Interview by Arthur Puotinen, July 14, 1973. Oral history interview transcript. Finnish American Historical Archive, Finlandia University, Hancock, Michigan.

Heritage Quest Online. *Thirteenth Census of the United States, 1910.* www.heritageque-stonline.com/hqoweb/library/do/index. Accessed May 2008.

———. *Fourteenth Census of the United States, 1920.* www.heritagequestonline.com/hqoweb/library/do/index. Accessed May 2008.

Hietala, Charles E., to Mr. Ernest Mills. Business correspondence, June 7, 1915. Papers of the Western Federation of Miners/International Union of Mine, Mill and Smelter Workers, box 1, University of Colorado-Boulder Archives, Boulder, Colorado.

Hilja Fräki-Regan Collection. Personal correspondence. Manuscript box T-38a, Finnish American Historical Archive, Finlandia University, Hancock, Michigan.

Holmio, Armas K. E. *History of the Finns in Michigan.* Translated by Ellen M. Ryynanen. Detroit: Wayne State University Press, 2001.

———. "Notes on the Finnish Anti-socialist League." Anti-sosialistien Liitto, manuscript box O-43, Finnish American Historical Archive, Finlandia University, Hancock, Michigan.

Hoagland, Alison K. "The Boardinghouse Murders: Housing and American Ideals in Michigan's Copper Country in 1913." *Perspectives on Vernacular Architecture: The Journal of the Vernacular Architecture Forum* 11 (2004).

Hoglund, A. William. *Finnish Immigrants in America: 1880–1920.* Madison: University of Wisconsin Press, 1960.

———. "Breaking with Religious Tradition: Finnish Immigrant Workers and the Church, 1890–1915." In *For the Common Good,* ed. Michael G. Karni and Douglas J. Ollila Jr. Superior, Wisc.: Työmies Society, 1977.

Houghton County, Articles of Association, Books 4–6. Copper Country Historical Archive, Michigan Technological University, Houghton, Michigan.

Houghton County Court. *S. Juntilla v. Työmies Publishing Company,* 1907. Microfilm. Copper Country Historical Archive, Michigan Technological University, Houghton, Michigan.

Houghton County, State of Michigan. "Coroner's Inquest Transcript," December 31, 1913. Labor and Political Collection, Italian Hall Materials, manuscript box K-17, Finnish American Historical Archive, Finlandia University, Hancock, Michigan.

Houghton County Tax Records. First Ward of Hancock, 1909. Copper Country Historical Archive, Michigan Technological University, Houghton, Michigan.

———. First Ward of Hancock, 1911. Copper Country Historical Archive, Michigan Technological University, Houghton, Michigan.

———. First Ward of Hancock, 1914. Copper Country Historical Archive, Michigan Technological University, Houghton, Michigan.

Hummasti, P. George. "The Workingman's Daily Bread: Finnish-American Working Class Newspapers, 1900–1921." In *For the Common Good,* ed. Michael G. Karni and Douglas J. Ollila Jr. Superior, Wisc.: Työmies Society, 1977.

Huss, Richard E. *The Developments of the Printers' Mechanical Typesetting Methods, 1822–1925*. Charlottesville: University Press of Virginia, 1973.

Hyde, Charles K. *Historic American Engineering Report: Quincy Mining Company*. Washington, D.C.: Department of the Interior, 1978.

Ilmonen, Salomon. "Raittiusseura Pohjantähden 25–Vuotis Historia." Translated by E. Olaf Rankinen, 1994. In *Raittius Kalenteri 1911*. Hancock, Mich.: Suomalais-Luteerilaisen Kustannusliikkeen Kirjapaino, 1910.

Institute of Migration. "Passenger and Passport Records for Maria and Laina Ollila." Turku, Finland. Accessed August 17, 2006.

———. "Passenger and Passport Records for Evert Björklund." Turku, Finland. www.migrationinstittute.fi/emreg/ml_enfdetail.asp?snimi=_QYH0Q7NZ9. Accessed August 17, 2006.

International Printing Pressmen and Assistants' Union. "Contract between the Työmies Publishing Company," September 18, 1911. Finnish American Historical Archive, Finlandia University, Hancock, Michigan.

Jussila, Osmo, Seppo Hentilä, and Jukka Nevakivi. *From Grand Duchy to Modern State: A Political History of Finland since 1809*. Translated by David and Eva-Kaisa Arter, 1999. Carbondale: Southern Illinois University Press, 1999.

"Kaleva Temple National Register of Historic Places Inventory—Nomination Form." Vertical Files, Keweenaw National Historical Park, Calumet, Michigan, 1977.

Kallungi, Herman. Interview by Harold L. Mathieu, July 18, 1973. Oral history interview transcript. Finnish American Historical Archive, Finlandia University, Hancock, Michigan.

Karni, Michael G. "For the Common Good." PhD diss. University of Minnesota, 1975.

———. "The Founding of the Finnish Socialist Federation and the Minnesota Strike of 1907." In *For the Common Good: Finnish Immigrants and the Radical Response to Industrial America*, ed. Michael G. Karni and Douglas J. Ollila Jr. Superior, Wisc.: Työmies Society, 1977.

Karni, Michael G., and Douglas J. Ollila Jr., eds. *For the Common Good: Finnish Immigrants and the Radical Response to Industrial America*. Superior, Wisc: Työmies Society, 1977.

Kivisto, Peter. "The Decline of the Finnish-American Left." *International Migration Review* 17, no. 1 (1983).

Klemetti, Mrs. Hugo. Interview by Eero Ranta, July 22, 1973. Oral history interview transcript. Finnish American Historical Archive, Finlandia University, Hancock, Michigan.

Koivisto, Edith A. Interview by Douglas Ollila, August 3, 1973. Oral history interview. Finnish American Historical Archive, Finlandia University, Hancock, Michigan.

Kolehmainen, John I. *The Finns in America: A Bibliographical Guide to Their History.* Hancock, Mich.: Finnish Lutheran Book Concern, 1947.

———. "The Inimitable Marxists: The Finnish Immigrant Socialists." *Michigan History* 36 (1952).

Koski-Björklund, Libby. Interview by Gary Kaunonen, March 2006. Oral history interview. Finnish American Historical Archive, Finlandia University, Hancock, Michigan.

Kostiainen, Auvo. *The Forging of Finnish-American Communism, 1917–1924: A Study in Ethnic Radicalism.* Turku, Finland: Turun Yliopisto, 1978.

Lankton, Larry D. *From Cradle to Grave: Life, Work, and Death at Lake Superior Copper Mines.* New York: Oxford University Press, 1991.

Lankton, Larry D., and Charles K. Hyde. *Old Reliable: An Illustrated History of the Quincy Mining Company.* Hancock, Mich.: The Quincy Mine Hoist Association, 1982.

Lazarus, Emma. "The New Colossus." Accessed July 21, 2005.

Leiviska, Helen K. Interview by Arthur Puotinen, June 26, 1973. Oral history interview transcript. Finnish American Historical Archive, Finlandia University, Hancock, Michigan.

MacNaughton, James, to Alexander Agassiz. Personal correspondence, May 23, 1904. Copper Country Historical Archive, Michigan Technological University, Houghton, Michigan.

Markkanen, Kristiina. "K.A. Suvanto: Political Satirist." *Finnish Americana: A Journal of Finnish American History and Culture* 9 (1992).

McAlester, Virginia and Lee. *A Field Guide to American Houses.* New York: Alfred A. Knopf, 1994.

Mikkonen, Pirjo, and Sirkka Paikkala. *Sukunimet.* Helsinki, Finland: Otava, 1992.

Mimnaugh, Sarah. "The South Range Finnish Socialist Hall, National Register of Historic Places Nomination Form." Unpublished paper, 2008. Finnish American Historical Archive, Finlandia University, Hancock, Michigan.

Moran, James. *Printing Presses: History and Development from the 15th Century to Modern Times.* Los Angeles: University of California Press, 1978.

Nelson-Walkama, Daisy. Interview by Gary Kaunonen, July 20, 2006. Oral history interview.

Finnish American Historical Archive, Finlandia University, Hancock, Michigan.

Nesheim, Asbjörn. *Introducing the Lapps.* Oslo, Norway: Johan Grundt Tanum Forlag, 1963.

Niemi, Clemens. *Americanization of the Finnish People in Houghton County, Michigan.* Duluth, Minn.: Finnish Daily Publishing Company, 1921.

No. 5 to Quincy Mining Company. Business correspondence, August 10, 1906. Quincy Mining Company Collection, box 341, Copper Country Historical Collection, Michigan Technological University, Houghton, Michigan.

———. Business correspondence, August 20, 1906. Quincy Mining Company Collection, box 341, Copper Country Historical Archive, Michigan Technological University, Houghton, Michigan.

———. Business correspondence, September 7, 1906. Quincy Mining Company Collection, box 341, Copper Country Historical Archive, Michigan Technological University, Houghton, Michigan.

Ollila Jr., Douglas A. "The Work People's College: Immigrant Education for Adjustment and Solidarity." In *For the Common Good: Finnish Immigrants and the Radical Response to Industrial America,* ed. Michael G. Karni and Douglas J. Ollila Jr. Superior, Wisc.: Työmies Society, 1977.

Operative K, Thiel Detective Service Company to Quincy Mining Company. Business correspondence, September 7, 1906. Quincy Mining Company Collection, box 341, Copper Country Historical Archive, Michigan Technological University, Houghton, Michigan.

Operative P, Thiel Detective Service Company to Quincy Mining Company. Business correspondence, September 21, 1906. Quincy Mining Company Collection, box 341, Copper Country Historical Archive, Michigan Technological University, Houghton, Michigan.

Passi, Michael M. "Finnish Immigrants and the Radical Response to Industrial America." In *For the Common Good: Finnish Immigrants and the Radical Response to Industrial America,* ed. Michael G. Karni and Douglas J. Ollila Jr. Superior, Wisc.: Työmies Society, 1977.

Puotinen, Arthur. "Transitions for Finnish-American Workers in Temple and Marketplace." Unpublished paper, December 7, 1970.

———. "Early Labor Organizations in the Copper Country." In *For the Common Good: Finnish Immigrants and the Radical Response to America,* ed. Michael G. Karni and Douglas J. Ollila Jr. Superior, Wisc.: Työmies Society, 1977.

———. *Finnish Radicals and Religion in Midwestern Mining Towns.* New York: Arno Press, 1979.

Quincy Mining Company. Quincy Drawing 2019, "Scheme for Shanty Town," 1899. Copper Country Historical Archive, Michigan Technological University, Houghton, Michigan.

Quincy Mining Company. Quincy Hillside Addition Property Deeds. Copper Country Historical Archive, Michigan Technological University, Houghton, Michigan.

Riipa, Timo. "The Finnish American Radical Theatre of the 1930s." In *Finnish Americana*, vol. 9, *A Journal of Finnish American History and Culture*, ed. Michael Karni. New Brighton, Minn.: Finnish Americana, 1992.

R. L. Polk & Co. Houghton County Directories. Hancock and Red Jacket City Directories, 1899–1917. Copper Country Historical Archive, Michigan Technological University, Houghton, Michigan.

Roe, James A. "Virginia, Minnesota's Socialist Opera: Showplace of Iron Range Radicalism." In *Finnish Americana*, vol. 9, *A Journal of Finnish American History and Culture*, ed. Michael Karni. New Brighton, Minn.: Finnish Americana, 1992.

Ross, Carl. "Essays on the Finnish American Community: 1865–1914, Part 2, The Finnish American Community Matures, 1885–1900." Unpublished work in the Carl Ross Papers, Immigration History Research Center, University of Minnesota, Minneapolis, Minnesota.

Salminen, Jukka. "Behind Bars: Written in the Marquette County Jail." *Työmies*, April 2, 1914. Translated by Taisto T. Holm, *Työmies-Eteenpäin* (July 1998).

Sampson, N. A., Manager Thiel Detective Service Company to Quincy Mining Company. Business correspondence, September 4, 1906. Quincy Mining Company Collection, box 341, Copper Country Historical Archive, Michigan Technological University, Houghton, Michigan.

Sanborn Insurance Company. Hancock, Michigan Map, 1893, 1900, 1907, and 1917. Microfilm reel 24. Copper Country Historical Archive, Michigan Technological University, Houghton, Michigan.

———. Houghton (South Range), Michigan Map, 1907 and 1917. Digital Map Collection, Keweenaw National Historical Park, Calumet, Michigan.

———. Red Jacket (Calumet), Michigan Map, 1908. Digital Map Collection, Keweenaw National Historical Park, Calumet, Michigan.

Sarell, A. O. "The Copper Country Strike: Its Features So Far." *Työmiehen Joulu 1913*.

Translated by Jarno Heinilä, 2006. Hancock, Mich.: Työmies Publishing Company, 1913.

Schlereth, Thomas J. "Social History Scholarship and Material Culture Research." In *Material Culture: A Research Guide*. Lawrence: University Press of Kansas, 1985.

Smith, G. Walton. "Houghton County Census." Vertical File Collection: Finnish Immigration, Copper Country Historical Archive, Michigan Technological University, Houghton, Michigan.

Socialist Party of Michigan. *State Bulletin, July 1914*. Harbor Springs, Mich.: Socialist Party of Michigan, 1914.

Sulkanen, Elis. *Amerikan Suomalaisen Työväenliikkeen Historia*. Fitchburg, Mass.: Amerikan Suomalainen Kansanvallan Liitto ja Raivaaja Publishing Company, 1951.

Suomalaisten Sosialistijärjestön Edustajakokouksen, *Pöytäkirja 1912*. Fitchburg, Mass.: Suomalainen Sosialisti Kustannus Yhtiö, 1912.

———. *Pöytäkirja 1914*. Hancock, Mich.: Työmies Publishing Company, 1914.

———. *Pöytäkirja 1915*. Hancock, Mich.: Työmies Publishing Company, 1915.

———. "Työmies Kustannusyhtiön vuosi-ja tilikertomus, tiliuotena 1911–1912." In *Työmiehen Vuosikok: Pöytäkirjat 1912–1924*. Hancock, Mich., and Superior, Wisc.: Työmies Publishing Company, 1924.

———. "Työmies Kustannusyhtiön vuosi-ja tilikertomus, tiliuotena 1912–1913." In *Työmiehen Vuosikok: Pöytäkirjat 1912–1924*. Hancock, Mich., and Superior, Wisc.: Työmies Publishing Company, 1924.

T. H. "Työmihen uusi koti." In *Työmiehen Joulu VII*. Translated by Aino Utriainen, 2006. Hancock, Mich.: Työmies Publishing Company, 1910.

Thiel Detective Service to C. L. Lawton, Esq. Business correspondence, August 5, 1913. Quincy Mining Company Collection, box 341, Copper Country Historical Archive, Michigan Technological University, Houghton, Michigan.

Thiel Detective Service to Quincy Mining Company. Business correspondence, August 15, 1906. Quincy Mining Company Collection, box 341, Copper Country Historical Archive, Michigan Technological University, Houghton, Michigan.

———. Business correspondence, August 31, 1906. Quincy Mining Company Collection, box 341, Copper Country Historical Archive, Michigan Technological University, Houghton, Michigan.

———. Business correspondence, September 21, 1906. Quincy Mining Company Collection, box 341, Copper Country Historical Archive, Michigan Technological

University, Houghton, Michigan.

———. "Re: Employees," October 15, 1906. Quincy Mining Company Collection, box 341, Copper Country Historical Archive, Michigan Technological University, Houghton, Michigan.

Todd, Williams Parson. Interview by Ralph Jalkanen, October 1974. Oral history interview transcript. Finnish American Historical Archive, Finlandia University, Hancock, Michigan.

Torma, Fred. Interview by Douglas Ollila, August 3, 1973. Oral history interview transcript. Finnish American Historical Archive, Finlandia University, Hancock, Michigan.

Thurner, Arthur. *Rebels on the Range: The Michigan Copper Miners' Strike of 1913–14*. Hancock, Mich.: Book Concern Printers, 1998.

———. *Strangers and Sojourners: A History of Michigan's Keweenaw Peninsula*. Detroit: Wayne State University Press, 1994.

United States Circuit Court of Appeals for the Sixth Circuit, Cincinnati, Ohio. *The Työmies Publishing Company, John Nummivuori and John Salminen, Defendants in Error v. The United States Government*, filed January 6, 1914. Työmies Society Collection, Finnish American Historical Archive, Finlandia University, Hancock, Michigan.

United States Department of Commerce and Labor. *The 13th Census of the United States of America: Bulletin Population Michigan*. 1910. Vertical Files: Finnish Immigration, Copper Country Historical Archive, Michigan Technological University, Houghton, Michigan.

United States Department of Labor. *Michigan Copper District Strike: Bulletin of the United States Labor Statistics, 1914*. Washington, D.C.: Government Printing Office, 1914.

United States of America, Western District of Michigan, Northern Division. *People of the United States v. The Työmies Publishing Company, John Nummivuori and John Salminen*. Copy of indictment filed January 15, 1913. Työmies Society Collection, Finnish American Historical Archive, Finlandia University, Hancock, Michigan.

Walli, Frank. "The Midwest: Cradle of the LSU." In *Työmies 85: 1903–1988*. Superior, Wisc.: Työmies Society, 1988.

Wargelin Brown, K. Marianne. "Three Founding Mothers of Finnish America: Ida Pasanen: Socialist Agitator and Women's Advocate." In *Women Who Dared: The History of Finnish American Women*, ed. K. Marianne Wargelin Brown and Carl Ross. New York Mills, Minn.: Parta Printers, 1986.

Newspapers/Periodicals

Amerikan Matti

The Daily Mining Gazette

The Evening Copper Journal

The (Hancock, Mich.) Evening Journal

Köyhalestön Nuija

Lapatossu

The Miners' Bulletin

Pelto ja Koti

Soihtu

Työmies

Työmies-Eteenpäin

Työmies 10 Vuotias

Työmiehen Joulu

Työvaen Kalentari

Työvaen Laulukirja

Urheilu-Viesti

Uusi Työvaen Laulukirja

Vallankumous

Vappu

The Wage Slave

Index

W